LANCASTER COUNTY, PENNSYLVANIA

LAND RECORDS
1729-1750
AND
LAND WARRANTS
1710-1742

Marsha Martin

HERITAGE BOOKS
2008

HERITAGE BOOKS
AN IMPRINT OF HERITAGE BOOKS, INC.

Books, CDs, and more—Worldwide

For our listing of thousands of titles see our website
at
www.HeritageBooks.com

Published 2008 by
HERITAGE BOOKS, INC.
Publishing Division
100 Railroad Ave. #104
Westminster, Maryland 21157

International Standard Book Numbers
Paperbound: 978-1-58549-163-6
Clothbound: 978-0-7884-7198-8

The land operation would have been an immense one even with all the administrative resources of a later age. That it was accomplished literally by hand, with compass and chain, quill pen and ink, illuminated by candlelight in rough prairie offices, was in itself a herculean performance.

LEONARD WHITE

INTRODUCTION

The last proprietary province in America was Pennsylvania, founded by William Penn in 1682. When the 23-year old William Penn became a Quaker, his father, an admiral and friend of Charles II, was so disgusted with him, that he beat him and barred him from the family's London mansion. William would sometimes wander over the country preaching to all who would listen to him. Penn was converted to Quakerism by George Fox who was the founder of the Society of Friends. Fox preached that Christians should practice peace and brotherhood, never striking a blow, or swearing an oath, or engaging in lawsuits. He preached equality of women to men, low class to high. He told Friends it was wrong to show special respect to a person because of his rank or position, and therefore they would not take off their hats before rulers, or address people by any title, not even Mister. They addressed lord and peasant alike, familiarly as "thee" and "thou" and as "friend". They believed it was wrong to wear jewelry or fine clothes, or to follow the fashions. They did not believe in bishops or priests, and they refused to swear in court. What seems to be so contradictory to their beliefs was the fact the most Quakers, including Penn, owned slaves. It was not until almost fifty years after the death of Penn that the Quakers renounced Slavery.

In England things were not going well for the Quakers, infuriated officials confiscated their property when they refused to tithe. They laughed at the simply dressed zealots quaking and moaning in public prayer. Then they beat, jailed, tortured, and occasionally hanged them. Some people even thought them to be dangerous.

On a trip back to England, while George Fox was visiting his convert, William Penn, he must have sung the praises of Jersey land. For in 1670 the Quaker towns in West Jersey had adopted Penn's "Concessions and Agreements". This was a forerunner of the Constitution, it provided a democratic government, and many guarantees of civil rights, and religious freedom. Penn, after arbitrating a disagreement between two Quakers, John Fenwick and Edward Byllinge, who had purchased a large tract of land in New Jersey, became convinced of the virtue of single proprietorship.

By 1681 William's father had died. In spite of the fact that William was a Quaker, it is said King Charles II liked him. Charles II had agreed to settle his debts to Penn's father by giving his son a 300 by 160 mile tract of wilderness across the Delaware from West Jersey. Penn wanted it named Sylvania but the king insisted on honoring Admiral Penn and named it Pennsylvania, meaning "Penn's Woodland". In all reality the King was probably thrilled to get rid of the trouble making Quakers so cheaply. After all it was an easily transplantable religion, no priest, or bishops, no fancy churches. By Oct 1681 Penn had sold 320,000 acres to 259 buyers, and by the time he left England, headed for Pennsylvania, he had sold another 300,000 acres to 250 buyers. He also succeeded in having Delaware included in his territory, since Pennsylvania did not have any seacoast. In less then two years Penn created a colony that was self sustaining, but because of financial problems, he was to spend less then four years in Pennsylvania. When Penn left in August of 1684 he appointed a council of eleven, ten of whom were Quakers. By 1688 when Penn returned to Pennsylvania his finances were in such a mess that he deeded the entire colony to his business agent, Philip Ford, who deeded it back to him for £360 a year. By this time Philadelphia was a city of about 5,000. William Penn did not live in the city, but instead lived at an 8,4000 acre estate about 26 miles northeast of the city. In 1701 the Penns returned to England. William left behind James Logan who was clerk of the council and secretary of the province. He was to collect rents, taxes, and to sell land. Upon his return to England William found himself buried in debt. In January of 1709 he was sent to Fleet Prison for debts. In October he was released, and once again tried to sell the colony, but before he could, he died, it was 1718. William's sons, John, Thomas, and Richard inherited the colony along with all its debt. Richard and Thomas were minors.

Many of the English Quakers came to Pennsylvania, as well as Scotch, Irish and Welsh. Penn had especially encouraged farmers and craftsmen from the Rhine Valley, Switzerland and Sweden. Because of the skilled people Penn brought, the Colony did not suffer the terrible hardships that most of the early colonies suffered. This was because Penn managed the colonization so well. He made friends with the Indians. The Indians so respected him that when he died the Delaware sent his widow a cloak sewn from the skins of wild animals. They said it was "to protect her whilst passing through the thorny wilderness without her guide". The cause of all of Penn's problems was his colony. The colony had cost him his life and every penny he had. He had established the Quaker principles of pacifism and religious tolerance. He had introduced his "Concession and Agreements" and thus planting the seed of a Democratic government. He was unlike any of the other early colonial leaders.

Many of the early pioneers who settled on the Susquehanna River area were Quakers from the Delaware Valley. By 1723 the Germans and Scotch-Irish were streaming into Lancaster County. The Germans were settled in the center of the county and the Scotch-Irish and Welsh settled the land to the north and south The Proprietary Land Office was closed from 1718 to 1732. William's sons refused to let any grants be issued to land lying west of the Susquehanna River and south of Harris Ferry until the boundary dispute with Maryland was settled and the western land could be purchased from the Indians. By purchasing the land from the Indians the Penns hoped to avoid violence and any alliances with the French.

At this time the frontier was north and west of Philadelphia. For the new immigrants coming into Philadelphia the frontier represented freedom. It was some place where they could worship as they chose and live where they chose. No matter what else happened you could always go west and start over. The first peoples to move west were the Scotch and Irish. The hardships of the frontier, and the Indians were not an obstacle for them, they already knew that you had to fight for what you want, and to keep what you have. They were stubborn too, you could move them off the land one day, only to find the next day they were back. Most of them did not bother with the Land Office. By 1730 it was a common sight to see ships loaded with immigrants in Philadelphia. When a ship arrived no one was allowed off until he paid his passage. The other passengers stayed aboard until they were purchased. If you were sick when you arrived then most likely you would stay on board until you died. It was not usual to see parents selling their children. What ever kind of life the children would have, would be better then anything they had come away from. At this time Philadelphia was full of several different religions. There were Dunkers, Presbyterians, Catholics, Mennonites, and Lutherans only to name a few. Though there was great freedom in this America, there was also severe punishment. Many times both the offender, and informer were punished. But as fast as people were coming to Pennsylvania some were beginning to leave. The price of land was going up, in 1713 the quit-rent per 100 acres was 1 shilling. By 1732 the quit-rent was 4 shilling and 2 pence. Other reasons for moving on was the high cost of goods and the distaste for authority. Many of the second generation families began moving down into Virginia and some on to Carolina.

PREFACE

Pennsylvania was operated under the Feudal Land System. This meant that the land ownership was based on a system in which the King owned all the land but allowed certain individuals the use of it in exchange for services. The types of services a person rendered could be something such as military service, or the delivery of agricultural products. Churches could hold special prayers and masses, all of these were considered service. Gradually most services were changed to their cash equivalents. One of the requirements of the Feudal System was, that in order for you to acquire any land you were required, to take an oath of "Fidelity". This formed the basis for a legal relationship between you and the Proprietor. This entitled him to emergency taxes, along with the rent you're already paying, he also had the right to slap a special tax on your eldest son as your heir. In this system there were three types of ownership, first there was **Fee Simple**. This is as close as you can get to actually owning the land. It meant that the land could be handed down to your heirs. The second was called **Fee Tail**. This meant that the land could only be handed down to a "lineal" descendant. If there was not one then the land could revert back to the Proprietor. The third and most undesirable was called **Life Estate**. This meant that the land was granted only for your lifetime. The one good thing that has come from this system for family researchers is that the land titles, in the older colonies can usually be traced back to the first point of ownership.

The normal process for acquiring land was a four step process. First there was the **Entry**, which was a formal act of marking the boundaries of the land and notifying the appropriate government agency of your desire to acquire the land, along with the reason for acquiring it. It is not unusual to see **Claim** substituted for Entry.

Step two was the **Warrant**. When issued it entitled the holder to have so many acres of land surveyed. Pennsylvania did not require that a warrant be recorded until 1759, and that only lasted for about three years.

The third step in acquiring land was the **Survey**, or sometimes called the **Plat**. This was a descriptive drawing of the boundaries of the land. It was the job of the surveyor to pinpoint boundaries of the tract as accurately as possible. Often the boundaries are referred to in terms boarding land owners and creeks, since there were no permanent markers. This can be an important clue as so many of the early settlers married their neighbors. The surveyors were the first ones in the westward movement. They came carrying a compass with folding sights, and a tripod or Jacob's staff. The distances along sight lines were measured with fifty or hundred link chains made of brass or iron. They had triangular handles. A one hundred link chain measured sixty-six feet, and eighty chains made a mile. They carried paper and ink for their notes. The two pole, fifty link chain was for hilly country, and the four pole chain was for flatlands. To measure the ground, the forward chain man carried eleven tally pins, each with a red cloth tied to a ring at the top. After stretching the chain, he stuck a pin in the ground. At the eleventh pin, he would cry "Tally!" Then the rear chain man collected the pins and brought them up to the front and became the forward chain man for the next series of twelve stretches. Eight tallies with the thirty-three-foot chain made a half a mile. The measurements that are used in the early Lancaster deeds are perches, which is equal in measurement to rods or poles.

The fourth and final step in acquiring land was the **Grant**. This was made by the proprietary and a deed was issued. **Patent** is another term used for grant, although in the Lancaster deeds it is used to refer to the first grant of the land made by the proprietary.

Not all of the steps were followed. Some claims were sold or abandoned. Some others never bothered with a claim at all, and took possession of the land by squatting. Not all deeds were recorded. If a deed was between family members and there was no threat of it being questioned, why bother recording it? It also may have been too hazardous of a journey to get to the land office, or the deed could be lost or destroyed during Indian attacks.

The kinds of deeds you're going to find in the Lancaster Deeds are:

Deed of Sale, referred to as **Enfeoff** - It simply means the transfer of land from the person selling it to the person purchasing it.

Lease and Release - This is a two part transfer deed. Mr. Jones leases land to Mr. Smith, then Mr. Jones releases Mr. Smith from his obligation of the lease.

Gift Deed of Property Distribution - Most of these deeds are from parent to child. They will contain words such as "for love and affection", and "for his better advancement in the world". Some of these deeds have restrictions. They may be a parent giving his land to his child in exchange for shelter and care the rest of his natural life.

 Estate Settlement - These deeds were used when someone died and the property needed to be divided among the heirs. The widow would receive 1/3 of the property, refered to as **Dower Rights**, the rest was divided among the other heirs, with the oldest son receiving double the share. Sometimes a child would sell his share to a brother, brother-n-law or other interested person.

Mortgage Sale - These deeds are probably the hardest to detect. There are several different ways they can be worded. If you're lucky it will say in the beginning, "This deed of mortgage". If not its more difficult to detect, but most of these types of deeds have language something like "sale to be void if £'s or $'s are paid by 1 May 1735". Another clue to a mortgage in the Lancaster Deeds is that the forfeiture was double the actual amount of the mortgage. It may read, "Mr. Smith is bound unto Mr. Jones in the amount of £300, Mr. Smith in consideration of the debt and in consideration of the further sum of 5/ grants 150A". "Terms for payment of £150 as follows". The fact that the amount bound is double the amount owed tells you its a mortgage where the land was used as collateral. When a mortgage was paid off at the end of the deed it will say something like "Received Full Satisfaction", or "Satisfaction in Full", meaning the mortgage was paid off.

In 1752 the calendar was changed from the Julian to the Gregorian calendar. Before the change, February was the 12th month of the year and March was the first month of the year. Because of a miscalculation, 11 days had been lost in the Julian calendar. To make up the loss, the 11 days were skipped in September of 1752 and January became the first month of the year. Before the change the year in the first two months is shown as 1746/7. The early part of March was also shown as 1746/7.

These deeds were abstracted from LDS film number 0021382, a microfilm of original records in the Lancaster Courthouse. The warrants were taken from LDS film number 0020360, a microfilm of the original taken from the "Taylor Papers" at Franklin and Marshall College in Lancaster. The first book of Deeds was a type written copy so is subject to someone else's interpretation. The warrants were very hard to read as were some of the deeds, look for every possible spelling of your names. In some of the deeds the same name is spelled 3 different ways in the same deed. A copy of the original deed can be obtained by writing to the County Recorder of Deeds. The format used in the abstracts is first, the book, page number, Grantor, place of residence and occupation, then the Grantee, place of residence and occupation. Followed next by £'s, number of acres, location and neighbors. The order may vary a little depending on how much information is in the deed. Where there is a ? I could not make out the word, where there is a ___ it was blank in the deed. I have tried to duplicate a person's mark as best I can with the tools available on the keyboard. If I could not duplicate it exactly, then I have described it.

A few things to keep in mind when going through these deed abstracts is that a unnaturalized alien could not grant land. So anyone who sold land in his name had either taken an oath of allegiance to the King of England, become naturalized, or was a natural-born subject of the king. Everyone paid a quit rent to the Penns. In Lancaster Borough, James Hamilton was the proprietor, an annual rent of 7 shilling was paid to him on 1 May. In Plumton Manor John Page was the proprietor.

On the next few pages are some maps that will show the splitting off of new counties from Lancaster County. Below is a list of some of the Creeks mentioned through out the deeds, where they are located now, and the tributary.

Bermundian Creek - York County - Tributary is Conewago Creek
Cocalico Creek - Lancaster County - Tributary is Conestoga Creek
Cacoosing Creek - Berks County - Tributary is Tulpehocken Creek
Codorus Creek - York County - Tributary is Susquehanna River
Conewago Creek - Dauphin, Lancaster, and York Counties - Tributary is Susquehanna River
Conewago Creek - Adams County - Tributary is Conewago Creek
Conococheague Creek - Franklin County - Tributary Potomac River
Conodoguinet Creek - Cumberland County - Tributary is Susquehanna River

Little Conestoga Creek - Lancaster County - Tributary is Conestoga Creek
Tulpehocken Creek - Berks County - Tributary is Schuylkill River
Yellow Breeches - Cumberland and York Counties - Tributary Susquehanna River

The following township are mentioned often in the deeds, but are no longer located in Lancaster County:

Antrim - Franklin County
Bethel - Berks County
Cumru - Berks County
Derry - Dauphin County
Hanover - York
Hopewell - Cumberland County
Paxtang & Paxton - Dauphin County
Pennsboro - Cumberland County
Plumton Manor - in Heidelberg Township - Berks County
Robeson - Berks County
Tulpehocken - Berks County

Lancaster County
1729 - 1759

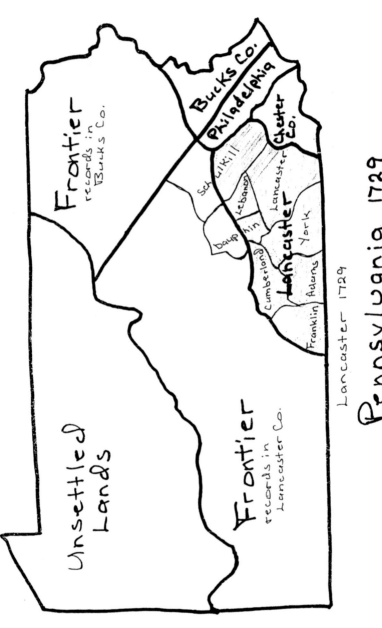

Pennsylvania 1729

Lancaster 1729

Bucks Co.

Philadelphia

Chester Co.

Frontier
records in
Bucks Co.

Schulkill

Lebanon

Lancaster

Dauphin

Lancaster

York

Cumberland

Franklin

Adams

Unsettled
Lands

Frontier
records in
Lancaster Co.

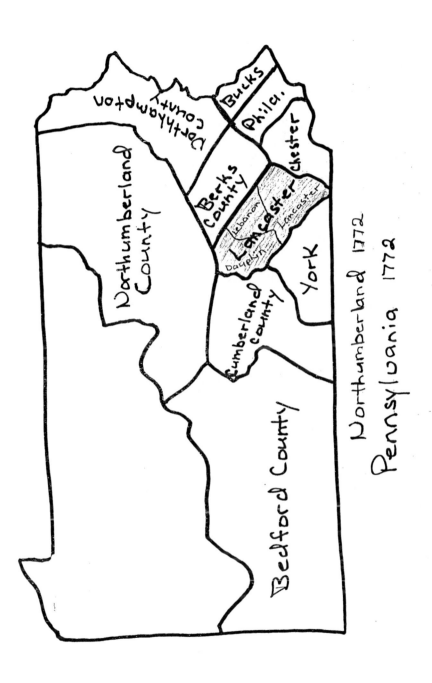

Northumberland 1772
Pennsylvania 1772

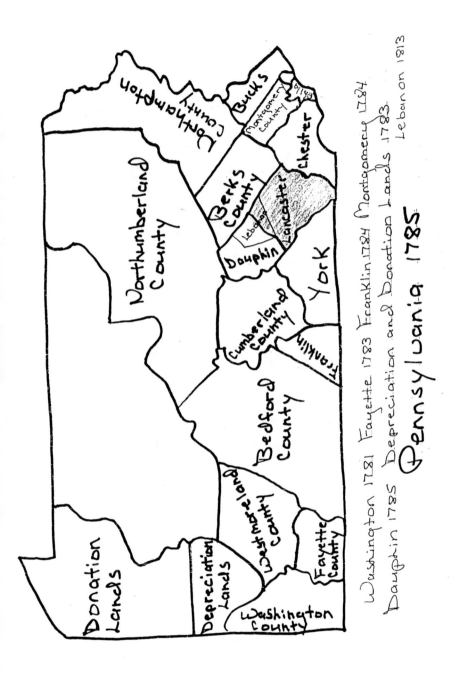

Pennsylvania 1785

Washington 1781 Fayette 1783 Franklin 1784 Montgomery 1784
Dauphin 1785 Depreciation and Donation Lands 1783
Lebanon 1813

Lancaster County Pennsylvania

Deed Book A 1729-1750

A-1 - THIS INDENTURE of mortgage - 3 May 1729 - Andrew Cornish of Conestoga Township in Chester Co., yeoman, and wife Elizabeth to James Logan of the city of Philadelphia, merchant. James paid £500 for 300A located on Conestoga Creek in Chester Co. Neighbors - none mentioned. Pay by 13 Apr 1731 ... Andrew Cornish, Elizabeth Cornish ... Signed in the presence of John Wright, and S. A. Blunston ... Ack'd none ... Rec'd Edwin L. Reinhold. See assignment of this mortgage by William Logan Esquire, James Logan, and John Smith executors of the last will of the mortgagee unto Mary Wright and James Burd: Book L, pg 266.

A-3 - THIS INDENTURE of mortgage - 17 Oct 1730 - I, Edmond Cartlidge of Lancaster Co., trader, by virtue of a warrant from commissioners of proprietary of the Province, ca 1717, obtained a survey of a tract situated on Mill Creek in Lancaster Co., containing 370A. James Logan of the city of Philadelphia, merchant, supplied me with £200 for building or rebuilding a mill, making other improvements, and paid the Proprietary the consideration money with interest due. The commission granted deed for land to Israel Pemberton of the city of Philadelphia, merchant. Deed was in trust for James Logan. Last Oct. with James permission, Israel assigned land to me, which I mortgaged in the loan office for £180. I paid out of the sum £150 and kept £38 for my own use. Land is now mortgaged for £188 in 16 yrs of payments of £11 15/ a year. James made first payment of £21 4/ with interest. I Edmond hold land in trust for James Logan. Two years to pay back ... Edmond Cartlidge ... Signed, sealed, and delivered in presence of John Wright, and George Stuart ... Ack'd none ... Witness - Samuel Blunston Esq. ... Rec'd 25 Mar 1731 Edwin L. Reinhold.

THIS INDENTURE - 28 Oct 1734 - Charles Jones of Conestoga Township, Lancaster Co., yeoman to Samuel Jones of Leacock Township, Lancaster Co., yeoman, £36 10/ for 250A. Land located in Leacock Township, neighbors - on east William Clark, on west Edward Woodwork. Land granted to Charles by warrant 27 Mar 1714. ... Charles Jones ... Sealed and delivered in the presence of Mary Postluhwait, William Mofortres, and Richard Marooned ... Ack'd none ... Witness: Tobias Hendricks 28 Oct 1734, entered 1 Oct 1735 ... Rec'd 31 Oct 1735 Edwin L. Reinhold.

A-4 - THIS INDENTURE of mortgage - 26 Jan 1735 - between Casper Wister of the city of Philadelphia, merchant, to the Honorable Thomas Penn Esq., one of the proprietors and Governors in Chief of Pennsylvania and Company, £1,818 3/, and 7d for 2 tracts containing 10,000A in Lancaster. First tract contains 9,740A and is located on a branch of Schuylkill River, called Tulpehocken Creek, neighbor - John Page. Second tract contains 260A, (except 190A which Casper granted to Jacob Leman,) located on a branch of the Swartara River, neighbors - Thomas Freams, Conrade Sharp, and Richard Penn Esq. (one

1

of proprietors) ... Casper Wistar ... Signed and sealed in the presence of Charles
Brockdon, James Steel Jr. and Tobias Showen ... Witness 5 May 1736 John Wright Esq.
justice ... Ack'd 6 May 1736 John Wright ... Received at date of indenture £1,818. 3/,
7d of Thomas Penn, Caspar Wistar ... Witness at signing Tobias Showen, Charles
Brockdon, and James Steel Jr. ... Rec'd 25 Jul 1736 Edwin L. Reinhold.

A-6 - THIS INDENTURE - 27 Jan 1735 - Honorable Thomas Penn Esquire, one of
proprietors and Governors in chief of PA and Casper Wistar of the city of Philadelphia
merchant. By an indenture dating 26 Jan between Thomas Penn and Casper Wistar, for
£1,818 3/ & 7d, and 1/2 penny sterling money of Great Britain did grant unto Casper 2
tracts of land containing 10,000A. The money is to be paid as specified - £303 7d & 1
farthing, part of principle sum of £1,818 3/ & 7d 1/2 penny together with £109 1/ 9d & 3
farthings sterling interest on 10 Nov next. Also £303 7d & 1 farthing more there of with
£90 18/ & 2d, and 1 farthing sterling interest on 10 Nov 1737. Then £303 7d & 1 farthing
more there of with £72 14/ & 6d sterling interest on 10 Nov 1738. Continuing with £303
7d 1 farthing more with £54 10/ & 1d, 1 farthing sterling interest on 10 Nov 1739.
Continuing with £303 7d & 1 farthing with £36 7/ & 3d 1 farthing sterling interest on 10
Nov 1740. Continuing with £303 7/ & 1 farthing, residue there of with £18 3/ & 7d 3
farthing sterling interest 10 Nov 1741 ... Thomas Penn ... Signed in the presence of C.
Brockdon, James Steel Jr., and Tobias Shewin ... Ack'd none ... Witness 5 May 1736 by
John Wright Esq., justice ... John Wright ... Rec'd 21 Jul 1736 Edwin L. Reinhold

A-9 - THIS INDENTURE - 2 Apr 1736 - Michael Meyer of Manheim Township,
Lancaster Co., yeoman, Barbara his wife to John Heer Jr. (alias Hair) of Donegal
Township, Lancaster Co., yeoman, 5/ for 294A of land located in Donegal Township on a
branch of the Chickaslunga Creek. Neighbor - Henry Saunders ... Michael (MM) Mires,
Barbara (B) Mires ... Signed in the presence of Christian Stoneman, and R. Marsdin ...
Ack'd 12 Sept 1737 by Samuel Blunston ... Rec'd Edwin L. Reinhold.

A-10 - THIS INDENTURE - 3 Apr 1736 - Michael Meyer of Manheim Township in
Lancaster Co. yeoman, Barbara wife to John Heer Jr. (alias Hair) of Donegal Township in
Lancaster Co. yeoman, 40/ for 294A. By virtue of a warrant from John, Thomas, and
Richard Penn Esqs., Proprietors and Governors of the Province, dated 21 May 1735,
surveyed on the 13 May unto John Hair Jr., land in Donegal Township on a branch of the
Chickaslunga Creek. Land contains 294A, and was patented on 20 Nov 1735. Under quit
rent of 1/2 penny sterling for every acre yearly. Recorded in Book A, vol 7, page 330, on
24 Nov 1735. ... Michael (MM) Mires, Barbara (B) Mires ... Signed in the presence of
Christian Stoneman, and R. Marsden ... Ack'd by Samuel Blunston justice 12 Sept 1737
... Rec'd no date Edwin L. Reinhold.

A-12 - THIS INDENTURE - 30 Oct 1730 - Thomas Gaill of Manheim Township in
Lancaster Co. to Andrew Miller of Aston Township in Chester Co., £120 for 200A. Land
located in Manheim Township on the south and east side of Conestoga Creek. Conestoga
Manor on the west side, neighbor - Jacob Ouarholtzars on the north side ... Thomas (TG)
Gail ... Signed in the presence of Tobias Hendricks, and Joshua Low ... Ack'd in
Hempfield 1737 by John Wright ... Rec'd no date Edwin L. Reinhold.

A-13 - THIS INDENTURE - 8 Nov 1722 - Alexander Bues of Conestoga Township in Chester Co. has sold to Thomas Gale of Conestoga Township, yeoman, £4 5/ for a building and tract of 200A. Land located on Conestoga Creek. Land was in the possession of John Vantine which he forfeited for £10 ... Alexander (A) Bues ... Witnessed by Isaac Shaddock, and George Gray ... Ack'd in Philadelphia 4 Jan 1737 by Andrew Hamilton ... Rec'd no date Edwin L. Reinhold.

THIS INDENTURE - 25 Mar 1737 - Felix Londus of Lampeter Township in Lancaster Co. yeoman, Rosanah his wife to John Pinkly of Lampeter Township, yeoman, £15 for 200A. Land located in Lampeter Township ... Fleix Landis, Rosanah (X) Landis ... Signed in the presence of Samuel Bethel, Dorick Updegraef ... Ack'd 14 Oct 1737 in Lancaster by Samuel Blunston ... Rec'd no date Edwin L. Reinhold.

A-14 - THIS INDENTURE - 26 Mar 1737 - Felix Londus of Lampeter Township in Lancaster Co., yeoman, and Rosanah his wife to John Pinkly of Lampeter Township, £100 for 400A. Where as Tobias Collet, Daniel Quare, Henry Gouldney of the City of London by lease and release on 19 & 20 Feb 1718 did sell to Felix Londus land in Strasburg now called Lampeter. Tract contains 400A with usual allowance, and was recorded Book E, vol 4, page 8-10 on 7 Aug 1719. This land is part of a tract of 5,553A which was patented to Tobias Collet, Daniel Quare, Henry Gouldney and the heirs of Michael Russell dec'd by William Penn Esq. Recorded in Book (none given), vol 5, pg 306. ... Felix Landis, Rosanah (X) Landis ... Signed in the presence of Samuel Bethel, and Dorick Updegraef ... Ack'd in Lancaster 14 Oct 1737 by Samuel Blunston, justice ... Rec'd no date Edwin L. Reinhold.

A-15 - THIS INDENTURE - 25 Mar 1737 - Felix Londus of Lampeter, Township Lancaster Co., yeoman, Rosannah wife to Felix Londus Jr. of Lampeter Township yeoman, son of the aforesaid Felix, 5/ for 200A, for 1 year. Land is located in Lampeter Township, neighbor - John Bundlys ... Felix Landis, Rosanah (X) Landis ... Sealed and delivered in the presence of Samuel Bethel, Dorick Updegraef ... Ack'd 14 Oct 1737 Samuel Blunston ... Rec'd no date Edwin L. Reinhold.

A-16 - THIS INDENTURE - 26 Mar 1737 - Felix Londus of Lampeter Township, yeoman, Rosanah his wife to Felix Jr. (son of Felix and Rosanah) of Lampeter Township, for love and affection and £75 for 200A. Whereas Tobias Collet, Daniel Quare, and Henry Gouldney of the city of London by their lease and release on 19 & 20 Feb 1718 to Felix Londus a tract in Strasburg, now Lampeter containing 400A recorded in Philadelphia, Bk F, vol 4, pgs 8-10 on 7 Aug 1719. The land is part of a tract of 5,553A owned by William Penn which he granted to Collet, Quare, Gouldney, and the heirs of Michael Russel, dec'd on 25 Jun 1718 recorded in Philadelphia in Bk A, vol 5, pg 306. Neighbors - John Bundly, Jacob Kindrick, Dorick Janson ... Felix Landis, Rosannah (X) Landis ... Signed in the presence of Samuel Bethel, and Dorick Updegraef ... Ack'd 14 Oct 1737 by Samuel Blunston ... Rec'd no date Edwin L. Reinhold.

3

A-17 - THIS INDENTURE - 10 Dec 1730 - between John Meilin of Lancaster Co. yeoman, (eldest son and heir of Hans Meilin dec'd), and Katherine his wife to John Howser of Lancaster Co., a weaver £12 for 200A, enfeoff. Tract is located in Strasburg and is part of a larger tract of 700A. The 700A was granted to Hans Meilin by William Penn Esq. late Proprietary of the Province dec'd by patent under commissioners, Richard Hill, Isaac Norris, and James Logan on 13 Aug 1717, under quit rent of 12/ sterling per 100A, recorded in Philadelphia in Bk A, vol 5, pg 220. Neighbors - Martin Meilin, Christian Jonce, and Martin Kendrick. Hans has died intestate, land descended to John Meilin. ... Hannis Meylin, Catherine K. Millin ... Signed in the presence of Andrew Cornish, Gabriel Davies ... Memorandum - possession of tract was taken by the within named John Milen and by him delivered to John Howser ... Emanuel Carpenter, Christian Meirr ... Ack'd 4 Aug 1736 Samuel Blunston ... Rec'd by Edwin L. Reinhold.

A-19 - THIS INDENTURE - 26 Apr 1738 - Casper Wister of the city of Philadelphia, brass button maker, and Catherine his wife to Peter Good of Lancaster PA, yeoman, 5/ for 165A. Land located on Pequea Creek, neighbor - John Swift dec'd, Samuel Boyors, and William Middletons. Indenture for 1 year ... Caspar Wistar, Catherine Wistar ... Signed in the presence of Thomas Lindley, and George Cryder ... Ack'd by Edward Smout, justice. ... Affirmed 1 May 1739, Edward Smout ... Rec'd none.

A-20 - THIS INDENTURE - 20 Apr 1738 - Casper Wister of Philadelphia, brass button maker, Catherine wife to Peter Good, yeoman of Lancaster Co., 165A for £49, 10/. Land is located on Pequea Creek, neighbors - John Swift dec'd, Samuel Boyor, and William Middletons. This land is part of 2 tracts granted by patent on 28 Mar last and recorded in Philadelphia in Bk A, vol 8, pg 334 to Casper in fee simple. ... Casper Wistar, Catherine Wistar ... Signed in the presence of Thomas Lindley, and George Cryder ... Received of Peter Good £49 and 10/, Casper Wister, Catherine Wister ... Ack'd and affirmed by Edward Smout 1 May 1739 ... Rec'd no date Edwin L. Reinhold.

A-21 - THIS INDENTURE - 25 Oct 1738 - Septimus Robinson of the city of Philadelphia Esq. to Peter Good of Lancaster Co., yeoman, £270 for 300A. Land located on Pequea Creek in Lancaster Co., neighbors - Samuel Boyers and land late of Ellis Jr. ... Septimus Robinson ... Signed in the presence of William Cundall and John Webbe ... Received £270, Septimus Robinson ... Witness - William Cundall and John Webbe ... Ack'd by John Wright 4 May 1739 ... Rec'd by Edwin L. Reinhold.

A-22 - THIS INDENTURE - 5 May 1739 - James Hamilton of the city of Philadelphia Esq. to Peter Good of Lancaster Co., yeoman, 250A for £163 13/, 2d. This is by virtue of bargain and sale for 1 year. Land located on east side of Pequea Creek in Lancaster Co., neighbors - William Sherralds, and Samuel Boyers. Hamilton received land from the proprieties who received land by patent on 9 Feb 1733, who in turn by indenture dated 14 June 1737 granted same land to Hamilton. The quit rent accruing for the land is subject to payment of Mortgage money with which the land is charged by virtue of an indenture of mortgage made by Septimus Robinson to the trustees of the General Loan Office ... James Hamilton ... Signed in the presence of Septimus Robinson and John Webbe ... Ack'd 5 May 1739 by John Wright ... Rec'd by Edwin L. Reinhold.

A-23 - THIS INDENTURE - 24 Feb 1738 - Michael Baughman of Manheim Township in
Lancaster Co., yeoman, Katherine wife to Abraham Stoner of Warwick Township,
Lancaster Co., blacksmith, 200A for £120. Land is located in Conestoga Township,
neighbors - Michael Baughman, and Abraham Heer. Land is part of a larger tract granted
to Michael by the proprietors on 20 Feb 1738. ... Michael Bachman, Kathrine Bachman
... Signed in the presence of Corneluis Verhulst, Roger Dyer (X) and John Taylor ...
Received of Abraham £120, unsigned ... Ack'd no date Thomas Cookson ... Rec'd 10
Mar 1740/1 by Edwin L. Reinhold.

A-25 - THIS INDENTURE - 6 Dec 1740 - Joseph Shippen Jr. of the city of Philadelphia,
merchant, (one of the sons of Joseph Shippen, who was one of the sons-in-law of Ester
Shippen, late of Philadelphia, widow dec'd) and Mary wife to Michael Shank of Lancaster
Co., yeoman. William Penn Esq. by indenture of 27 Sept 1681 granted to Charles Jones
the elder and Charles Jones the Younger, then of the city of Bristol, soap boilers, 2,000A
in PA. Charles Jones the younger departed this life without making any partition of the
premises. The whole vested in Charles Jones the Edler by right of survivorship who by
indenture dated 4 Nov 1711 granted 2,000 unto Esther Shippen with her husband, Edward
Shippen dec'd, grandfather of said Joseph Shippen. The whole vested in Ester by right of
survivorship. In Ester's will dated 4 Aug 1724, she devised; concerning the residue of
2,000A (over and besides 540A in will specified), unto Edward and Joseph Shippen, sons
of hers, son-in-law Joseph Shipppen of Philadelphia merchant and to Margaret Shippen
daughter of her son-in-law, Edward Shippen dec'd to divided among them equally. If
Edward and Joseph should die under age and unmarried the land goes to William their
brother. Shares equal 460 & 2/3A a piece. Joseph Shippen Jr. and Mary wife to Michael
Shank, 94 2/3A for £35. Land located on a branch of the Conestoga Creek in Lancaster
Co., land Michael is now living on, indenture for one year ago by virtue of proprietary
warrant dated 20 May 1725, surveyed on 20 Oct 1733 to Joseph Shippen Jr. in part of a
486 2/3A tract ... Joseph Shippen, Mary Shippen ... Signed in the presence of Edward
Jones and Samuel Kearny ... Ack'd 23 Mar 1740/1 by William Allen Esq. ... Received
from Michael Shank £35, Joseph Shippen ... Rec'd 11 May 1741 by Edward L.
Reinhold.

A-27 - THIS INDENTURE of mortgage - 22 Nov 1740 - James Musgrove of Sadsbury
Township, Lancaster Co., yeoman and Hannah wife to Daniel McConnell of Lancaster
Co., yeoman, 92A for £35. James is moving, land is located in Sadsbury Township,
neighbor William Smith. Quit rent, subject to a mortgage of £90 payable by indenture
bearing a date of 16 Nov 1739. Mortgage left is £53 ... James Musgrove, Hannah
Musgrove ... Witness and sealed in presence of Samuel Lightfoot, and Ben Lightfoot ...
Ack'd 25 Mar 1741 Samuel Blunston ... Rec'd 12 May 1741 Edwin L. Reinhold.

A-29 - THIS INDENTURE - 6 Dec 1740 - Joseph Shippen Jr. of Philadelphia, merchant
(one of the sons of Joseph Shippen, who was one of the sons-in-law of Ester Shippen, late
of Philadelphia, widow, dec'd) and Mary his wife to Oswalf Hostater of Lancaster Co.,
yeoman. William Penn Esq. proprietary of the Province of PA did by indenture dated 27
Sept 1681 grant unto Charles Jones the elder and Charles Jones the younger then of city of

5

Bristol, soapboilers, 2,000A. Charles the younger died without making partition of the premises, where as the land was vested in Charles elder by right of surivivorship who by indenture on 4 Nov 1711 granted the 2,000A to Ester Shippen with her husband Edward Shippen, grandfather of said Joseph Shippen. Edward Shippen, grandfather also departed this life, all land was vested in Ester by right of survivorship. Her will dated 4 Aug 1724 - concerning all the rest and residue of 2,000A (over and besides 540A in will specified) I devise unto Edward and Joseph sons of her, son-in-law Joseph Shippen of Philadelphia, merchant. Also to Margaret Shippen daughter of her son-in-law, Edward Shippen dec'd and to their heirs and assigns forever, to be equally divided amongst them. If Edward and Joseph should die under age and unmarried then their shares are to go to William Shippen their brother - Edward, Joseph, and Margaret are married and of age and have made partition of the land in shares of 486 2/3A's. Warrant for Joseph Jr. dated 20 May 1725 and surveyed on 20 Oct 1733 as part of his share. Joseph Shippen Jr. and Mary to Oswald Hostater, £35 for 100A. Land Oswald is now in possession of by indenture of lease dated 1 year ago. Land is located on a branch of the Conestoga Creek in Lancaster Co., neighbor Michael Shanks ... Joseph Shippen, Margaret Shippen ... Witness in the presence of Edward Jones, Samuel Kearny ... Ack'd 23 Mar 1740/41 by William Allen Esq. ... Received of Oswald Hostater £35, Joseph Shippen ... Rec'd 11 May 1741 Edwin L.Reinhold.

A-31 - THIS INDENTURE - 31 Dec 1739 - Andrew Hamilton Esq. of the city of Philadelphia to Michael Baughman of Lancaster Co. yeoman, £1,000 for 1,500A, enfeoff. Land already in Michael's possession by indenture dated 1 year before. Land is located in the Manor of Conestoga. Land was first granted to Andrew Hamilton by patent dated 13 Dec 1735. Land is subject of quiet rent of 1/ for 100A also sum of 6d paid to Andrew Hamilton on 10 April annually forever. ... Pr. Andrew Hamilton ... Signed in the presence of James Steel and James Sanders ... Received of Michael Boughman £1,000, Andrew Hamilton ... Witness James Steel and James Sanders ... Ack'd 13 Jan 1739 by Thomas Edwards ... Rec'd 9 Dec 1741 Edwin L. Reinhold.

A-32 - THIS INDENTURE - 24 Feb 1738 - Michael Baughman of Manheim Township, Lancaster Co. yeoman, and Katherine wife to Abraham Stoner of Warwick Township, Lancaster Co., blacksmith, £120 for 200A. Land now in Abrahams possession by indenture dated 1 year earlier. Land is located in the Manor of Conestoga, neighbor Michael Baughman and Abraham Heer. ... Michael Bachman, Katherine Bachman ... Sealed in presence of Cornelius Verhulst, Roger Dyer (X), and Jno Taylor ... Ack'd 17 Dec 1739 by Thomas Cookson ... Rec'd 11 Dec 1741 Edwin L Reinhold.

A-34 - THIS INDENTURE - 1 Jun 1741 - Martin Wypreight of Lancaster Co., blacksmith, and Margaret wife to Emanuel Carpenter Esq. and Sebastian Groffe of Lancaster Co., shopkeepers, £133 13/ for 275A. Land is located on Conestoga Creek - neighbor - Fredrick Oihleberger, Jacob Stoner, Benjamin Webbe. Land was granted to Margaret Wypreight by patent dated 11 Dec 1739 and recorded in Bk A, Vol 10, pg 153. ... Martin Weybrecht, Margaret (X) Weybrecht ... Ack'd by Thomas Cookson, no date ... Received 1 Jun 1741 £130, Martin Weybrecht ... Witness M. Byerly ... Rec'd 14 Dec 1741 Emanuel Carpenter ... Full satisfaction 8 Dec 1763, Eve Groffe, Jno Hopson.

A-35 - THIS INDENTURE - 18 Jan 1739 - Hans Henry Neff of Lancaster Co., physician, and Franca wife to Sebastian Groffee of Lancaster Co., shopkeeper, £250 for 150A. Land is in the possession of Sebastian by indenture. Land is located on the west side of Conestoga Creek, neighbor - Henry Funk. The land is part of a larger tract of 5,553A belonging to Tobias Collet, Daniel Quare, and Henry Goldney, which they conveyed 300A of tract to Hans Henry Neff by lease and release dated 13 & 14 Mar 1722. The 5,553A tract was granted to Tobias, Daniel, Henry, and heirs of Michael Russell by patent under hands of Richard Hill, Isaac Norris, and James Logan on 25 Jan 1718, recorded in Bk A, vol 5, pg 306. ... Henrieus Neff, Franca (F) Neff ... Witness and signed in the presence of Jacob Beyerley, Frantz Neff, and Abraham Neff ... Ack'd 24 Jan 1738/9 by Thomas Cookson ... Rec'd 18 Dec 1741 Edwin L. Reinholder.

A-37 - TO ALL PEOPLE - no date - Andrew Hamilton, Jeremiah Langhorne, Richard Hayes, trustees of the General Loan Office of PA Greetings - John Ross of Donegal Township in Lancaster Co., yeoman by his indenture dated 27 Apr 1734 for £69 paid by Andrew Hamilton, Charles Read, Jeremiah Langhorne, Richard Hayes and John Wright pursuant to direction of an Act of General Assembly entitled Act for Remitting, sold 230A located on Susquehanna River. Whereas John Ross did not pay the sum of £69, the land was sold to Thomas Ewing of Lancaster Co. yeoman at Margaret Wilkins house on 22 Mar 1738, who was the highest bidder, £175 ... Andrew Hamilton, Jeremiah Langhorne, Richard Hayes ... Signed in the presence of Joseph Breintnall, and John Webb ... Ack'd 7 May 1738 by John Wright ... Rec'd 25 Dec 1741 Edwin L. Reihold.

A-38 - THIS INDENTURE - 20 May 1749 - John Middleton of Donegal Township, Lancaster Co., yeoman (eldest son of Robert Middleson, late of Donegal Township, yeoman, dec'd who was the eldest brother of George Middleston of Martic Township also dec'd) to George Gibson of the Lancaster borough, tavernkeeper 83A for £140 George Middleston during his life and at death was seized with 200A on Pequea Creek. He died leaving a widow, but no children, widow died soon afterwards. He received the land by patent from Thomas Penn Esq. on 3 May 1740, recorded in Bk A, Vol 10, pg 134. He also had another tract in Martic Township adjoining the other track containing 83A. ... John Middleton ... Signed in the presence of George Smith, Gordon Howard, and Isaac Whitelock ... Received of George Gibson £140, John Middlton ... Witness: George Smith, and Isaac Whitelock ... Ack'd by Thomas Cookson, no date ... Rec'd 22 May 1749 Edwin L. Reinhold.

A-39 - THIS INDENTURE - 2 Nov 1748 - Thomas Cox of Manchester Township Lancaster Co. yeoman and Mary wife to Joshua Low and Caleb Low of Manchester Township, £225 for 186A, enfeoff. Land located in Manchester, part of an Island on the west side of Susquehanna, neighbor - James Logan Esq. Land was granted to Thomas Cox by Thomas and Richard Penn Esq. by patent under the hand of the honorable Anthony Palmer Esq., President of the council, dated 19 Sept 1748, recorded in Bk A, Vol 14, pg 73 on 20 Sept last. ... Thomas Cox, Mary Cox ... Signed in the presence of Christian Crawl and Jacob __ ... Ack'd 8 Jun 1749 by George Swoope ... Received £225, Thomas Cox ... Rec'd 17 Jun 1749 Edwin L. Reinhold.

A-40 - THIS INDENTURE of mortgage - 28 Apr 1749 - Elizabeth Cadoogan widow of Thomas Cadoogan dec'd of Nantmeal Township in Chester Co. to John Potts Esq. of Colebrook, Dale Township, Philadelphia Co., 47/ & 2d for 103 A. Land located in Robinson Township, Lancaster Co. ... Elizabeth (E) Cadoogan ... Signed and sealed in the presence of David Evans, and George Taylor ... Ack'd 23 May 1749 by Thomas Cookson Esq. ... Rec'd 24 May 1749 Edwin L. Reinhold.

A-41 - THIS INDENTURE of mortgage - 16 May 1749 - James Johnson of Drumore Township in Lancaster Co., yeoman to Thomas Falkner of Salisbury Township in Lancaster Co., yeoman, £800 for 280 3/4A. James is bound unto Thomas Falkner in the sum of £800. To better secure payment and in consideration of the further sum of 5/ grants 3 tracts. First tract is located in Salisbury Township and contains 100A, neighbors - Thomas Falkner was Ezakiel Harlan, and William Jones. Second tract is also located in Salisbury Township and contains 100 3/4A, neighbors - Francis Jones, Samuel Garrette, Aaron Jackson, and Christian Griffitts. Third tract contains 80A no location no neighbors. Conditions for repayment of £400 on 16 May 1750 are as follows - £100 on 16 May 1751, £100 on 16 May 1752, and £100 on 16 May 1753. ... James Johnson ... Signed in the presence of Thomas Edwards, and James Whitehall ... Sealed and delivered by Calvin Cooper, and Andrew Moore ... Ack'd no date James Whitthill Esq. ... Rec'd 25 May 1749 Edwin L. Reinhold.

A-42 - THIS INDENTURE of mortgage - 1 Apr 1749 - Christopher Shope of Cocalico Township in Lancaster Co., yeoman, and Susanna wife to John Ruble of Bethlehem Township in Bucks Co., yeoman, £319 for 220A. Land is located in Cocalico Township, neighbors - George Hedgis, Peter Hollars, Conrad Miller, and William Bird. Land granted to John Ruble by George Thomas Esq., Lieutenant Governor on 28 Oct 1746, then by several conveyances came to be vested in Christopher Shope by fee and patent recorded in Bk A, Vol 13, pg 145. ... Christopher Shop ... Sealed and delivered by Peter Harter and John Renshaw ... Ack'd by Thomas Cookson Esq. 3 Apr 1749 ... Received from Christopher Shope full satisfaction of mortgage, Johannes Rubel ... Rec'd 9 May 1758 Edwin L. Reinhold.

A-44 - THIS INDENTURE - 26 Apr 1749 - Joseph Steer of Lampeter Township in Lancaster Co., yeoman, and Grace his wife to William Evans, James Webb, and John Kirk, of Lampeter Township, yeomen, 5/ for 1A, enfeoff. Land located in Lempeter Township and is part of a tract of 200A. Joseph Steer lives on the tract and was granted land by patent. (no date, or book) ... Joseph Steer, Grace Steer ... Sealed and delivered by John Evans and James Evans ... No ack'd ... Rec'd 27 May 1749 Edwin L. Reinhold.

A-45 - THIS INDENTURE - 25 Apr 1749 - John McNabb of Lampeter Township in Lancaster Co., yeoman, _____ wife to William Evans, James Webb, and John Kirk of same, yeomen, 5/ for 2A, enfeoff. Land located in Lampeter Township, 1/2A of the 2A is near the first tract. Land is part of a larger tract of 200A granted by patent to William McNabb late of Lampeter Township, yeoman, dec'd and father of John McNabb, dated 5 Mar

1735, rec'd Bk A, Vol 7, pg __. William McNabb by will dated 11 Mar, now last past devised 200A to John McNabb. ... John McNabb ... Sealed and delivered by John Evans, and James Evans ... No ack'd ... Rec'd 28 May 1749 Edwin L. Reinhold.

A-47 - THIS INDENTURE of mortgage - 6 May 1749 - Daniel Hister of Upper Sulford in Philadelphia Co., tanner, and Katherine his wife to William Bingham of the city of Philadelphia, merchant, £1,000 for 500A. Daniel is bound unto William Bingham in the sum of £1,000. To better secure payment and in consideration of the further sum of 5/ grants 500A. Land is located on Tulpehocken Creek in Lancaster Co., neighbors - none mentioned. William Binghamn and wife Mary by indenture to Daniel dated 5 May 1749. Terms for repayment of £500 with interest in portions, £100 on 1 Oct next, £124 on 1 Oct. 1750, £118 on 1 Oct 1751, £112 on 1 Oct 1752, £106 on 1 Oct 1753. ... Daniel Hister, Katharine Hister ... Sealed in presence of James Brown and John Reily ... Ack'd and release of dower by Thomas Greene Esq. 6 May 1749 ... Satisfaction of Mortgage ack'd before Thomas Greene ... Rec'd 21 Jun 1749 Edwin L. Reinhold.

A-48 - THIS INDENTURE - 8 May 1749 - Emanuel Herman of Lampeter Township in Lancaster Co., yeoman and Mary wife to Daniel Herman the younger of Lampeter Township, yeoman, £350 for 146A. Land located in Lampeter Township, neighbors - William Evans, Jacob Tenlingers, and Daniel Hermans. Land was acquired by 2 deeds, one between Daniel Herman the elder, Mary wife and Emanuel Herman, dated 15 Feb 1739. The other tract between Daniel Herman the younger and Emanuel Herman dated 18 Jan 1749, conveyed to Emanuel in fee and recorded in Bk B, pgs 585&589. ... Emanual (EH) Heiman, Mary (X) Heiman ... Sealed and delivered in the presence of Thomas Cookson and John Renchaw ... Ack'd no date Thomas Cookson ... Rec'd 20 Jun 1749 Edwin L. Reinhold.

A-50 - THIS INDENTURE - 11 Jul 1748 - George Hoofman, of Lancaster Borough, Lancaster Co., sadler, and Mary Magadlena wife to Jacob Hoover, of Lancaster Borough, yeoman, £260 for lot in Lancaster Borough, enfeoff release. Land is now in the possession of Solomon Hirm Bonn and is located on the south side of Kings St., neighbor - Daniel Cohon, and Jacob Hoofman of George Hoofman. ... George Hoffman, Mary Magdaline (X) Hoffman ... Sealed in the presence of Peter Worral and David Stout ... Ack'd 8 May 1749 by Thomas Cookson ... Rec'd 23 Jun 1749 Edwin L. Reinhold.

A-51 - THIS INDENTURE - 9 Jul 1748 - George Hoofman of the Lancaster Borough, Lancaster Co., sadler and Mary Magdalena wife to Jacob Hoover of same, yeoman, £350 for a lot in Lancaster Borough. This lot is where George Hoofman now lives and is located on the south side of Kings St. Neighbors - Soloman Hirm Bonn, Joseph Simons. ... George Hoffman, Mary Magdalena (X) Hoofman ... Sealed in the presence of Peter Worrall, and David Stout ... Ack'd 8 May 1749 by Thomas Cookson Esq. ... Rec'd 23 Jun 1749 by Edwin L. Reinhold.

A-52 - TO ALL PEOPLE - 10 Dec 1742 - John Bumbarger son of Christian Bumbarger late of Warwick township in Lancaster Co., yeoman, dec'd, John Coffman and Ann his wife, John Bowman and Margaret his wife, Christian Hersha and Barbara his wife, Martin

Bouher and Elizabeth his wife. (the said Ann, Margaret, Barbara, and Elizabeth being daughters of Christian Bumbarger, dec'd) By the last will and testament of Christian Bumbarger dated 30 Jan 1741/42 did bequeath to his son Christian Bumbarger the plantation and tract of land where he lived containing about 246A. It is to be appraised and he is to get no more than one equal share with the rest of the children. Neighbors - John Bumbarger, Martin Boohers. For the purpose of preventing any disputes that might arise about the boundaries, Christian Bumbarger Jr. paid 5/ to John Bumbarger, John Coffman and Ann his wife, John Bowman and Margaret his wife, Christian Hersha and Barbara his wife, Martin Bouher and Elizabeth his wife. They have released quit claim. ... John (JB) Bumbarger, John Coffman, Ann (A) Coffman, John Bowman, Margaret (X) Bowman, Christian Hersha, Barbara Hersha, Martin Bouher, Elizabeth (L) Bouher ... Sealed in the presence of Alexandar McCollough, and Henry Rode ... Ack'd 3 May 1749 by Emanuel Carpenter .. Rec'd 24 Jun 1749 Edwin L. Reinhold.

A-54 - 10 Dec 1742 - TO ALL PEOPLE - John Bumbarger and Christian Bumbarger sons of Christian Bumbarger, late of Warwick Township in Lancaster Co., yeoman dec'd, John Coffman and Ann his wife, John Bowman, and Margaret his wife, Christian Hersha and Barbara his wife. (said Ann, Margaret, and Barbara being daughters of Christian Bumbarger dec'd) Whereas Christian Bumbarger by his will dated 13 Jan 1741/42 gave to Martin Bouher of Warwick Township a tract of land: "I give and bequeath to my son-in-law Martin Bouher who married my daughter Elizabeth all that tract of land where he now lives containing 160A." The land is part of a greater tract of 551A. When Martin's land was marked off from the larger tract it contains 113A. To prevent disputes about the boundaries, 5/ is paid by Martin Bouher to John Bumbarger, Christian Bumbarger Jr., John Coffman and Ann his wife, John Bowman and Margaret his wife, Christian Hersha and Barbara his wife. They have released quit claimed. ... Christian Hersha, Barbara (B) Bumbarger, John Bumbarger, Christian Bumbarger, John Coffman, Ann ( ) Coffman, John Bowman, Margaret Bowman ... Sealed in the presence of Alexandar McCullough and Henry Rode ... Ack'd 3 May 1749 by Emanuel Carpenter ... Rec'd 24 Jun 1749 Edwin L. Reinhold.

A-55 - 10 Dec 1742 - TO ALL PEOPLE - Christian Bumbarger Jr., (son of Christian Bumbarger, late of Warwick Township, yeoman dec'd) John Coffman and Ann his wife, John Bowman and Margaret his wife, Christian Hersha and Barbara his wife, Martin Bouher and Elizabeth his wife. (Ann, Margaret, Barbara, and Elizabeth are daughters of Christian Bumbarger dec'd) Whereas Christian Bumbarger by last will dated 30 Jan 1741/42 did bequeath to son John a tract in Warwick Township, part of a greater tract, land which he now lives on containing 189A. Neighbors - John Kingry. To prevent any boundary disputes, for the sum of 5/, Christian Bumbarger Jr., John Coffman, and Ann his wife, John Bowman and Margaret his wife, Christian Hersha and Barbara his wife, Martin Bouher and Elizabeth his wife have released quit claim. ... Christian Hersha, Barbara (B) Hersha, Martin Bouher, Elizabeth Bouher, Christian Bumbarger, John Coffman, Ann Coffman, John Bowman, Margaret (X) Bowman ... Signed in the presence of Alexandar McCullough, and Henry Rohdy ... Ack'd 3 May 1749 by Emanuel Carpenter ... Rec'd 26 Jan 1749 Edwin L. Reinhold.

A-56 - THIS INDENTURE of mortgage - 27 Jun 1749 - George Croghan, of Lancaster, merchant, to Richard Peters of the city of Philadelphia Esq., £1,000 for 629A. George is bound unto Richard Peters in the sum of £2,000. Condition for payment of £1,000 with interest on 26 Jul next ensuing. George to better secure payment and in consideration of the further sum of 5/ grants 4 tracts. First - 354A, all land on Conodoguinet Creek in Pennsboro Township, neighbor - John Law. Patent on 17 Oct 1744 and recorded in Philadelphia in Bk A, Vol 12, pg 197, granted in fee to William Walker of Lancaster who sold by indenture on 7 Oct 1745 to William Trout of Lancaster, merchant and George Croghan. William conveyed his share to George on 4 Jul 1746. Second - 171A located in Pennsboro, neighbors - William Walker, James Silvers. Patented on 19 Apr 1740, recorded in Philadelphia Bk A, vol 12, pg 370, granted in fee to George Croghan. Third - 104A located on Conodogwainas Creek in Pennsboro, neighbor - John Scott, __ Robb, Joseph Thompson. Patented 25 Jun 1748 and recorded in Philadelphia Bk A, Vol 14, pg 323, granted to George Croghan. Fourth - 200A located in Hopewell Township in Lancaster Co., neighbor - Michael Killpatrick. Patented 23 Jan 1749 to George Croghan. ... George Croghan ... Sealed in the presence of John Callahan, and William Hamilton ... Ack'd 27 Jun 1749 by John Kinsey Esq. ... Rec'd 30 Jun 1749 Thomas Cookson.

A-59 - THIS INDENTURE of mortgage - 12 Nov 1748 - Patrick McCamish of Marple in Chester Co., mason, and Ann his wife to Thomas Stamper of the city of Philadelphia, mariner, £125 for 321A. Where as McCamish by obligation is bound to Stamper for £250. Condition for payment of £125 on 12 Nov 1749. Patrick and Ann to better secure payment and in consideration of the further sum of 5/ grant 321A located on Conococheague Creek in Lancaster Co., neighbor - Robert Black. ... Patrick McCamish, Ann McCamish ... Sealed in the presence of Samuel Rhoade, and Robert Levers ... Ack'd 17 Nov 1745 by John Kinsey Esq. ... Satisfaction ack'd on this mortgage ... Rec'd 10 Jul 1749 Thomas Cookson.

A-60 - THIS INDENTURE of mortgage - No date - I, James Silver of Lancaster Co., yeoman, whereas by indenture of mortgage dated 17 Aug 1744, I did grant unto Richard Peters of Philadelphia Esq. 530A located in Pennsboro Township, neighbor James Laws. Land was patented to me 12 May 1743 in fee and recorded in Bk A, Vol 12, pg 1. Land redeemable on payment of £300 and interest on a certain day long past. I, James Silver have borrowed from Richard £100 more for which I have executed a bond bearing equal date herewith penalty of £200. Condition for payment to Richard of £100 on 17 Jun next. In consideration of the further bond of £100 lent me by Richard, that all said tract of 530 A in the indenture of mortgage shall stand as security for payment of this bond as well as first bond. Payment of £400 due 17 Jun next. ... James Silver ... Sealed in the presence of William Peters, and John Callahan ... Ack'd 7 Jun 1749 George Croghan Esq. ... I hereby ack'd satisfaction on this mortgage 19 Jun 1750, Richard Peters ... Ack'd no date Thomas Cookson ... Rec'd none.

A-61 - THIS INDENTURE - 1 Jun 1749 - Melchor Snyder of Lancaster Co., yeoman, Margaret his wife to Lodovick Trucka Miller Lancaster Co., yeoman, £160 for 150A, enfeoff release. Melchor and Margaret are moving. Land is located on Conestoga Creek in Lancaster, neighbor - Leonard Pendals. Melchor received land by indenture dated 26

May now last past from Jacob Miller, yeoman and Agnes his wife. Granted and released by fee, recorded Bk __. ... Melchor Snyder, Margaret Snyder ... Sealed in the presence of Thomas Cookson, and John Renshaw ... Received £160 of Lodovick Trucka Miller, Melchor Snyder ... Signed in the presence of John Renshaw ... Ack'd no date Thomas Cookson Esq. ... Rec'd 4 Jul 1749 Edwin L. Reinhold.

A-63 - THIS INDENTURE - 14 Jun 1746 - Charles Cookson of Lancaster Co., yeoman to Daniel Cookson Lancaster Co., yeoman, £280 for 230A. Land located in Sadsbury Township in Lancaster Co., neighbor - Joseph Jervis, William Clark. Land was granted to Charles on 11 Dec 1745 by Samuel Smith formerly Sheriff of Lancaster and John Kinsey, Thomas Chandler, and John Wright, trustees of the General loan office. ... Charles Cookson ... Sealed in the presence of Thomas Cookson, John Renshaw ... Received £280 from Daniel Cookson, Charles Cookson ... Witness: Thomas Cookson, and John Renshaw ... Ack'd no date Thomas Cookson Esq. ... Rec'd 11 Jul 1749 Edwin L. Reinhold.

A-65 - THIS INDENTURE - 10 Apr 1749 - James Patterson of Donegal Township Lancaster Co., yeoman, and Mary wife to Lazarus Lowry of Donegal Township, yeoman, £190 for 152A, enfeoff. James and Mary are moving. Land located in Donegal Township, neighbors - William Michael, James Logan, and James Harris. This is the same land James Logan and wife Sarah did grant to Peter Haig by indenture dated 16 May 1747. Peter and wife Elizabeth granted to James Lowry by indenture dated 17 May 1748. James by indenture of lease and release, lease date 9 Sept, release date 10 Sept now last past, sold land to James Patterson in fee. ... James Patterson, Mary Patterson ... Sealed in the presence of Thomas Cookson and Robert Thompson ... Received from Lazarus Lowry the sum of £190, James Patterson ... Ack'd no date Thomas Cookson Esq. ... Rec'd 12 Jul 1749 Edwin L. Reinhold.

A-66 - THIS INDENTURE - 24 Jun 1749 - Christian Hean of Heidelberg Township, Lancaster Co., yeoman, Peter Hean of Heidelberg, yeoman, Adam Hean of Heidelberg yeoman, George Hean of Heidelberg yeoman, Frederick Hean of Heidelberg, yeoman, Henry Hean of Heidelberg yeoman, they being sons of George Hean late of Heidelburg Township yeoman, dec'd. Jacob Frymeir of Cumru Township in Lancaster Co., yeoman and Anna Sibilla his wife, William Fisher of Heidelberg Township, yeoman and Elizabeth his wife, Anna and Elizabeth being the daughters of said George Hean dec'd to Caspar Hean of Heidelberg yeoman, another son of George Hean dec'd. George died intestate, by law eldest son gets double share. Brothers and sisters are entitled to 1 undivided tenth part of land and premises. The brothers and sisters, and husbands for the sum of 5/ a piece have sold unto Casper their parts in the division of their fathers land. Land is located in Heidelberg Township and contains 102A. The tract is part of a larger tract of 227 1/2A which was patented to George, now dec'd, 10 Nov 1741 and recorded in Philadelphia in Bk A, vol 10, pg 343. ...Christian Hean, Peter Hean, Adam Hean, George Hean, Frederick Hean, Henry Hean, Jacob Frymier, Anna Sibilla Frymier, William Fisher (no signature for Elizabeth, she is listed in the acknowledgment) ... Ack'd 24 Jun 1747 Conrad Weiser ... Rec'd 13 Jul 1749 Edwin L. Reinhold.

A-68 - THIS INDENTURE - 24 Jun 1747 - Christian Hean of Heidelberg Township Lancaster Co., yeoman, Peter Hean of Heidelberg yeoman, George Hean of Heidelberg yeoman, Frederick Hean of Heidelberg yeoman, Henry Hean of Heidelberg yeoman and Caspar Hean of Heidelberg yeoman, they being the sons of George Hean dec'd, Jacob Frymeir of CumruTownship yeoman and Anna Sibilla his wife, William Fisher of Heidelberg Township yeoman and Elizabeth his wife, Anna and Elizabeth being daughters of George Hean dec'd to Adam Hean of Heidelberg yeoman another son of George Hean dec'd. George died intestate leaving issue only to said Christian the oldest. Oldest son gets double share. Children are entitled to 9 full equal and undivided tenth parts. Christian, Peter, George, Frederick, Henry, Caspar, Jacob Frymeir, and Anna his wife, William Fisher and Elizabeth his wife for the sum of 5/ a piece have sold their shares to Adam Hean. Land located in Heidelberg Township and contains 200A, neighbor - William Allen. Land is part of a 400A tract which was patented 26 Nov 1735 to George Hean dec'd, and recorded in Philadelphia in Bk A, vol 7, pg 341. ... Christian Hean, Peter Hean, George Hean, Frederick Hean, Henry Hean, Caspar Hean, Jacob Frymeir, Anna Sibilla Frymeir, William Fisher, Elizabeth Fisher ... Sealed in the presence of James Quin and Conrad Weiser ... Ack'd 24 Jun 1747 Conrad Weiser ... Rec'd 13 Jul 1749 Edwin L. Reinhold.

A-70 - THIS INDENTURE - 24 Jun 1747 - Christian Hean of Heidelberg Township, Lancaster Co., yeoman, Peter Hean of Heidelberg, yeoman, Adam Hean of Heidelberg, yeoman, George Hean of Heidelberg, yeoman, Frederick Hean of Heidelberg, yeoman and Caspar Hean of Heidelberg, yeoman, all sons of George Hean late of Heidelberg Township yeoman dec'd, Jacob Frymeir of Cumru Township yeoman, and Anna Sibilla his wife, William Fisher of Heidelberg yeoman and Elizabeth his wife, Anna and Elizabeth being daughters of George Hean dec'd, to Henry Hean of Heidelberg also a son of George Hean dec'd, 5/ for all of their 9 full equal parts in the land left by their father, 162A, neighbor - William Allen. Land is part of a 292A tract patented to George Hean dec'd on 2 Sept 1742 and recorded in Bk A, vol 10, pg 177. ... Christian Hean, Peter Hean, Adam Hean, Caspar Hean, Jacob Frymeir, Anna Sibilla Frymeir, William Fisher, Elizabeth Fisher ... Ack'd 24 Jan 1747 Conrad Weiser ... Rec'd 14 Jul 1749 no name.

A-72 - THIS INDENTURE - 10 Oct 1740 - Michael Schmell of Heidelberg Township yeoman to William Fisher, same, 2 1/2A for £5. Land is located on a branch of Tulpehocken Creek and is part of 203A patent granted to John Jones on 12 Jul 1736 and recorded in Philadelphia in Bk A, vol , pg . John sold to Michael Schmell on 10 Oct 1740. ... Michael Schmell ... Ack'd no date Conrad Weisner Esq. ... Rec'd 14 Jul 1749 no name.

THIS INDENTURE - 24 Jun 1747 - Christian Hean of Heidelberg Township, Lancaster Co., yeoman, Peter Hean of Heidelberg, yeoman, Adam Hean of Heidelberg, yeoman, George Hean of Heidelberg, yeoman, Frederick Hean of Heidelberg, yeoman, Henry Hean of Heidelberg, yeoman, Caspar Hean Heidelberg, yeoman, all sons of George Hean late of Heidelberg Township dec'd, Jacob Frymeir of Cumru Township Lancaster Co., yeoman, and Anna Sibilla his wife, Anna being a daughter of George Hean dec'd, to William Fisher of Heidelberg Township yeoman and Elizabeth his wife, Elizabeth being a daughter of George Hean dec'd. George Hean died intestate leaving above children. William and

Elizabeth have paid 5/ for 130A, the other children's 9 full equal and undivided tenths parts of the land. Land is located on the 3 Creeks in Heidelberg Township, and is part of a 292A tract patented to George Hean dec'd on 2 Sept 1742 and recorded in Bk A, vol 10, pg 477. ... Christian Hean, Peter Hean, Adam Hean, George Hean, Frederick Hean, Henry Hean, Casper Hean, ___, Anna Sibilla Frymeir ... Ack'd 24 Jun 1747 Conrad Weiser ... Rec'd 14 Jul 1749 Edwin L. Reinhold.

A-74 - THIS INDENTURE - 21 Mar 1748 - Christian Hean of Heidelberg Township Lancaster Co., yeoman, and Mary Barbara his wife to William Fisher Heidelberg yeoman £500 for 50A, enfeoff release. Christian is firmly bound unto William by obligation dated 24 Jun 1747 in the sum of £500 The condition is as such that Christian and wife, for 5/, and at the request of William Fisher convey and assure unto William all the land situated near the Western Branch of Cacoosing Creek containing 50A. The land is part of a tract containing 200A that was granted to George Hean dec'd by patent dated 26 Nov 1735 and recorded in Philadelphia in Bk A, vol 7, pg 341. It was conveyed to Christian by the heirs of the dec'd by indenture dated 24 Jun 1747. ... Christian Hean, Mary Barbara Hean ... Sealed in the presence of Peter Wim and Valentine Smith ... Ack'd 21 Apr 1749 Conrad Weiser ... Rec'd 15 Jul 1749 Edwin L. Reinhold.

A-76 - THIS INDENTURE - 25 Mar 1748 - Caspar Hain of Heidelberg Township Lancaster Co., yeoman to William Fisher of Heidelberg, 5/ for 74A. Casper moving. Land is located in Heidelberg Township, neighbor - George Hain, and William Fisher. Land was patented 18 Feb 1747 and recorded in Bk A, vol 13, pg 344, 20 Feb 1747/8. ... Casper Hean (his mark) ... Sealed and delivered by Francis Reynolds, and Conrad Weiser ... Ack'd 25 Mar 1748 by Conrad Weiser ... Rec'd 17 Jul 1749 Edwin L. Reinhold.

A-77 - THIS INDENTURE - 10 Nov 1747 - Joseph Brinton Esq. of Thornbury Township Chester Co., to James Brinton of Leacock Township in Lancaster Co., James is son of Joseph. Richard Hill, Isaac Norris, James Logan, Thomas Griffitts, Commissioners of Property of Province of PA and counties of New Castle, Kent, Sussex, and attorneys of Josha Gee of the city of London, Silkman Thomas Oad of city of Bristol and John Wood of the city of London merchant, surviving mortgagees and Trustees of said Province and Counties by a grant or patent under the hand of Isaac Norris, James Logan, Thomas Griffitts dated 23 Oct 1728 did grant to Joseph Brinton 650A. Land is located on Mill Creek then reputed to be in Chester Co., but since division has been found to be in Lancaster Co., neighbor - Elizabeth Whartnaby. Patent recorded in Bk A, vol 6, pg 109. Joseph Brinton for the natural love and affection he bears for his son James Brinton gives to him the land located in Lecock Township, Lancaster Co. containing 200A, enfeoff. ... Joseph Brinton ... Sealed in the presence of John Brinton, and Mary Elgar ... Ack'd 1 Nov 1748 Thomas Cookson ... Rec'd 17 Jul 1749 Edwin L. Reinhold.

A-79 - THIS INDENTURE - 14 May 1748 - Michael Reis of Bethel Township Lancaster Co., wheelwright and Margaret his wife to George Miller of Heidelberg Township Lancaster Co., yeoman, £425 for 440A enfeoff release. Land is now in George's possession and is located in Bethel Township, neighbor - Thomas Freame dec'd, Rudolph Meirs, and Henry Smith. Land was patented to Michael in fee on 4 Mar 1742 and

14

recorded in Philadelphia in Bk A, vol 11, pg 105. Yearly quit rent is 1/ per 100A. ...
Michael Reis, Margaret (X) Reis ... Sealed in the presence of William Parsons, and
Phillip Weiser ... Received of George Miller £425, Michael Reis ... Ack'd 14 May 1748
Conrad Weiser ... Rec'd 18 Jul 1749 Edwin L. Reinhold.

A-80 - THIS INDENTURE - 22 May 1749 - Henry White of Rapho Township Lancaster
Co., yeoman and Johanna his wife to Jacob Heistand of Hempfield Township Lancaster
Co., yeoman, £250 for 131A enfeoff release. Land is located in Donegal Township.
Henry and Johanna moving, neighbors - Hugh White dec'd and Moses White. Land was
patented to Henry White on 10 Jun 1741 and recorded in Bk A, vol 10, pg 315. ... Henry
White, Johanna S. (X) White ... Sealed in the presence of John Ferry and R. John
Renshaw ... Received from Jacob Heistand £250, Henry White ... Ack'd 22 May 1749
Thomas Cookson ... Rec'd 18 Jul 1749 Edwin L. Reinhold.

A-82 - THIS INDENTURE - 11 Jul 1749 - John Snevely of Manheim Township
Lancaster Co., yeoman and Frena his wife to Ann Snevely of Manheim Township, spinster
and sister of John Snevely. Whereas John Snevely late of Manheim Township aforesaid
yeoman dec'd died intestate leaving issue the above John and Ana Snevely. At his death
John had 2 plantations and tracts of land located in Manheim Township containing 613A
by 2 patents. John made application to Orphans Court 10 Jul in Lancaster praying that a
person appraise the value of the land for the purpose of being vested in one payment. Ann
pursued an Act for Better Settling Estates causing Michael Baughman, Martin Cryder,
Henry Neff and Michael Carver to be chosen to appraise and value the land. They
appraised its value to be £2,000. Ann's share is £666, 13/ & 4d. John Snevely gave
sufficient security to Ann, the whole of the tracts and premises were vested in said John.
John has paid £666 13/, & 4d for 300A, enfeoff release. John shall provide and maintain
for Anna, his mother and widow of dec'd during her life in exchange for her dower,
neighbors - Robert Ears, and John Coghanouis ... John Snevely, Frena (F) Snevely ...
Sealed and delivered in the presence of John Renshaw, Thomas Cookson, Frena Snevely,
Michael Baughman, and Ulrick Springer ... Ack'd 2 Aug 1749 Thomas Cookson Esq. ...
Rec'd 2 Aug 1749 Edwin L. Reinhold.

A-84 - THIS INDENTURE - 24 Aug 1745 - John Gilcrest of Little Brittian in Lancaster
Co., to William Gilcrest, son of John, of Little Brittian, £80 for 150A, enfeoff release.
Land is part of a 300A tract, no location, neighbor - Henry Reynolds. In the year 1704 by
warrant a tract called Miloom Island on the west side of Octoraro Creek was surveyed for
1,000A by virtue of the original grant made by the Governor William Penn unto John
Wilmer who conveyed the same unto Randal Jonny who in turn conveyed unto John Budd
and Sarah Murry. John and Sarah being dissatisfied with the location and survey of the
land did in 1745 resign to the proprietors who granted them like quantity of land in County
of Philadelphia. Part of the land was surveyed unto Elisha Gatche Esq. for 600A, who
sometime after assigned a moiety (half) unto Henry Reynolds. The division being by
mutual satisfaction they obtained a warrant on 13 Apr 1737. Elisha Gatchett Sr. obtained a
deed bearing the date 8 Jul 1737 signed by Thomas Penn Esq. by virtue granted by John
and Richard Penn. For the sum of £46 10/, paid by Elisha for yearly quit rents the said
300A was sure and confirmed to him. Elisha Gatchet and Rachel his wife sell 300A for

£165 to John Gilcrest. ... John Gilcrest ... Sealed and delivered in the presence of Elisha Gatchett, and John Cartrill ... Ack'd 4 Jul 1749 by James Gillespie ... Rec'd 26 Jul 1749 Edwin L. Reinhold.

A-85 - THIS INDENTURE of mortgage - 15 Jul 1749 - Hans Zimmerman otherwise called John Carpenter of Cocalico Township Lancaster Co., yeoman to Casper Wister of the city of Philadelphia, merchant, £268 15/ & 5d for 900A. Hans by certain obligation is bound to Casper in the sum of £537 10/ & 10d. Payable by 14 Jul 1749. Hans for the debt of £268 15/ & 5d and for better securing payment and in consideration of the further sum of 5/ grants 900A in Cocalico Township. Neighbors - Woolrick Carpenter and Peter Buckers. Land is also subject to payment of £400 payable to Israel Pamberton of the city of Philadelphia, merchant, by indenture dated 17 May 1748 and recorded in Bk B, pg 518. ... Hans Zimmerman ... Signed in the presence of ___ (blank) ... Ack'd no date Thomas Cookson ... Rec'd 26 Jul 1749 Edwin L Reinhold.

A-87 - THIS INDENTURE of mortgage - 31 Jul 1749 - Melchor Fortinee of Lancaster Borough Lancaster Co., butcher to Casper Wister of the city of Philadelphia merchant, £177 for lot in Lancaster Township. Melchor is bound unto Casper in the penal sum of £354. Condition for payment of £177 on 31 Jul 1749. Melchor in consideration of the debt and for better securing payment and the further consideration of 5/ does release a lot located in the town of Lancaster on King St. Neighbors - formally Roger Hunt now Andreas Beverly, formally Herman Updegraeff now Sebastian Greaffe. The lot was granted to Frederick Elverset by James Hamilton on 24 Nov 1736, then by several conveyances became vested in Melchor Fortinee. ... Melchor Fortinee ... Sealed in the presence of Thomas Cookson, and John Renshaw ... Ack'd by no date Thomas Cookson ... Rec'd 26 Jul 1749 no name.

31 May 1793 - I, Bartholomew Wiester acting executor of the last will of Catherine Wiester dec'd who was executrix of her late husband Casper Wiestar, dec'd: I can not find any bond to show that this was unsatisfied, must have been paid off during Caspers lifetime. ... B. Wiester

A-88 - THIS INDENTURE - 16 Mar 1748/9 - William White late of Cecill Co., but now of the Township of Nottingham in Chester Co., cordwainer to Roger Kirk of Nottingham Township, weaver, £30 for 111A, enfeoff release. Land is located in the Township of Little Brittain in Lancaster Co., neighbors - John Crumptons, James Morris and John Scott. The land was granted to William on 13 Mar 1748/9 and recorded in Bk A. vol 14, pg 163. ... William White ... Sealed in the presence of Timothy Kirk, Elisha Hughes and Elizabeth Mitchell ... Received of Roger Kirk £30, William White ... Ack'd 7 May 1749 by Elisha Gatchell ... Rec'd 22 Aug 1749 Edwin L. Reinhold.

A-89 - THIS INDENTURE - 3 Mar 1749 - Michael Baughman the elder of Manheim Township Lancaster Co., yeoman and Catherine his wife to Michael Baughman the younger and Peter Whitmore both of Manheim Township, yeomen, 5/, love and affection for 311A, enfeoff release. Michael and Catherine for the love and affection for their son John and for settling the lands and for the further sum of 5/ paid by Michael the younger

16

and Peter Whitmore, grant 311A, enfeoff release. Land is located in Lebanon Township in Lancaster Co., neighbor - Michael Baughman the elder. Land is for the use of John Baughman, son during his natural life. Michael Baughman, Catherine (KB) Baughman ... Sealed in the presence of Thomas Cookson, and Samuel Gifford ... Ack'd and release of dower by Thomas Cookson no date ... Rec'd no name 24 Aug 1749.

A-91 - THIS INDENTURE - 21 Mar 1749 - Michael Baughman of Manheim Township in Lancaster Co., yeoman, and Katherine his wife to Elizabeth Baughman, daughter. Michael and Katherine for the natural love and affection for their daughter Elizabeth and for her advancement in the world, along with 5/ paid by Christian Baughman and John Baughman, sons of Michael, they grant 200A enfeoff release. The land is located on a branch of Conestoga Creek. The land was granted to Michael on 10 Jun 1734 and recorded in Bk A, vol 6, pg 405. The land is for the use of Elizabeth Baughman during her natural life. ... Michael Baughman, Katherine (KB) Baughman ... Sealed in the presence of Thomas Cookson and Samuel Gifford ... Ack'd and release of dower by Thomas Cookson no date ... Rec'd 25 Aug 1749 no name.

A- 93 - THIS INDENTURE - 1 Jun 1749 - Michael Baughman of Manheim Township of Lancaster Co., yeoman and Katherine his wife to Maudeline, their daughter, 5/, love and affection for 449A. Michael and Katherine for the love and affection they bear for their daughter, Maudeline and for her further advancement in the world, along with 5/ paid by John Baughman and Christian Baughman, sons, grant 449A, enfeoff release. Land is located on a branch of the Conestoga called Middle Creek. Land was patented to Michael 7 Dec 1739 and recorded in Bk A, vol 9, pg 219. This is a special trust for the use of Maudeline during her natural life. ... Michael Baughman, Katherine (KB) Baughman ... Sealed in the presence of Thomas Cookson and Samuel Gifford ... Ack'd and release of dower by Thomas Cookson no date ... Rec'd 26 Aug 1749 Edwin L. Reinhold.

A-94 - THIS INDENTURE - 1 Jun 1749 - Michael Baugham of Manheim Township in Lancaster Co., yeoman and Katherine his wife to Frena Baughman, their daughter, 5/, love and affection for 267A. Michael and Katherine for the love and affection they bear for their daughter, and for her further advancement in the world, along with the further consideration of 5/ paid by John Baughman and Christian Baughman, sons, grant 267A, enfeoff release. Land is located in Lebanon Township in Lancaster Co., neighbors - John Baughman, Balthazar Vats, Michael Baughman. This is a special trust for Frena during her natural life. ... Michael Baughman, Katherine (KB) Baughman ... Sealed in the presence of Thomas Cookson, and Samuel Gifford ... Ack'd and release of dower by Thomas Cookson no date ... Rec'd 29 Aug 1749 Edwin L. Reinhold.

A-96 - THIS INDENTURE - 7 Aug 1749 - James Mitchell of Donegal Township in Lancaster Co., yeoman, (one of the sons of James Mitchell late of Donegal Township dec'd) to Henry Musselman of Hempfield Township, Lancaster Co., yeoman, £270 for 150A, enfeoff release. James is moving. James Mitchell dec'd, at the time of his death was seized in fee with a certain tract of land, 300A in Donegal Township. Patented to him on 14 Mar 1742 and recorded in Bk A, vol 11, pg _. In James's will dated 17 Feb 1746/7, he made John Noble and Nathaniel Little executors, he also bequeathed to his son James

17

150A which is part of the 300A tract. Neighbors - John Stewart, Nathaniel Little, John Galbreaths, and Thomas Mitchell. ... James Mitchell ... Sealed in the presence of Samuel Gifford and John Renshaw ... Received from Henry Musselman £270, James Mitchell ... Signed in the presence of Samuel Gifford and John Renshaw ... Ack'd by Thomas Cookson no date ... Rec'd 30 Aug 1749 Edwin L. Reinhold.

A-98 - THIS INDENTURE - 1 May 1749 - Joseph Cruncleton the elder of Antrim Township in Lancaster Co., yeoman, and Mary his wife to Joseph Cruncleton the younger of Antrim Township, one of the sons of Joseph Sr., 5/, love and affection for 234A. Joseph and Mary for the love and affection they bear for their son and for the further consideration of 5/ grant 234A, enfeoff release. Land is part of a larger tract of 469A located in Antrim Township. Neighbors - Jacob Snevely, and George Gibson ... Joseph Cruncleton, Mary Cruncleton ... Signed and sealed in the presence of John Dotter and John Cruncleton ... Ack'd and release of dower by Samuel Smith no date ... Rec'd 31 Aug 1749 Edwin L. Reinhold.

A-100 - THIS INDENTURE - 1 May 1749 - Joseph Cruncleton of the Antrim Township, Lancaster Co., yeoman and Mary his wife to John Cruncleton, same, son of Joseph and Mary, 5/, love and affection for 234A. Joseph and Mary for the love and affection they bear for their son John and for the further consideration of 5/ grant 234A, enfeoff release. Land is located in Antrim Township and part of a larger tract containing 469A. Land was granted to Joseph 14 Aug 1741. Neighbors - George Gibson, Jacob Snevely. ... Joseph Cruncleton, Mary (H) Cruncleton ... Sealed in the presence of John Potter, and Joseph Cruncleton ... Ack'd by Samuel Smith no date ... Rec'd 2 Sept 1749 by Edwin L. Reinhold.

A-101 - THIS INDENTURE - 8 Sept 1749 - John Lowry of Donegal Township in Lancaster Co., and Elizabeth his wife to Joseph Symons of Lancaster Borough in Lancaster Co., shopkeeper, £250 for 288A, enfeoff release. John received the land from his father Lazarus Lowry by gift deed dated 16 Sept 1747. Lazarus received land by grant on 6 Aug 1744 and recorded in Bk A, vol 11, pg 514 on 3 Jul 1745. ... John Lowry, Elizabeth Lowry ... Signed in the presence of Thomas Cookson and John Galbreath ... Ack'd 11 Sept 1749 Thomas Cookson ... Rec'd 11 Jun 1749 Edwin L. Reinhold.

A-103 - THIS INDENTURE of mortgage - 5 Sept 1749 - George Charles Meyer of Lancaster Borough, Lancaster Co., joiner and Barbara his wife to George Coalrider of Sadsbury Township yeoman, £86 19/, and 9d for a lot located on King St. George and Barbara are moving. Neighbor - Casper Persinger. Lot is under subject to payment of £32 interest on 12 Aug, now last past between George and Barbara and Michael Grouse, shopkeeper. Conditions for payment are as follows - £20 on 1 May next, £20 on 1 May 1751, £20 on 1 May 1752, £26 19/ and 9d the residue on 1 May 1753. ... Charles Meyer, Barbara (X) Meyer ... Sealed in the presence of Adam Simon Kuhn, and John Renshaw ... Ack'd 9 Sept 1749 by Conrad Haltsbaum ... Rec'd Thomas Cookson no date ... Satisfaction of mortgage on 13 Jun 1752, Conrad Haltsbaum.

A-105 - THIS INDENTURE of mortgage - 1 May 1749 - Henry Walter of Cocalico Township of Lancaster Co., yeoman to John Carpenter alias Hans Zimmerman of Cocalico Township, yeoman, £170 for 136 1/2A. Henry is bound unto John in the amount of £340. Condition for payment is £170 on 1 May next. Henry to better secure payment and for the further consideration of 5/ grants 136 1/2A. Land is located in Cocalico Township, neighbors - Peter Shoemaker and Ulrick Ily. ... Henry Walter ... Sealed in the presence of Thomas Cookson, and John Renshaw ... Ack'd Oct 1749 by Thomas Cookson ... Rec'd 25 Oct 1749 Edwin L. Reinhold ... Satisfaction of mortgage on 30 Jan 1753, Hans Zimmerman.

A-107 - THIS INDENTURE of mortgage - 11 Nov 1749 - John Balthazar Pidser (alias Beitzer) of Earl Township in Lancaster Co., yeoman to Patrick Baird of the city of Philadelphia, gentleman, £150 for 128 1/2A. John is bound to Patrick in the sum of £300. Condition for payment of £150 on 11 Sept 1750. To better secure his debt and in consideration of the further sum of 5/ grants 128 1/2A in Earl Township, neighbors - Evan Davids, John Mucklewain, and Michael Ranks. ... John Balthazar Pidser ... Sealed and delivered in the presence of C. Brockden and Paul Isaac Voto ... Ack'd 11 Sept 1749 Thomas Greene Esq. ... Rec'd 8 Nov 1749 Edwin L. Reinhold.

A-108 - THIS INDENTURE - 7 Sept 1748 - Maria Katherine Ensmonger of Lancaster Co., widow to Jacob Hershberger of Lancaster Co., yeoman, £300 for 200A. Whereas Sylvester Goldney, now late of Chippenham in Wills Co., in England, relict of Adam Goldney late of Chippenham gentleman dec'd, Adam Goldney and Henry Goldney of same gentlemen and sons of Adam Goldney dec'd, Mary Goldney, Jane Goldney, Sarah Goldney, Ann Goldney, daughters of Adam dec'd by their indenture of lease and release dated 15 & 16 of Apr 1737, they did grant unto Jane, wife of Joseph Hoskins, by name of Jane Fenn 1,500A. The land is contained in 3 tracts in Lancaster and Chester Co., by virtue of several warrants dated 22 Mar 1733/4 recorded 6 Apr 1734. Joseph and Jane did convey to Jacob Beyerly of Lancaster Co., 200A which is located in Lancaster Co. and is one of the tracts mentioned above and granted to Jane, now wife of Joseph Hoskins. Jacob Beyerly and his wife Maria Rosina sold the last mentioned tract to Maria Katharine Ensmonger. ... Marie Katherine Ensmonger ... Sealed and delivered in the presence of Michael (MM) Moyer and George Smith ... Received of Jacob Hersberger £300, Marie Katherine Ensmonger ... Ack'd 7 Sept 1740 Emanuel Carpenter ... Rec'd 1 Dec 1749 Edwin L. Reinhold.

A-111 - THIS INDENTURE of mortgage - 23 Nov 1749 - Hans Zimmerman of Lancaster Co., yeoman to Patrick Baird of the city of Philadelphia, £150 for 278A. Hans is bound to Patrick in the sum of £300. Condition for payment of £150 on 27 Nov 1750. Hans in consideration of the aforesaid debt, to better secure payment, and in consideration of the further sum of 5/ grants 6 tracts totaling 278A. The land is located in Cocalico Township - First tract contains 42A, second tract contains 20A, third tract contains 50A, neighbors - Peter Carpenter and Samuel Harnis. Fourth tract contains 25A, fifth tract contains 22A, neighbor Ulrick Carpenter, Sixth tract contains 119A, neighbor - Peter Brickers. Hans received the land by patent dated 20 May 1740 and recorded in Bk A, vol 13, pg 408. ... Hans Zimmerman ... Sealed and delivered in the presence of William

Peters, and James Biddle ... Ack'd by Thomas Cookson no date ... Rec'd 15 Dec 1749 Edwin L. Reinhold.

A-113 - THIS INDENTURE of mortgage - 23 Nov 1749 - Hans Zimmerman of Lancaster Co., yeoman to William Allen Esq. of the city of Philadelphia, £400 for 467A. Hans is bound unto William Allen in the amount of £800. Condition for payment of £400, on 22 Nov 1750. Hans to better secure his debt and in consideration of the further sum of 5/ grants 2 tracts. The first tract contains 150A and is located in Earl Township, Lancaster Co., neighbors - Edward Edwards, Thomas Edwards, Nicholas Redson. The second tract contains 317A and is located in Carnarvon Township, Lancaster Co., neighbors - Edward Edwards, Nicholas Redson, William Hazlette, Hugh Davis, and Morgan Evans. ... Hans Zimmerman ... Sealed and delivered in the presence of William Peters and Alexandar Stuart ... Received of William Allen £400, Hans Zimmerman ... Signed in presence of William Peters, and Alexandar Stuart ... Ack'd 24 Nov 1749 - Thomas Cookson ... Rec'd 16 Dec 1749 Edwin L Reinhold.

A-115 - THIS INDENTURE of mortgage - 5 Dec 1749 - Abraham Bear of Leacock Township, Lancaster Co., yeoman and Frany his wife to Patrick Carigan, £200 for 210A. Abraham is bound unto Patrick in the sum of £400. Abraham and Frany to better secure payment and in consideration of the further sum of 5/ grants 2 tracts in Leacock Township. The first contains 113A, neighbors - Casper Walters, John Johnson, and Henry Carpenter. The second contains 97A, neighbors - Henry Carpenter, and Casper Walters. Condition for repayment of £200 is as follows - £12 on 5 Dec 1750, £12 & £200 on 5 Dec 1751. ... Abraham Bear, Frany (F) Bare ... Sealed and delivered in the presence of Thomas Cookson and Thomas Dayl ... Ack'd and release of dower by Thomas Cookson 18 Dec 1749 ... We, John Wilson and Margaret Wilson, late Margaret Carrigan, administrators of the estate of Patrick Carrigan have received full satisfaction, 15 Feb 1769, John Wilson, Margaret Wilson ... Ack'd Edwin Shippen no date.

A-116 - THIS INDENTURE - 9 Dec 1749 - William Evans Sr. of Lampeter Township in Lancaster Co., yeoman to William Evans Jr. of Lampeter Township, yeoman. (one of the sons to William Evans Sr.) William Sr. for the love and affection he bears for his son as well as for the sum of £20 paid to him by William Jr., he grants 150A. The land is located in Lampeter Township and is part of a tract of 1,000A granted to William Evans Sr. by John Moore by indenture dated 4 Sept 1730 and recorded in Philadelphia in Bk F, vol 5. pg 437. ... William Evans ... Sealed and delivered in the presence of James Webb and Arthur Forster ... Received of William Jr. £20, William Evans Sr. ... Witness - James Webb and Arthur Forster ... Ack'd 19 Dec 1749 - Thomas Cookson ... Rec'd 12 Dec 1749 Edwin L. Reinhold.

A-118 - THIS INDENTURE - 9 Dec 1749 - William Evans of Lampeter Township, Lancaster Co., yeoman to John Evans of Lampeter Township, one of the sons of William Evans. William for the love and affection he bears for his son John and for the sum of £20, he grants 150A. The land is located in Lampeter Township and is part of a tract of 1,000A granted to William by John Moore by indenture on 4 Sept 1730 and recorded in Bk F, vol 5, pg 437. ... William Evans ... Sealed and delivered in the presence of James

Webb and Arthur Forster ... Ack'd 19 Dec 1749 Thomas Cookson Esq. ... Rec'd 22 Dec 1749 Edwin L. Reinhold.

A-119 THIS INDENTURE of mortgage - 6 May 1749 - James Lennox of Norrington Township, Lancaster Co., yeoman to Joseph Parker of the Borough of Chester, Chester Co., yeoman, £150 for 235A. Land is located on a branch of Beaver Creek, on the west side of the Susquehanna River in Lancaster Co. James is to pay to Joseph the sum of £150 by 6 May 1751 and £150 by 6 May 1752. ... James Lennox ... Sealed and delivered in the presence of Daniel Calvert, James McCandles, and Henry Graham ... Ack'd 31 Jul 1749 Matthew Dyll Esq. ... Rec'd 22 Dec 1749 Edwin L. Reinhold.

A-120 - THIS INDENTURE - 10 May 1748/9 - Reverend Adam Boyd, Thomas Clark, both of Chester Co., yeomen and executors of the will of William Clark late of Lancaster Co., yeoman dec'd, to William Clark of Lancaster Co., yeoman and eldest son of William Clark dec'd, 200A. On 16 Oct 1715 there was surveyed to William Clark, the father 350A on Pequea Creek in Sadsbury Township, neighbor - Joseph Jarvis. William died leaving his will dated 17 Sept 1732 in which he devised the tract to and for the use of his widow and children. The will did appoint his brother Thomas Clark and Adam Boyd executors. By a patent dated 22 May 1744 the widow received full satisfaction for her interest. Now all or most of the children are of age and want division to be made of the tract according to the direction of their fathers will. Warrant was issued to Thomas Clark and Adam Boyd dated 27 May 1743 and patent was granted for 350A so executors could make division of the land amongst the children. Patent is recorded in Bk A, vol 11, pg 360. William Clark, son was given 200A, the part of the tract where Robert McClure formally lived. Neighbors - late of Joseph Jervis now James Whithill, Hugh Jenkins, Robert Mosser and Andrew Campbell. Part of the tract was allotted to Prisellia Clark, Sarah Clark, and Esther Clark, sisters of William, amounting to 211A. The Presbyterian Congregation of Pequea received 2A for a meeting house and burying ground. ... Thomas Clark, Adam Boyd ... Sealed and delivered in the presence of John Miller and Abigs Miller ... Ack'd 10 Mar 1748/9 James Whithill ... Rec'd 23 Dec 1749 Edwin L. Reinhold. (widow is not named)

A-123 - THIS INDENTURE of mortgage - 12 Aug 1749 - George Charles Mayer of Lancaster Borough the, Lancaster Co., joiner and Barbara his wife to Michael Grouse of Lancaster Borough, merchant, £32 for lot on King St. in Lancaster Borough. George is bound unto Michael Grouse in the sum of £62. Condition for payment of £32 before 12 Feb 1750. George and Barbara in order to better secure the payment and in consideration of the further sum of 5/ grants a tenement and half a lot lying in Lancaster Borough on King St. Neighbors - Caspar Persinger, George Apleman. Lot was granted to Grabriel Imble and by several conveyances came to George. Yearly rent of 3/ & 6d. ... Charles Myer, Barbara (Q) Myer ... Sealed and delivered in the presence of John Jones and John Renshaw ... Ack'd 29 Oct 1749 Thomas Cookson ... Rec'd 6 Feb 1749 Edwin L. Reinhold ... Satisfaction received 9 Jun 1752, Thomas Cookson.

A-126 - TO ALL PEOPLE - 12 Feb 1741 - Catherine Hickinbottom of Lancaster Township, Lancaster Co., widow of Thomas Hickinbottom, during Thomas's life he contracted for a lot on Queen St. in Lancaster Township. On this lot he built a house.

Thomas died before lease or the conveyance was made. He left only one child named Lucy. After his death Catherine was granted administratrix and paid debts and took title from James Hamilton for the lot on Queen St. Neighbors - Caspar Lochman, and Martin Harness. Lease dated 12 May 1735. For the love and affection I bear for my daughter Lucy, I give the lot located on Queen St. ... Catherine (O) Hickenbottom ... Sealed and delivered in the presence of Samuel Blunston, Sarah Blunston, Mary Patterson ... Ack'd 31 Jan 1749 Thomas Cookson ... Rec'd Edwin L. Reinhold (no date)

A-127 - THIS INDENTURE of mortgage - 11 Jan 1749 - Melchor Fortinee of Lancaster Borough. Lancaster Co., butcher and Barbara his wife to John Wister of the city of Philadelphia, shopkeeper, £600 for 10A. Melchor is bound unto John in the sum of £1,200. Condition for payment of £600 by 11 Jan 1750. Melchor and Barbara to better secure payment and in consideration of the further sum of 5/ grant 10A located in Lancaster Township. Neighbors - Rhoday Myer, James Hamilton Esq., and Peter Worralls. One moiety (a half, or a share) granted to Melchor Fortinee by one Michael Fortinee by indenture dated 10 Mar 1748 and the other moiety by Francis Fortinee by indenture dated 14 Feb 1748. Also a lot on King St., this is the same lot which James Hamilton by indenture dated 24 Nov 1736 granted to Frederick Elverset, who in turn granted on 25 Nov 1736 to Sebastian Graffe. Sebastian granted it to Melchor Fortinee on 16 Mar 1745. Neighbors - late of Roger Hunt now Andrew Bierly, late of Herman Updegraeff now Sebastian Graff. ... Melchor Fortinee, Anna Barbara Fortinee ... The words "Barbara his wife" being first underlined through out, Sealed and delivered in the presence of Henry Keppely, and Martin Brand ... Ack'd and release of dower by Emanuel Carpenter 87 Feb 1749 ... Rec'd 9 Feb 1749, no name ... Satisfaction ack'd of £100 on 8 Feb 1751, John Wister ... Satisfaction ack'd £100. 9 May 1751 John Wister ... Full satisfaction ack'd 6 Feb 1763, John Wistar.

A-128 - THIS INDENTURE - 14 May 1748 - Hans Good of Lancaster Township, Lancaster Co., yeoman to Patrick Carrigan gentleman, £300 for 200A, enfeoff release. Land is located in Leacock Township. Of the 200A, 125A of it is part of a larger tract granted to Hans on 16 Oct 1740. The other 75A is part of another large tract granted to Hans 25 Jun 1748. Neighbors - John Bares, John Stumps, and Hans Rudolph Negerly. ... Hans (HG) Good ... Sealed and delivered in the presence of Abraham Bear, and John Bear ... Ack'd 14 May 1748 by Emanuel Carpenter ... Rec'd 29 Mar 1750 Edwin L. Reinhold.

A-130 - THIS INDENTURE - 19 Dec 1747 - Hans Good of Leacock Township, Lancaster Co., yeoman to John Bear of Leacock Township, yeoman £350 for 239A, enfeoff release. Land is located in Leacock Township, neighbors - James Miller, Martin Myxell, widow Moyer, Jacob Good, and John Stump. Land is part of 2 tracts, first 225A tract granted to Hans on 16 Oct 1740 and recorded in Bk A, vol 9, pg 205. Second 216A granted to Hans on 25 Jan 1740 and recorded in Bk A, vol 9, pg 264. ... Hans (H) Good ... Sealed and delivered in the presence of Abraham Bear, and Hans Gerber ... Ack'd 19 Dec 1747 by Emanuel Carpenter ... Rec'd 15 May 1750 Edwin L. Reinhold.

A-132 - THIS INDENTURE - 23 Apr 1750 - Michael Byerle of Lancaster Borough, Lancaster Co., yeoman and Catherine his wife to Michael Fortinee of Lancaster Borough, Lancaster Co., butcher £30 for 5A. Land is located in Lancaster Township, neighbors - Michael Meyer. This land was first granted to Cornelius Vechulst by James Hamilton on 20 May 1735. Cornelius and Joanna his wife assigned their right and title to Michael Byerle in fee, no date. ... Michael Byerle, Catherine (X) Byerle ... Sealed and delivered in the presence of Thomas Cookson, and Arthur Forster ... Ack'd 25 Apr 1750 by Thomas Cookson ... Rec'd 14 May 1750 Edwin L. Reinhold.

A-133 - THIS INDENTURE of mortgage - 17 May 1749 - Benjamin Lightfoot of the city of Philadelphia, merchant to Peter Turner of the city of Philadelphia, merchant, £320 for 781A. Benjamin is bound to Peter in the amount of £640. Condition of payment is £320 on 17 Mar 1750/51. Benjamin in order to secure a better payment and in consideration of the further sum of 5/ grants 2 tracts. First is in Maiden Creek Township, Philadelphia Co. The tract contains 497A, neighbors - Nehemiah Hutton, Moses Starr, Robert Perrose, Joseph Wiley, Robert Jones and Richard Sundays. Land was granted to Benjamin on 18 Nov 1748 and recorded in Bk A, vol 15, pg 142. The second tract contains 284A and is in Bern Township, Lancaster Co., neighbors - Adolph Henry, Francis Pawin and Phillip Boyers. Benjamin received this land by patent dated 28 Feb 1749 and recorded in Bk A, vol 14, pg 392. ... Benjamin Lightfoot ... Sealed in the presence of C. Brockden, and John Simms ... Ack'd 17 Mar 1749/50 by John Kinsey ... Rec'd 22 Mar 1749\50 C. Brockden ... Cert'd deed was recorded 24 May 1750 Edwin L. Reinhold.

A-136 - THIS INDENTURE - 27 Jan 1749 - Ulrick Houser of Strasburg Township, Lancaster Co., yeoman and Frena his wife to Jacob Houser one of the sons of Ulrick, £350 for 150A. Land is located in Strasburg Township, neighbors - late of John Funk now Henry Haines, Christopher Franciscus, and Hans Weber. Land is part of a 500A tract granted to Johannes Rudlophus Bendelin on 13 Jun 1711 and recorded in Bk A, vol 4, pg 231. Johannes sold to Ulrick and Hans Weber by indenture dated 13 Oct 1717. Ulrick received 2 fifths equal parts and Hans 3 fifth parts, they in turn granted the land to John Wister on Oct 1740. John by indenture dated 13 Oct 1740 granted 245A unto Ulrick Houser. Ulrick and Hans by indenture dated 7 Nov 1720 granted 101A, part of Ulricks share of the 500A unto John Funk. The quantity of the land conveyed by John Wister to Ulrick should have been no more than 150A. ... Ulrick (UH) Houser, Frena (M) Houser ... Sealed and delivered in the presence of John Liman, and James Webb Jr. ... Received of Jacob Hauser £350, Ulrick (UH) Houser ... Ack'd and release of dower by James Webb Esq. 31 Mar 1750 ... Rec'd 25 May 1750 Edwin L. Reinhold.

A-138 - THIS INDENTURE - 13 Oct 1740 - John Wister of the city of Philadelphia, shopkeeper to Ulrick Hauser of Strasburg Lancaster Co., yeoman, £50 for 245A, enfeoff. Land is located in Strasburg Township, neighbors - John Funk, Christopher Franciscus, Hans Weber, and Isaac Lefevr. Part of the 245A tract, 200A was first granted to Johannes Rudolphus Bundelin by patent dated 13 Jun 1711 and recorded in Bk A, vol 4, pg 231. Johannes by indenture on 13 Oct 1717 granted to Ulrick Hauser and Hans Weber: 2 equal fifths parts to Ulrick and 3 equal fifth parts to Hans. They in turn granted by indenture Oct 1740 to John Wister. ... John Wister ... Sealed and delivered in the presence of Christian

Carpenter and Matthias Yung ... Received of Ulrick Hauser £50, John Wister ... Witness - Christian Carpenter and Matthias Yung ... Ack'd 6 Nov 1740 by Emanuel Carpenter ... Rec'd 25 May 1750 Edwin L. Reinhold.

A-139 - THIS INDENTURE - 31 Jul 1747 - Thomas Musgrove of Lampeter Township, Lancaster Co., yeoman and Hannah his wife to Abraham Whitmore of Lampeter Township, Lancaster Co., yeoman, £52 for 25A, enfeoff. Land is located in Lampeter Township and is part of a tract of 600A. When the tract was first granted it was located in Chester Co. on Conestoga Creek. It was granted to John Musgrove, by lease and release dated 13 Mar 1722, by Tobias Collet of London, haberdasher, Daniel Quare of London, watchmaker, Henry Goldney of London, linen draper, and the heirs of Michael Russell dec'd. The 600A is part of a tract containing 5,553A and was granted to said Collet, Quare, Goldney by William Penn among others on 25 Jun 1718 and recorded in Bk A, vol 5, pg 300. Of the 600A John granted 450A to Thomas Musgrove by lease and release dated 10 & 11 Oct 1740. ... Thomas Musgrove, Hannah Musgrove ... Sealed and delivered in the presence of Theophilus Owen and Abraham Musgrave ... Witness - Theophilus Owen and Abraham Musgrave 1 Jul 1747 ... Ack'd 5 Aug 1747 by Peter Worrall ... Rec'd 25 May 1750 Edwin L. Reinhold.

A-141 - THIS INDENTURE - 12 Aug 1746 - Benjamin Whitmore of Lancaster Co., yeoman to John Whitmore of Lancaster Co. and son of Benjamin, for love, affection and 5/ for 250A, enfeoff. Land is located in Lampeter Township, neighbors - formally Hans Snyder, late of Hans Graffe, and late of Jacob Landus. Land was granted to Benjamin by indenture of lease and release from Tobias Collet, Daniel Quare, and Henry Goldney on 13 & 14 Mar 1722. ... Benjamin (Z) Whitmore ... Sealed and delivered in the presence of Thomas Cookson ... Ack'd 11 May 1750 by Adam Simon Kuhn Esq. ... Rec'd 27 May 1750 Edwin L. Reinhold.

A-143 - THIS INDENTURE - 17 Apr 1750 - John Jones of Strasburg Township, Lancaster Co., yeoman and Elizabeth his wife to John Feiree of Strasburg Township, Lancaster Co., yeoman £825 for 195A. Land is lying in Strasburg Township, neighbors - late of Thomas Story, Isaac Lefever, and John Ferree. This is the same land that Thomas Falkner and Jane his wife granted to John Jones on 7 May 1745. It is part of 2 tracts received by Falkner containing 380A on 6 & 20 Dec 1744. Falkner received land from Daniel Feiree and Isaac Lefevre. It is part of a tract of 2,000A which they received from John, Thomas, and Richard Penn on 29 Oct 1734. ... John Jones, Elizabeth (B) Jones ... Sealed and delivered in the presence of William McCauslan, and Samuel Jones ... Received of John Ferrie £825, John Jones ... Ack'd and release of dower by James Whitehill on 20 Apr 1750 ... Rec'd 29 May 1750 Edwin L. Reinhold.

A-145 - THIS INDENTURE - 7 May 1745 - Thomas Falkner of Salisbury, Lancaster Co., yeoman and Jane his wife to John Jones of Strasburg, Lancaster Co., yeoman, £200 for 195A, enfeoff release. Land is located in Strasburg, neighbors - Thomas Story, Isaac Lefever, and John Ferree. This land is part of a tract of 380A granted to Falkner by Daniel Ferree and Isaac Lefevre dated 6 & 20 Dec 1744. The 380A is part of a larger tract of 2,000A that was granted to Daniel and Isaac by John, Thomas, and Richard Penn by patent dated 29 Oct 1734. ... Thomas (S) Farkner, Jane (F) Farkner ... Sealed and delivered in the presence of George Duffell, Robert Stockton, and James Whithill ... Ack'd 11 May 1745 by James Whitehill ... Rec'd 29 May 1750 Edwin L. Reinhold.

A-148 - THIS INDENTURE - 16 Jul 1733 - John Musgrave of Sadsbury Township, Lancaster Co., yeoman to Abraham Whitmore of Sadsbury Township, Lancaster Co., yeoman, £88 for 150A, enfeoff release. Land is located in Lancaster Co., neighbors - Jacob Landaus, and John Musgrave. Land is part of a tract containing 600A granted to John on the 13 & 14 Mar 1722 by Tobias Collet of London, haberdasher, Daniel Quare of London, watchmaker, Henry Gouldney of London, linen draper, and the heirs of Michael Russell dec'd. The 600A is part of a larger tract containing 5,553A and granted to the aforesaid by William Penn among others on 25 Jun 1718 and recorded in Bk A, vol 5, pg 306. ... John Musgrove ... Sealed and delivered in the presence of Samuel Irwin, Edward MacConnell, and Thomas Musgrave ... Ack'd 29 Oct 1742 Emanuel Carpenter ... Rec'd 31 May 1750 Edwin L. Reinhold.

A-150 - THIS INDENTURE - 14 Sept 1739 - John Funk of Orange Co. VA, yeoman to Henry Haines the younger of Lancaster Co., yeoman, £75 for 101A, enfeoff release. Land is located in Strasburg Township, neighbors - Isaac Lefevre, and Ulrick Houser. John received the 101A of land from Hance Webber and Barbara his wife on 7 Feb 1721. Land was part of a larger tract containing 500A. The 500A was conveyed to Hance Webber and Ulrick Houser on 13 Oct 1717, from John Rudloph Bundelin. John received the land from William Penn by patent under the hands of Edward Shippen, Griffth Owen and Thomas Story on 13 Jan 1711. ... John Funk ... Sealed and delivered in the presence of Michael (MM) Moyer, Leonard Lutz, and John Funk ... Received of Henry Haine £75 14 Sept 1739, John Funk ... Witness: John Funk and Thomas Cookson ... Ack'd 14 Sept 1739 Thomas Cookson ... Rec'd 1 Jun 1750 Edwin L. Reinhold.

A-152 - THIS INDENTURE - 7 Feb 1720 - Hance Webber of Strasburg Township, Chester Co., yeoman and Barbara his wife, Ulrick Houser of Strasburg Township, Chester Co., yeoman and Agnes his wife to John Funk of Strasburg Township, Chester Co., yeoman, £18 for 101A, enfeoff release. Land is located in Strasburg Township, neighbors - Isaac Lefeavers, formerly Vandalye Boman, now John Funk. The 101A is part of a larger tract of 500A granted to Hance and Ulrick by John Rudolph Bundelin on 30 Oct 1717 and recorded in Bk E-7, vol 10, pg 401. John received the tract from William Penn, proprietary by a certain patent under the hands of Edward Shippen, Griffith Owen and Thomas Story, gentlemen on 30 Jun 1711 and recorded in Bk A, vol 4, pg 231. Neighbors - Vendaylen Bowman, and Stoffal Franciscus. ... Hance (HW) Webber, Barbara (B) Webber, Ulrick (U) Houser, Agnes (C) Houser ... Sealed and delivered in the presence of Henry (HC) Carpenter, Henry (HW) Webber, and Edmund Cartlidge ... Ack'd 1 Oct 1733 Thomas Edwards ... Rec'd no date Edwin L. Reinhold.

A-155 - THIS INDENTURE - 1 Jun 1750 - William Morrison of Derry Township, Lancaster Co., yeoman and Margaret his wife to Jacob Stoner of Lebanon Township, Lancaster Co., yeoman and Barbara his wife, £310 for 157A. On 6 Dec 1742 John, Thomas, and Richard Penn granted to William 157A located in Derry Township. Deed is recorded in Bk A, vol 11, pg 5. neighbors - Thomas Wilson, Patrick Hayes, William Hayes, Charles Clark, and James Miller. ... William Morrison, Margaret (X) Morrison ... Sealed and delivered in the presence of Thomas Cookson and Arthur Forster ... Ack'd 1 Jun 1750 Thomas Cookson Esq. ... Received of Jacob Stoner £310, William Morrison ... Witness - Thomas Cookson, and Arthur Forster ... Rec'd 4 Jun 1759 Edwin L. Reinhold.

A-157 - THIS INDENTURE of mortgage - 1 Jun 1750 - Isaac Hall of Earl Township, Lancaster Co., yeoman to Patrick Carrigan of Leacock Township Lancaster Co., yeoman, £100 for 164A. Isaac is bound unto Patrick Carrigan in the sum of £200, condition for payment of £100 1 Jun 1751. Isaac to better secure payment and in consideration of 5/ from Patrick has granted 2 tracts totaling 164A. The first tract contains 100A and is located in Earl Township, neighbors - Andrew Mosmann, and Hance Graff. Second tract is also located in Earl Township and contains 64A, neighbor - John Adis. ... Isaac Hall ... Sealed and delivered in the presence of Thomas Cookson and Arthur Forster ... Ack'd 1 Jun 1750 Thomas Cookson ... Rec'd 4 Jun 1750 Edwin L. Reinhold.

A-159 - THIS INDENTURE of mortgage - 17 May 1750 - Hans Zimmerman, alias John Carpenter of Cocalico Township Lancaster Co., yeoman and Sallome his wife to Thomas Lawrence Esq., Peter Delage, and Andrew Read of the city of Philadelphia, merchants, Rachel Bowes widow and executors of Francis Bowes last will and testament late of the city of Philadelphia dec'd, £400 for 623A. Hans is bound unto the Thomas, Peter, Andrew, and Rachel in the sum of £800. To better secure payment of debt and in consideration of 5/ grants 2 tracts, containing 442A and 181A. Condition for payment of £400 on 16 May 1751. Hans was granted 2 tracts by patent on 8 Dec 1739 recorded in Bk A, vol 10, pg 155. They are located on branches of Cocalico Creek in Lancaster Co. The first tract contains 1,042 A, second contains 181A, neighbor - Ulrick Carpenter. Hans has since conveyed to his brother Peter a tract containing 600A, which was surveyed by Samuel Lighton. ... Hans Zimmerman ... Signed in the presence of Lewis Gordon and William Tea ... Sealed and delivered in the presence of Sollome Zimmerman, it being first declared by all parties that the sum of £400 is proper money and estate of Sarah Bowes, Mary Bowes, Esther Bowes and John Bowes, infants under 21 yrs and children of Francis Bowes ... Salome (Z) Zimmerman ... Signed in the presence of Martin (X) Datweiler, Conrad Weisner ... Received from Thomas Lavrena, Peter Delage, Andrew Read and Rachael Bowes, £400 ... Hans Zimmerman ... Signed in the presence of Lewis Gordon, and William Fea ... Ack'd 16 Jul 1750, no signature ... Rec'd 14 Aug 1750 Edwin L. Reinhold.

A-161 - THIS INDENTURE of mortgage - 15 Jun 1750 - Christian Stoner of Lampeter Township Lancaster Co., yeoman to Thomas Doyle of Lancaster Borough Lancaster Co., hatter, £200 for 163A. Christian is bound unto Thomas Doyle in the sum of £400. Condition for payment of £200 on 15 Jun 1751. Christian to better secure payment of debt and in consideration of the further sum of 5/ grants 2 tracts. Both tracts are located in Lampeter Township, first tract contains 110A, neighbor - Martin Kendrick. Second tract contains 53 A, neighbor - Christian Herr, Martin Kendrick and Martin Miley. ... Christian Stoner ... Sealed and delivered in the presence of Adam Simon Kuhn, and Arthur Forster ... Ack'd 15 Jun 1750 Adam Simon Kuhn Esq. ... Rec'd 14 Aug 1750 no name ... Received 27 Dec 1759 full satisfaction of mortgage, Thomas Doyle ... Witness - Edward Shippen.

A-163 - TO ALL PEOPLE - 26 Dec 1749 - Jacob Shelly of Lancaster Co., yeoman and Anna his wife, Hans Kugle of Lancaster Co., yeoman and Barbara his wife, Christian Shelly of Lancaster Co., yeoman and Magdalen his wife, Elizabeth Peelman and Eve Peelman both of Lancaster Co., spinsters. (they the said Anna, Barbara, Magdalen, Elizabeth and Eve being five of the children of Christian Peelman late of Manor Township Lancaster Co., yeoman dec'd) to Jacob Segrist, £500 for 219A. Christian Peelman in his lifetime received a patent on 13 Oct 1735, recorded in Bk A, vol 7, pg 313 for 2 tracts located in Manor Township. The first tract contains 200A, neighbor - John Whitmore. The second tract contains 19A and joins the first tract. Christian died intestate. Land descended unto his six children, Anna, Barbara, Magdalen, Elizabeth, Eve, and Mary being the oldest and now the wife of Jacob Segrist of Lancaster Co., yeoman. At orphans court held in Lancaster on 20 Dec 1749 before Edward Smout, Adam Simon Kuhn, and James Webb Esqs. justices, upon application of Jacob Segrist that he is willing to hold the same undivided land and pay the younger children their shares. All parties consented. Jacob Shelley, Benjamin Hersey, Michael Segrist, and Michael Baughman are appointed to appraise the 2 tracts. The tracts were appraised at £500. Each child receiving £83 & 8d. ... Jacob Shelly, Anna Shelly, Hans (HK) Kugle, Barbara (X) Kugle, Christian Shelly, Magdalene (X) Shelly ... Sealed and delivered in the presence of Christian Stoneman, Johannes Newcomeatt, and Jacob Niff ... Ack'd 26 Jul 1750 Thomas Cookson ... Release of dowers for Anna, Barbara, Magdalen, Elizabeth, and Eve Dec 1749, Anna, Barbara, and Magdalen being of full age, Thomas Cookson ... Rec'd 15 Aug 1750 Edwin L. Reinhold.

A-165 - THIS INDENTURE of mortgage - 1 May 1750 - Jacob Klyne of Lancaster Borough Lancaster Co., waggoner and Catherine his wife to Leonard Billmire of Lancaster Co., yeoman, £43 for a lot in Lancaster Township. The lot is located on King St., neighbor - Graft Reasor. Lot was first granted to Melchor Soliday on 14 Jan 1740. Melchor granted the lot to Jeremiah Milton on 4 Jun 1740. Jeremiah and Elizabeth his wife granted lot to Jacob Klyne on 20 Jun 1747. ... Jacob (H) Klyne, Catherina (C) Klyne ... Sealed and delivered in the presence of David Stout and Jacob Billmayer ... Ack'd 6 Aug 1750 Thomas Cookson ... Rec'd 15 Aug 1750 no name ... Received full satisfaction from Jacob Klyne, Leonard Billmayer ... Ack'd 5 Dec 1754 Edwin Shippen.

A-166 - THIS INDENTURE - 24 Jun 1747 - Christian Hean of Heidelberg Township Lancaster Co., Adam Hean of Heidelberg Township, yeoman, George Hean of Heidelberg Township, yeoman, Fredrick Hean of Heidelberg Township, yeoman, Henry Hean of Heidelberg Township yeoman, Casper Hean of Heidelberg Township, yeoman (they being the sons of George Hean late of Heidelberg Township, yeoman dec'd) Jacob Frymeir of Cumru Township Lancaster Co., yeoman and Anna Sibila his wife, and William Fisher of Heidelberg Township, yeoman and Elizabeth his wife (Anna Sibila and Elizabeth daughters of George Hean dec'd) to Peter Hean of Heidelberg Township, yeoman, the other son of George Hean dec'd, 5/ for 125 1/2A. George died intestate, Christian Hean being the oldest son receives double the share of land. The other children receive 9 full and

27

undivided 10th parts, neighbors - Ulrick Michael. The land is part of a 227 1/2A tract granted to George Hean on 10 Nov 1741 and recorded in Bk A, vol 10, pg 343. ... William Fisher, Elizabeth (X) Fisher, Jacob (I) Frymeir, Anna Siblila (T) Frymeir, Henry (HH) Hean, Casper (KH) Hean, Frederick (FH) Hean, Christian Hean, Adam (AH) Hean ... Ack'd 24 Jun 1747 Conrad Weiser ... Rec'd 15 Aug 1750 Edwin L. Reinhold.

A-169 - THIS INDENTURE of mortgage - 6 Aug 1750 - Philip Graber of Tulpehocken Township Lancaster Co., yeoman to Valentine Unruh of Tulpehocken Township, £99 17/ & 11d for 183A. Philip is bound unto Valentine in the sum of £199 15/, 10d. Condition of payment, on 6 Aug 1751. Philip in order to better secure payment and in consideration of 5/ grants 183A located on the north east branch of Swartara Creek in Lancaster Co. Neighbors - Barthol Deisinger, Christian Moyer, John Moyer, Mathes Dapeler, John Wolfant, George Brosius, and George Tollinger ... Philip Graber ... Sealed and delivered in the presence of Christian Daniel Claus, and Conrad Weiser ... Ack'd 6 Aug 1750 Conrad Weiser ... Rec'd 16 Aug 1750 Thomas Cookson ... Satisfaction received on mortgage 28 Mar 1752, Thomas Cookson.

A-170 - THIS INDENTURE of mortgage - 6 Aug 1750 - Martin Triester of Bethel Township in Lancaster Co., yeoman to George Tollinger of Tulpehocken Township, £82 12/ & 11d for 148A. Martin is bound unto George in the sum of £165 5/ & 10d. Condition for payment of £82 12/ & 11d on 6 Aug 1750. Martin in order to better secure payment and in consideration of 5/ doth grant 148A. Land is located on the north east branch of the Swartara Creek in Lancaster Co. Neighbors - Christopher Ulrich, Adam, Daniel, and Nicholas Simon, Sebastian Stone, and Michael Axah. ... Martin Triester ... Sealed and delivered in the presence of Christian Daniel Claus and Conrad Weiser ... Ack'd 6 Aug 1750 Conrad Weiser ... Rec'd 16 Aug 1750 Edwin L. Reinhold.

A-172 - THIS INDENTURE - 21 Jul 1749 - Joseph Steer of Lampeter Township in Lancaster Co., inn-holder to John James of Lampeter Township, cooper, 2 1/2A to farm. Land is near Mill Creek, neighbor - John McKnab. John is to pay £1 rent to Joseph yearly. John can not retail any Liquors and can not cut down any timber. ... Joseph Steer ... Witness - Francis McCulloch, Archibald Wilson, and Thomas Parker Jr. ... Ack'd 23 Apr 1750 James Smith ... Rec'd 16 Aug 1750 Edwin L. Reinhold.

A-174 - THIS INDENTURE - 14 Jul 1750 - Samuel Smith Sr. of Lancaster Co., yeoman to Samuel Smith Jr. of Lancaster Co., yeoman, £400 for 217A, enfeoff release. Land is located in Donegal Township, neighbors - Thomas Wilkins, Joseph Work, Thomas Bagley, Gordon Howard. Land was granted to Samuel Smith Sr. by patent dated 11 Jan 1738 and recorded in Bk A, vol 9, pg 61. ... Samuel (S) Smith ... Sealed and delivered in the presence of Peter Worrall, David Stout and Gordon Howard ... Ack'd 17 Aug 1750 Thomas Cookson ... Rec'd 17 Aug 1750 Edwin L. Reinhold.

A-176 - THIS INDENTURE of mortgage - 6 Aug 1750 - Barthol Deisinger of Tulpehocken Township in Lancaster Co., yeoman to Conrad Weiser of Heidelberg Township in Lancaster Co., Esq., 5/ for 200A. Barthol is bound unto Conrad in the amount of £190 19/ & 4d. Condition for payment of £95 9/ & 8d on 20 Aug 1750.

Barthol to better secure payment and in the consideration of the further sum of 5/ has granted 200A. Land is located on the north east branch of the Swartara Creek in Lancaster Co. Neighbors - Catherine Reed, Henry Boyer, George Dellingers, and Christian Moyer. ... Barthol Deisinger ... Sealed and delivered in the presence of Christian Daniel Claus, and George Doelinger ... Ack'd 8 Aug 1750 William Parsons Esq. ... Rec'd 17 Aug 1750 no name ... Received of Barthol Deisinger full satisfaction on mortgage, 7 Aug 1752, Conrad Weiser.

A-177 - THIS INDENTURE of mortgage - 6 Aug 1750 - Sebastian Stein, otherwise called Stone, of Bethel Township in Lancaster Co., yeoman to Conrad Weiser of Heidelberg Township, £79 2/ & 4d for 139A. Sebastian is bound unto Conrad in the amount of £158 4/ & 8d. Condition for payment of £79 2/ & 4d by 6 Aug 1751. Sebastian to better secure payment and in consideration of the further sum of 5/ does grant 139A. The land is located on the north east branch of Swartara Creek in Lancaster Co. Neighbors - Hans Adam Suntag, Nicholas Simon, Martin Shipe, and Adam Fisher. ... Sebastian Stein ... Sealed and delivered in the presence of Christian Daniel Claus, and George Dollinger ... Ack'd 8 Aug 1750 William Parsons ... Rec'd 18 Aug 1750 Edwin L. Reinhold.

A-179 - THIS INDENTURE of mortgage - 13 Jun 1750 - Jacob Kline of Lancaster Borough Lancaster Co., yeoman to Melchior Fortinee of Lancaster Borough, butcher, £60 for lot on King St. in Lancaster Borough. Jacob is bound unto Melchior in the amount of £120. Condition for payment of £60, on 13 Jun 1751. Jacob to better secure payment and in consideration of the further sum of 5/ grants a lot on King St. in Lancaster Borough. Neighbor - Graft Beaver. ... Jacob (H) Kline ... Sealed and delivered in the presence of Tetrich Besch and Arthur Forster ... Ack'd 18 Aug 1750 Thomas Cookson ... Rec'd 10 Aug 1750 Thomas Cookson ... We, Michael Fortanee, Casper Shaffner and John Barr executors of the will of Mulchor Fortunee dec'd do certify that full satisfaction was received, Michael Fortinee, Casper Shaffner, and John Barr.

A-181 - THIS INDENTURE - 23 Mar 1749 - Sebastian Graffe of Lancaster Township Lancaster Co., yeoman and Eve his wife to Michael Byerle of Lancaster Borough Lancaster Co., yeoman, £5 for 6A. Land is located in Lancaster Township, neighbor - Andrew Miller. The 6A is part of a larger tract of 150A which Hans Henry Neff and Franca his wife did by indenture on 18 Jan 1738/9 grant to Sebastian Graffe. Recorded in Bk A, vol 1, pg 35. ... Sebastian Graffe, Eve Graffe ... Sealed and delivered in the presence of Arthur Forster, and James Smith ... Ack'd and release of dower by Thomas Cookson on 31 Mar 1750 ... Rec'd 20 Aug 1750 Edwin L. Reinhold.

A-182 - KNOW ALL MEN - 9 Jun 1750 - George Gibson of Lancaster Borough Lancaster Co., inn-holder to Richard Peters of the city of Philadelphia Esq., £10 for 520A. Land is located in Antrim Township, Cumberland Co. Land was surveyed for George on 20 Oct 1746. ... George Gibson ... Sealed and delivered in the presence of Thomas Cookson and Robert Thompson ... Ack'd 20 Aug 1750 Thomas Cookson ... Rec'd 20 Aug 1750 Edwin L. Reinhold.

A-183 - KNOW ALL MEN - 9 Jun 1750 - Arthur Forster of Lancaster Borough Lancaster Co., to Richard Peters, £5 for a tract in Peters Township Cumberland Co. Neighbors - William McDowell, William Clark, and Mathias Patten. Land was surveyed to Arthur on 20 May 1750. ... Ack'd 20 Aug 1750 Thomas Cookson ... Rec'd 20 Aug 1750 Edwin L. Reinhold.

A-184 - KNOW ALL MEN - 20 Jun 1750 - Robert Thompson of Lancaster Borough Lancaster Co., physician to Richard Peters of the city of Philadelphia, Esq. £5 for 368A. Land is located in Boiling Springs on Yellow Breeches creek in Cumberland Co. ... Robert Thompson ... Sealed and delivered in the presence of Thomas Cookson and George Gibson ... Ack'd 20 Aug 1750 Thomas Cookson ... Rec'd 20 Aug 1750 Edwin L. Reinhold.

A-185 - THIS INDENTURE of mortgage - 11 Jul 1750 - Hans Zimmerman, alias John Carpenter, of Cocalico Township Lancaster Co., yeoman to John Moland of the city of Philadelphia Esq., 5/ for 900A. Hans is bound unto John in the amount of £200. Condition for repayment of £100 on 10 Jul 1751. Hans to better secure payment and in consideration of the further sum of 5/ grants 900A. Land is located in Cocalico Township, neighbors - Woolrick Carpenter and Peter Brickers. This land was also mortgaged to Israel Pemberton of the city of Philadelphia, merchant on 17 May 1748 and recorded in Bk B, pg 516. ... Hans Zimmerman ... Sealed and delivered in the presence of Christian Daniel Claus, and Conrad Weiser ... Ack'd 8 Aug 1750 Conrad Weiser Esq. ... Rec'd 20 Aug 1750 Edwin L. Reinhold.

A-187 - THE INDENTURE - 24 Jun 1747 - Christian Hean of Heidelberg Township Lancaster Co., yeoman, Peter Hean of Heidelberg Township, yeoman, Adam Hean of Heidelberg Township, yeoman, Frederick Hean of Heidelberg Township, yeoman, Henry Hean of Heidelberg Township, yeoman, Casper Hean of Heidelberg Township, (They all sons of George Hean of Heidelberg Township, yeoman dec'd) Jacob Frymeir of Cumru Township Lancaster Co., yeoman and Anna Sibilla his wife, William Fisher of Heidelberg Township, yeoman and Elizabeth his wife (Anna Sibilla and Elizabeth being daughters of George Hean, dec'd) to George Hean (other son of George Hean dec'd) of Heidelberg Township, yeoman, 5/ for 122A. George died intestate leaving issue to the above children. The oldest son, Christian gets double the share leaving 9 full undivided 10ths parts to the other children. George had paid the other children 5/ a piece and they have granted all their shares in the land amounting to 122A. The land is located in Heidelberg Township near Goshen Hill. Neighbor - Hugh Jones. The land is part of a 222A tract granted to George Hean on 27 Nov 1735 and recorded in Bk A, vol 7, pg 339. ... William Fisher, Elizabeth (L) Fisher, Jacob (JF) Frymeir, Anna Sibilla (X) Frymeir, Henry (H) Hean, Adam (AH) Hean, Christian Hean, Casper (KH) Hean, Frederick (FH) Hean, Peter (FH) Hean. ... Ack'd 24 Jun 1747 Conrad Weiser ... Rec'd 27 Aug 1750 Edwin L. Reinhold.

A-189 - THIS INDENTURE - 25 Mar 1748 - Casper Hein of Heidelberg Township Lancaster Co., yeoman to George Hean of Heidelberg Township, yeoman, 5/ for 63 3/4A. Casper is moving. Land is located in Heidelberg Township, neighbors - Philip Philsmoyers. Land was granted to Casper Hein by patent on 18 Feb 1747/48 and recorded in Bk A, vol 13, pg 344. ... Casper (HK) Hain ... Sealed and delivered in the presence of Francis Reynolds and Conrad Weiser ... Ack'd 25 Mar 1745 Conrad Weiser ... Rec'd 27 Aug 1750 Edwin L. Reinhold.

A-191 - THIS INDENTURE - 18 Dec 1749 - Archibald Douglas, Edward Douglas both of Lancaster Co., yeomen, Edward Barwick of Lancaster Co., Esq., executors of the will of Andrew Douglas of Lancaster Co., yeoman dec'd, to George Douglas the eldest son of Andrew Douglas, £333 6/ 8d for 254A. At the time of his death, Andrew had 202A which was part of a 500A tract located in Salisbury Township. He shared this tract with James and Archibald Douglas viz: Archibald 207A, James 100A, and Andrew 202A. The tract was divided by Samuel Lightfoot on 20 Aug 1740. Shortly after the division James and Andrew died. Archibald and Edward Douglas being the eldest sons of James applied for a warrant. it was granted and dated 13 Aug 1743. (The original survey for the land was made for Joseph Cloud, it became void because Joseph did not comply with the conditions in the warrant) The warrant was for the use of Archibald and Edward Douglas, also the children of Andrew Douglas. A warrant which was dated 23 Mar 1738 was surveyed to and for Andrew Douglas. This land was located in Salisbury Township and contained 52 1/2A. Andrew Douglas by his last will, dated 1 Jan 1741/42, after appointing Archibald and Edward Douglas, with Edward Barwick as executors, ordered as follows: executors to sell estate and all other goods in the hands of the executors. Executors to consult with the oldest son, being George. The two tracts are valued at £500. George gets tracts by paying Andrew Douglas, his brother, and Mary Douglas, his sister, both being minors making George the only surviving child. Executors agreed to sell and convey the 2 tracts to George. This indenture, Archibald Douglas, Edward Douglas and Edward Barwick for £333, 6/, 8d to them paid by George Douglas, to and for Andrew and Mary Douglas and to be divided equally among them. Also for and in consideration of 5/ a piece paid to said Archibald Douglas, Edward Douglas and Edward Barwick by George Douglas, 202A in Salisbury Township, neighbors - John Miller. Also the other tract of 52A in Salisbury Township, neighbors - James Douglas and Andrew Douglas. ... Archibald Douglas, Edward Douglas, Edward Barwick ... Sealed and delivered in the presence of Thomas Cookson and William Peters ... Ack'd 18 Dec 1749 Thomas Cookson ... Rec'd 28 Aug 1750 Edwin L. Reinhold.

A-194 - THIS INDENTURE - 8 May 1749 - Michael Meyer the younger of Manor Township Lancaster Co., yeoman to John Miller of Lancaster Co., £600 for 217A, enfeoff release. The land is located in the Manor of Conestoga, neighbor - Andrew Hamilton. Michael Meyer Sr. was granted the land on 16 Oct 1738, recorded in Bk A, vol 1, pg 124 on 17 Oct 1738. Michael Sr. and Elizabeth his wife granted the land to Michael the younger on 22 Jun 1745. ... Michael Maier ... Sealed and delivered in the presence of Jacob Slaugh, and David Stout ... Rec'd of John Miller £600, Michael Maier ... Witness - Jacob Slaugh, and David Stout ... Ack'd 6 Sept 1750 Thomas Cookson ... Rec'd 6 Sept 1750 no name.

A-196 - THIS INDENTURE - 31 Aug 1750 - Christian Stoneman of Hempfield Township Lancaster Co., yeoman to John Jacob Brubaker and Ulrick Roadt of Hempfield Township. yeomen (elders of and trustees for the Society of Mennoists in Lancaster Co.)

5/ for 1A. Christian to promote worship, and for the Mennoists to have a burial place, also in consideration of 5/ grants 1A. Meeting house is already erected on the land. The land is located in Hempfield Township near the Little Conestoga Creek. Neighbors - Melchor Erishan, Christian Stoneman, and John Mieres. The land is part of a parcel containing 150A which was granted to Christian on 13 May 1729 by Hans Brubaker and Ann his wife. The 150A is part of a much larger tract containing 1,000A which was granted to Hans Brubaker (there in called Pupather) and Christian Hersey. The deed is recorded in Bk A, vol 5, pg 271. The 1,000A was later divided equally between Hans and Christian. ... Christian Stoneman, J. Jacob Brubaker, Ulrick Roadt ... Sealed and delivered in the presence of Peter Worrall, and Abraham Myer ... Ack'd 1 Sept 1750 Thomas Cookson ... Rec'd 15 Sept 1750 Edwin L. Reinhold.

A-198 - THIS INDENTURE of mortgage - 14 May 1750 - Mauritz Bond of Lancaster Borough, yeoman to Andreas Persinger of Lancaster Borough, yeoman, £123 for lot in Lancaster Borough. Mauritz is bound unto Andreas in the amount of £246. Condition of payment of £123 on 14 May 1751. To better secure payment and in consideration of the further sum of 5/ paid by Andrew, Mauritz grants a lot in Lancaster Borough located on Queen St. Neighbor - Peter Walmar on the south side. ... Mauritz Bond ... Sealed and delivered in the presence of Adam Simon Kuhn and Arthur Forster ... Ack'd 14 May 1750 Adam Simon Kuhn Esq. ... Rec'd 15 Sept 1750 Edwin L. Reinhold.

A-200 - THIS INDENTURE - 4 Oct 1750 Abraham Neff of Lancaster Township, gentleman, and Mary his wife to Sebastian Graffe of Manheim Township, gentleman, £100 for 26 1/2A. The land is located in Lancaster Township, neighbor - Abraham Neiff. This tract is part of a larger tract containing 300A which Tobias Collett, Daniel Quare, and Henry Goldney did by indenture of lease and release on 13 & 14 Mar 1722 grant to Hans Henry Neiff (father of Abraham) in fee. Abraham received the land from his fathers will receiving 1/2 of 300A being 150A subject of payment of certain sums of money to the daughters of Hans Henry Neiff. ... Abraham Neiff, Maria Neiff ... Sealed and delivered in the presence of Thomas Cookson, and Arthur Forster ... Received of Sebastian Graff £100, Abraham Neff ... Ack'd and release of dower 5 Oct 1750 Thomas Cookson ... Rec'd 6 Oct 1750 Edwin L. Reinhold.

A-201 - THIS INDENTURE - 28 Nov 1747 - Joseph Jervis of Salisbury Township, Lancaster Co. yeoman and Esther his wife to Solomon Jervis one of the sons of Joseph Jervis by his wife Esther. For the natural love and affection and the sum of £200 paid by Solomon we grant 71 3/4A and 39 perches to our son Solomon. The land is located in Salisbury Township and contains a water grist mill or corn mill. Neighbors - James Clemson, Thomas Clemons, William Clarke, and Daniel Cookson. The land is part of a 658A tract which John Marsh, the elder, of Netherheyford, in the County of Oxon, carpenter and Joseph Turkbride his attorney did by indenture dated 3 Jan 1711/12 grant unto Joseph Jervis. Recorded in Bk C7, vol 8, pg 162. ... Joseph Jervis, Esther (E) Jervis ... Sealed and delivered in the presence of Charles Cookson, and John Jervis ... Ack'd and release of dower 22 Nov 1747 James Whithill ... Rec'd 17 Oct 1750 Edwin L. Reinhold.

A-203 - THIS INDENTUE of mortgage - 16 Oct 1750 - Solomon Jervis of Salisbury Township, Lancaster Co., yeoman to Isaac Richardson of Salisbury Township, yeoman, £200 for 71 3/4A and 39 perches. Solomon is bound unto Isaac in the sum of £400. Solomon to better secure payment of his debt and in consideration of the further sum of 5/ does grant 71 3/4A and 39 perches. The land is located in Salisbury Township. Neighbors - James Clemson, Thomas Selmon, William Clark, Daniel Cookson, and Joseph Jervis. Condition for repayment of £200 is - £62 on 16 Oct 1751, £59 on 16 Oct 1752, £56 on 16 Oct 1753, £53 on 16 Oct 1754. ... Solomon Jervis ... Sealed and delivered in the presence of Arthur Forster, and Charles Morse ... Ack'd 16 Oct 1750 Thomas Cookson ... Rec'd 17 Oct 1750 Edwin L. Reinhold.

A-205 - THIS INDENTURE - 17 Mar 1749/50 - Adam Simon Kuhn of Lancaster Borough, Lancaster Co., physician and Mary Sabena his wife to the Honorable James Hamilton of the city of Philadelphia, £400 for 15A. Whereas by sale dated 17 Sept 1744 between Hans Moser of Lancaster Co., yeoman and Phrona his wife to Adam Simon Kuhn, Adam purchased a 15A tract located in Lancaster Borough. Neighbors - James Hamilton Esq., and John Moser. The tract is part of a large tract of 300A granted to Hans Moser by patent dated 16 Nov 1737 by Thomas Penn Esq. Deed is recorded in Bk A, vol 8, pg 314 on 3 Jan 1737. Adam had the 15A divided into 46 lots, he has granted all lots, except lot # 45 which he reserved for himself, to James Hamilton. The lots have been purchased as follows:

Lot # 1 - Martin Walse on 15 May 1747, rent is 15/
Lot # 2 - Michael Stump, no date, rent is 12/
Lot # 3 - Tater Granor on 13 May 1747, rent is 15/
Lot # 6 - Michael Hubly on 22 Aug 1748, rent is 15/
Lot # 7 - Daniel Debus on 16 Nov 1744, rent is 7/
Lot # 8 - Jehoiakem Borger on 14 Nov 1744, rent is 7/
Lot # 9 - Paul Rider on 16 Nov 1744, rent is 7/
Lot # 10 - Michael Shriach on 31 Dec 1744, rent is 7/
Lot # 11 - Bernard Hubley on 14 Nov 1744, rent is 7/
Lot # 12 - Mathias Buch on 14 Nov 1744, rent is 7/
Lot # 13 - Nicholas Schnell on 16 Nov 1744, rent is 7/
Lot # 14 - Charles Myers on 16 Nov 1744, rent is 7/
Lot # 15 - Jacob Spancilor on 16 Nov 1744, rent is 7/
Lot # 16 - Michael Shryach on 16 Nov 1744, rent is 7/
Lot # 17 - John Shankmire on 9 Jan 1746, rent is 7/
Lot # 18 - William Kable on 16 Nov 1744, rent is 7/
Lot # 19 - Jeremiah Milton on 16 Nov 1744, rent is 7/
Lot # 20 - William Kyger on 13 Aug 1747, rent is 7/
Lot # 21 - Lawrence Opmyer on _ _ 1744, rent is 3/ 6d
Lot # 22 - Lawrence Opmyer on 10 Dec 1744, rent is 5/
Lot # 23 - Lawrence Thorstanson Nyberg on 16 Nov 1744, rent is 5/
Lot # 24 - George Oyler on 14 Aug 1744, rent is 7/
Lot # 25 - George Andrew Mehler on 15 Nov 1744, rent is 7/
Lot # 26 - William Sower on 15 Nov 1744, rent is 7/
Lot # 27 - George Seehk on 15 Nov 1744, no rent amount listed

Lot # 28 - Phillip Quedoll on 15 Nov 1744, rent is 7/
Lot # 29 - Conrad Hefft on 15 Nov 1744, rent is 7/
Lot # 30 - Daniel Duboos on 18 Sept 1747, rent is 7/
Lot # 31 - Jacob Teeker on 16 Nov 1744, rent is 7/
Lot # 32 - Henry Mool on 16 Nov 1744, rent is 7/
Lot # 33 - no name or date, rent 7/
Lot # 34 - Nicholas Kunze on 14 Nov 1744, rent is 7/
Lot # 35 - Conrad Kohl on 15 Nov 1744, rent is 7/
Lot # 36 - John Oldenbarger on 14 Nov 1744, rent is 7/
Lot # 37 - John Henneberger on 14 Nov 1744, rent is 7/
Lot # 38 - Mathias Rozer on 14 Nov 1744, rent is 7/
Lot # 39 - Daniel Debus on 14 Nov 1744, rent is 7/
Lot # 40 - Jacob Lulman on 14 Nov _, rent is 7/
Lot # 41 - George Black on 14 Nov 1744, rent is 7/
Lot # 42 - Nicholas Shyer on 10 Jul 1749, rent is 7/
Lot # 43 - Peter Rausch on 16 Nov 1744, rent is 7/
Lot # 44 - Edward Smout Esq. on 18 Feb 1744, rent is 7/
Lot # 46 - George Gross on 23 Jan 1747, rent is 7/
Lots on plan numbered 4 & 5 are in possession of Adam and are to be granted to him in fee, rent 17/, 6d, by deed from James Hamilton. All rents are payable 1 May. ... Adam Simon Kuhn, Mary Sabena Kuhn ... Sealed and delivered by Adam Simon Kuhn in the presence of William Peters and William Tea ... Sealed and delivered by Mary Sabia Kuhn in the presence of Joseph Rose and William Peters ... Received of James Hamilton Esq. £400, no signature ... Witness - William Peters, William Tea ... Ack'd 10 May 1750, no name ... Rec'd 16 Oct 1750 Edwin L. Reinhold.

A-212 - THIS INDENTURE - 6 Mar 1749 - Adam Simon Kuhn of Lancaster Borough, physician to the Honorable James Hamilton of the city of Philadelphia Esq., 5/ for all yearly rents amounting to £17 sterling arising out of the 15A tract now divided into 46 lots. Refer to A-205 for a listing of lot owners and rent amounts. ... Adam Simon Kuhn ... Sealed and delivered in the presence of William Peters, and William Tea ... No ack'd ... Rec'd 16 Oct 1750 no name.

A-215 - THIS INDENTURE - 7 Aug 1750 - Abraham Hare of Conestoga Township Lancaster Co., yeoman to Michael Myer Jr. of Manheim Township Lancaster Co., yeoman, £1,200 for 250A. Land is located in Conestoga Township, neighbors - Michael Baughman, John Hare, and Jacob Martin. Land is part of a larger tract of 424A. Land was surveyed to Abraham on an agreement for payment of £60 for each 100A. (greatest part has already been paid) ... Abraham Hare ... Sealed and delivered in the presents of John Renshaw and Arthur Forster ... Received of Michael Meyer, £1,200, Abraham Hare ... Signed in the presence of John Renshaw ... Ack'd 29 Oct 1750 Thomas Cookson ... Rec'd 30 Oct 1750 Edwin L. Reinhold ... Full satisfaction received 13 Aug 1751, Michael Maier ... Ack'd Thomas Cookson.

A-216 - TO ALL PERSONS - 20 Apr 1750 - James Hamilton of the city of Philadelphia granted on 21 Jul 1742 unto John Hare of Lancaster Co., a lot lying in Lancaster

Township on Queen St., neighbor - Samuel Bethel, and James Hamilton. Also by another indenture dated 21 Jul 1742, James granted to John Hare another lot in Lancaster Township also located on Queen St., neighbors - the other lot of John Hare and the Quaker meeting house. Each lot rents for 7/. John has not built on the lots. James Hamilton appoints William Peter of Philadelphia, gentleman his attorney. ... James Hamilton ... Sealed and delivered in the presence of Sarah Hyde and Matthais Sandham ... Memorandum - 5 May 1750, William Peters did take possession of the two lots. ... Witness: Thomas Cookson, Isaac Whitelock ... Be it remembered 18 Oct 1750 before me Conrad Weiser Esq. personally appeared Mrs. Sarah Hyde of Philadelphia spinster, Mathias Sandham of Philadelphia, Thomas Cookson Esq., and Isaac Whitelock, tanner of Lancaster Co. Sarah and Isaac both Quakers affirmed and Mathias Sandham and Thomas Cookson made oaths: They were present when William Peters took possession of the lots in the name of James Hamilton 18 Oct 1750. ... Rec'd 14 Nov 1750 Edwin L. Reinhold

A-219 - 1 Nov 1746 - James Hamilton of Philadelphia Esq. did by deed dated 21 Jul 1743 sell to Patrick Campbell of Lancaster Co., merchant, since dec'd, 3 lots in the town of Lancaster on Prince St. Rent of 21/, also a condition of the deed was that a house with a chimney be built on the lots within 2 years. Nothing was built. James Hamilton appointed John Moland of Philadelphia Co. Esq. his attorney to act in place of him in this matter concerning the above 3 lots. ... James Hamilton ... Sealed and delivered in the presence of Patrick Baird and Samuel Carson ... On 4 Nov 1746 John Moland did enter upon the lots by virtue of power of attorney ... Witness: Thomas Cookson and George Smith ... Ack'd 18 Oct 1750 Conrad Weiser Esq. George Smith since dec'd ... Rec'd 14 Nov 1750 Edwin L. Reinhold.

A-222 - THIS INDENTURE of mortgage - 6 Nov 1750 - John Miller of Manor Township Lancaster Co., blacksmith and Elizabeth his wife to Peter Turner of the city of Philadelphia, merchant, £330 for 217A. John bound unto Peter Turner in the sum of £660. Condition for repayment of £330 on 6 Nov 1751. John and Elizabeth for and in the consideration of the above debt and to better secure payment, also in consideration of the further sum of 5/ paid by Peter, has granted 217A. Land is located in Conestoga Manor Lancaster Co., neighbor - Andrew Hamilton. ... John Miller, Elizabeth (X) Miller ... Sealed and delivered by John Miller in the presence of C. Brockden and Peter Miller Jr. ... Sealed and delivered by Elizabeth Miller in the presence of Arthur Forster and Charles Morse ... Ack'd and release of dower by Thomas Cookson 25 Nov 1750 ... Ack'd 6 Nov 1750 William Allen Esq. ... Rec'd 28 Nov 1750 no name ... Received of John Miller £330 on 25 May 1763, P. Turner ... Sealed and delivered in the presence of George Stevenson and Deborah Claypole ... Ack'd 25 May 1764 Emanuel Carpenter Esq.

A-224 - THIS INDENTURE - 12 Jun 1750 - Daniel Fiere of Strasburg Township Lancaster Co., yeoman to Salome Wistar of the city of Philadelphia, spinster, and a daughter of John Wistar of the city of Philadelphia, merchant, £10 for 32A. Land located in Cocalico Township, neighbor - Henry Stover. Tract is part of a 102A tract which by patent on 21 Apr 1750 was granted unto Daniel Fiere and recorded in Bk A, vol 15, pg 390. ... Daniel Fierree ... Sealed and delivered in the presence of Gabriel Zimmerman and Henry Carpendon ... Received from Salome Wistar the sum of £10, Daniel Ferree ...

Present at signing Gabriel Zimmerman ... Salome may put damn on a branch of water on the tract on Cocalico Creek ... Ack'd 7 Jul 1750 Emanuel Carpenter ... Rec'd 23 Nov 1750 Edwin L. Reinhold.

A-228 - THIS INDENTURE - 24 Jun 1747 - Christian Hean of Heidelberg Township in Lancaster Co., yeoman, Peter Hean of Heidelberg Township, yeoman, Adam Hean, of Heidelberg Township, yeoman, George Hean of Heidelberg Township, yeoman, Henry Hean of Heidelberg Township, yeoman, and Caspar Hean of Heidelberg Township, yeoman (they all being sons of George Hean late of said Township, yeoman dec'd) Jacob Frymeir of Cumru Township Lancaster Co., yeoman, and Anna Sibila his wife, William Fisher of Heidelberg Township, yeoman, and Elizabeth his wife (Anna Siblia and Elizabeth being daughters of George Hean late of Heidelberg Township dec'd) to Frederick Hean of Heidelberg Township, yeoman and other son of George Hean dec'd. George died intestate, law states oldest of the sons receives double share of land, while other children receive 9 full equal undivided 10th parts. In consideration of 5/ a piece to brothers and sisters paid by Frederick, they have granted all their shares, 9 full equal and undivided 10th parts of the tract left by their father. Land is located on Great Spring Creek and contains 198A, neighbors - William Allen, and Christian Hain. Land was granted to their father on 19 Nov 1741 and recorded in Bk A, vol 10, pg 341. ... William Fisher, Elizabeth (L) Fisher, Jacob (JF) Frymeir, A. Sibila (X) Frymeir, Henry (HH) Hean, Casper (KH) Hean, Adam (AH) Hean, George (GH) Hean, Christian Hean, Peter (PH) Hean ... Ack'd 24 Jun 1747 Conrad Weiser ... Rec'd 24 Nov 1750 Edwin l. Reinhold ... Delivered to Fredrick Hain 5 Nov 1753.

A-231 - THIS INDENTURE - 25 Mar 1747 - Casper Hain of Heidelberg Township, yeoman to Frederick Hain of Heidelberg Township, 5/ for 17 3/4A. Land is located in Heidelberg Township, Casper is moving. Neighbor - William Allen, George Hain. This land was granted to Casper along with several other tracts on 18 Feb 1747, and recorded in Bk A, vol 13, pg 344 on 20 Feb 1747. ... Casper (KH) Hain ... Sealed and delivered in the presence of Francis Reynolds and Conrad Weiser ... Ack'd 25 Mar 1748 Conrad Weiser ... Rec'd 5 Nov 1753 Edwin L. Reinhold.

A-233 - THIS INDENTURE - 16 Oct 1745 - Wolrick Shively of Lancaster Co., yeoman and Elizabeth his wife, late Elizabeth Thomas daughter and heir of Jacob Thomas dec'd, to John Garber of Lancaster Co., yeoman, £105 for 92A, enfeoff release. Land is located in Leacock Township, neighbors - Caspar Walter, John Meir, Andrew Maxwell and Mathias Sneider. The tract was granted to Jacob Thomas by patent on 16 Aug 1743 by the Honorable George Thomas Esq., Lieutenant Governor for John, Thomas, and Richard Penn Esqs. It is recorded in Bk A, vol 11, pg 215 on 16 Sept 1743. ... Wolrick Shively, Elizabeth (E) Shively ... Sealed and delivered in the presence of George Lain ... Rec'd from John Garber £105, no signature ... Ack'd 19 Oct 1745 Emanuel Carpenter ... Rec'd 11 Dec 1750 Edwin L. Reinhold.

A-236 - THIS INDENTURE of mortgage - 22 Nov 1750 - Christian Showalter of Earl Township, yeoman and Catherine his wife to Joseph Sims of Philadelphia, merchant, and guardian of Sarah Woodrop of the city of Philadelphia, a minor under 21, £120 for 274A.

Christian Showalter is bound unto Joseph Sims as guardian in the sum of £240. Condition for repayment of £120, being the proper moneys of the said Sarah Woodrop on 22 Nov 1751. Christian and his wife Catherine in consideration of the above debt and to better secure payment also in consideration of the further sum of 5/ paid by Joseph they grant 2 tracts. The first contains 150A and is located in Earl Township, neighbors - George Brown, John Evans, Robert Shankland, Hans Witware, Edward Owen, and Rees Morgan. The second tract contains 124A also located in Earl Township, neighbors - John Evans, George Brown, Rees Morgan and Patrick Wilson. ... Christian Showalter, Catherine (X) Showalter ... The words Sept and Catherine his wife twice underlined. ... Sealed and delivered in the presence of Lewis Gordon and William Tea ... Received of Joseph Sims £120, Christian Showalter ... Witness - Lewis Gordon, and William Tea ... Ack'd and release of dower 26 Nov 1750 Emanuel Carpenter ... Rec'd 13 Dec 1750 Edwin L. Reinhold.

A-240- THIS INDENTURE - 28 Aug 1750 - John Mencencope of Lancaster Borough Lancaster Co., yeoman and Elizabeth his wife to Jacob Stoner and Melchor Prenniman of Lancaster Borough, yeomen, £56 for a lot located in Lancaster Borough on the south side of King St. Neighbor - on the east side Charles Meyer. ... John Menzencope, Elizabeth (X) Menzencope ... Sealed and delivered in the presence of Margaret Stout and Dave Stout ... Ack'd and release of dower 28 Aug 1750 Adam Simon Kuhn ... Rec'd 18 Dec 1750 Edwin L. Reinhold.

A-242 - THIS INDENTURE of mortgage - 18 Dec 1750 - Abraham Neff of Lancaster Township Lancaster Co., gentleman to Sebastian Graffe of Manheim Township, £300 for 124A. Abraham is bound unto Sebastian in the penal sum of £600. Condition for repayment of £300, on 18 Dec 1751. Abraham in consideration of the debt and to better secure payment, also in consideration of the further sum of 5/ paid by Sebastian has granted 124A. Land is located on Conestoga Creek in Lancaster Township, no neighbor mentioned. Included in the 124A is a small tract of 2 1/2A belonging to Sebastian Graffe. The 124A is part of a larger tract of 300A which was granted by lease and release dated 13 & 14 Mar 1722 to Hans Henry Neff, the father of Abraham, by Tobias Collett, Daniel Quare, and Henry Goldney. Hans Henry died and in his will gave 150A being the moiety (half) of 300A to Abraham, subject to the payment of certain sums of money to the daughters of said Hans Henry Neiff. Abraham had given security for payment. ... Abraham Neiff ... Sealed and delivered in the presence of Archibald Taite and Charles Morse ... Ack'd 16 Dec 1750 Thomas Cookson ... Rec'd 27 Dec 1750 no name ... Full satisfaction received on the mortgage 9 Dec 1751, Sebastian Graffe ... Witness - Thomas Cookson.

A-245 - THIS INDENTURE - 4 Jan 1750 - Michael Sharer of Lancaster Co., yeoman and Magdalen his wife, Isaac Bare of Lancaster Co., yeoman and Barbara his wife, Abraham Bare of Lancaster Co., yeoman and Frena his wife to Michael Myer, £1,400 for 182A. Whereas Michael Sharer, Isaac Bare, and Abraham Bare at time of a certain indenture on 5 Oct 1750 made between Jacob Bare Jr. of Lancaster Co., yeoman and Barbara his wife of the first part and Michael Sharer, Isaac, and Abraham Bare of the other part are seized of the Grist Mill, Oyl Mill and Saw Mill and 2 pieces of land. Jacob Bare stood seized.

Michael Myer has contracted with Michael Sharer, Isaac, and Abraham Bare for absolute purchase for the sum of £1,400 receiving 2 tracts of 137A and 45A. Neighbors - John Davis, David Reidy, John Long, Isaac Bare. The 45A tract is located in Manheim Township, neighbors - John Long, George Nicholas Bucher, Isaac Bare, and Jacob Bare, except for 7A which was surveyed and parceled out from the larger grant and conveyed to Michael Myer by Jacob Bare. ... Abraham Bare, Frana (F) Bear, Jacob Bare, Barbara (B) Bear, Michael Sharer, Magdalen M. Sharer ... Received of Michael Myer £1,400, no signature ... Ack'd and release of dowers 5 Jan 1750 Emanuel Carpenter ... Rec'd 15 Jan 1750 Edwin Reinhold.

A-250 - THIS INDENTURE - 22 Jun 1745 - Michael Moyer of Manheim Township Lancaster Co., yeoman and Elizabeth his wife to Michael Moyer, one of the sons of Michael and Elizabeth, of Manheim Township, yeoman. For the natural love and affection they bear their son and for £50 do grant 217A, enfeoff release. Land is located in the Manor of Conestoga, neighbors - Andrew Hamilton. Tract was granted to Michael by John, Thomas, and Richard Penn under the hand of Thomas Penn 16 Oct 1738 and recorded in Bk A, vol 1, pg 124. ... Michael (MM) Meyer, Elizabeth (LI) Meyer ... Sealed and delivered in the presence of John Hart and David Stout ... Received of Michael Moyer the sum of £50, Michael (MM) Meyer ... Ack'd 22 Jun 1745 Adam Simon Kuhn ... Rec'd 19 Jan 1750 Edwin L. Reinhold.

A-252 - THIS INDENTURE of mortgage - 20 Jul 1750 - Abraham Hare of Lancaster Co., yeoman and Anna his wife to Christian Hare of Lancaster Co., yeoman, £300 for 150A. The land is located on little Conestoga Creek in Manor Township, neighbors - surveyed to Samuel Overholts and Henry Killhover, Abraham Hare, John Shank, Joshua Low and Michael Meyer. The tract was granted to Michael Myer by patent under the hand of George Thomas Esq., late Lieutenant Governor on 25 Jul 1742 and recorded in Bk A, vol 10, pg 469. Michael and Barbara his wife did by deed grant to Edward Taylor on 18 Jan 1747. Edward and his wife Ann did by deed grant on 6 May 1749 to Abraham Hare. ... Abraham Hare, Anna (I) Hare ... Sealed and delivered in the presence of David Stout and Michael (MM) Meyer ... Ack'd 19 Jan 1750 Thomas Cookson ... Rec'd 23 Jan 1750 ... Received full satisfaction on the mortgage, Christian Hare ... Ack'd 13 Aug 1750 Thomas Cookson.

A-256 - WE THE SUBSCRIBERS - 13 Oct 1750 - have been elected and chosen on part and behalf of Christopher Graffert and Paul Whitsall to award and order concerning a dispute between parties in relation to a certain well of water in the lot of Christopher Graffert. We order that a fence be made by Christopher Graffert, that shall leave the half of the pump standing in the said well open to the half lot adjoining to the said Christopher Graffert by a space of 6' in length from the eastward to westward, meaning 2' to the westward from the center of the pump as it now stands and 4' from the said center to the eastward and that Paul Whitsall, his heirs and assigns of that half lot which he purchased of Robert Lee and adjoining to the said Christopher Graffert, shall for ever hereafter have the use and benefit of the said well. And that the said Christopher Graffert his heirs and assigns, of the half lot he lives on shall for ever hereafter have the use and benefit of the said well, and that neither the said Paul Whitsall or Christopher Graffert shall permit any other family to make use of the said well without the consent of the other. We farther award and order that Paul Whitsall shall on Monday next ensuing the date hereof put the fence in the same or as good order as it was before he pulled or broke it down. And that Christopher Graffert shall on the same day remove the wood that he piled up to obstruct the passage to the said well, so that the passage for the said Paul Whitsall be open to fetch water as usual. We farther award that the said Christopher Graffert shall at or before the expiration of 21 days next ensuing the date hereof make up the said fence and fix the pump with a double handle in the manner above mentioned. Which fence and pump we award to remain in the above mentioned manner for ever hereafter, and to be kept in repair at the equal charge and expense of both parties and their assigns for ever. And that the said Paul Whitsall shall (when the fence and pump is put in order) pay to the said Christopher Graffert the full half part of the expense of doing it. And that the costs of the suits or actions brought by Paul Whitsall against Christopher Graffert shall be paid off and discharged by Paul Whitsall. And that the costs in the action brought by Christopher Graffert shall be discharged by the said Christopher Graffert. And that the said Paul Whitsall selling or leasing the said half lot his own particular right, shall cease and go to his assignee or assignees, lessee or lessees and the said Christopher Graffert selling or leasing his half lot his own particular right to cease and go to his assignee or assignees, lessee or lessees and lastly that the cost of this administration to be equally de frayed between them. ... In witness whereof we have hereto set our hands and seals the 13 Oct 1750 ... Thomas Poultney, David Stout, Caspar ___, Berned Hubley ... Signed and sealed in presence of us, "the above raiser in the 17th line from the top being first made", "The words leasing and the words lessee or lessees" being first interlined in two places, and also the words "with a double handle". ... Lodwick Stone ... Rec'd 25 Jan 1750 Edwin L. Reinhold.

Finis Book A

Joseph Shippen Jr.

1753

Deed Book B: 1741 - 1750

B-1 - THIS INDENTURE of mortgage - 13 Oct 1741 - Walter Newman of Lancaster Co.
to James Steel, Richard Peters, and Lynford Lardner all of the city of Philadelphia,
gentlemen, £25 for 234A. Walter to secure payment of £25 to John, Thomas, and Richard
Penn Esqs. proprietors and in consideration of the further sum of 5/ has granted 2 tracts
containing 234A. Tracts are located in Lancaster Co., first tract contains 100A, neighbor -
John Sellers. Second tract contains 134A, neighbors - David Evin, Walter Newman, and
Frederick Capp. Conditions for repayment of £25, ___ on 13 Oct 1742, £5.18 on 13 Oct
1744, £5.12 on 13 Oct 1745, 5.6 residue on 13 Oct 1746. John Kinsey authorized to act
in court of common pleas in the event of default ... Walter (IO) Newman ... Sealed and
delivered in the presence of William Peters and John Callahan ... Ack'd 24 Dec 1741
Thomas Cookson ... Rec'd Thomas Cookson 20 Dec 1741 ... Mortgage discharged and
paid in full 13 Oct 1743, Richard Peters ... Witness - Thomas Cookson.

B-3 - THIS INDENTURE of mortgage - 15 Aug 1741 - Joseph Cruncleton of Lancaster
Co., to James Steel, Richard Peters, and Lynford Lardner all of the city of Philadelphia
gentlemen. Joseph to secure payment of £76 13/ 10d due to John, Thomas and Richard
Penn Esqs. proprietors and in consideration of the further sum of 5/ has granted 469A &
92 perches. Land is located in Lancaster Co., neighbor - Jacob Snivley. Conditions of
repayment £76 13/ 10d in the following manner - £16 18/ on 15 Aug 1742, £16 2/ 4d on
15 Aug 1743, £15 6/ 9d on 15 Aug 1744, £14 11/ 2d on 15 Aug 1745, £13 15/ 7d residue
on 15 Aug 1746. John Kinsey has been authorized to act in court of common pleas in the
event of default. ... Joseph Crekelton (German) ... Sealed and delivered by William
Peters and John Callahan ... Ack'd 22 Dec 1741 Thomas Cookson ... Rec'd 22 Dec
1741 Thomas Cookson ... Full satisfaction received 12 Feb 1744/5, Thomas Cookson.

B-6 - THIS INDENTURE of mortgage - 15 Aug 1741 - Robert Cruncleton of Lancaster
Co., to James Steel, Richard Peters, and Lynford Lardner all of the city of Philadelphia
gentlemen. Robert to secure payment of £88 10/ due to John, Thomas, and Richard Penn
Esqs. proprietors and in the consideration of the further sum of 5/ has granted 524 3/4A.
Land located in Lancaster Co., neighbors not mentioned. Condition of repayment of the
sum of £88 10/ as follows - £19 10/ on 15 Aug 1742, £18 12/ on 15 Aug 1743, £17 14/ on
15 Aug 1744, £16 16/ on 15 Aug 1745, £15 18/ residue on 15 Aug 1746. John Kinsey
Esq. authorized to act in court of common pleas in the event of default. ... Robert
Crunkilton ... Sealed and delivered in the presence of William Peters, and John Callahan
... Ack'd 24 Dec 1741 Thomas Cookson ... Rec'd 29 Dec 1741 Thomas Cookson ...
Satisfaction in full 12 Feb 1744/5 Thomas Cookson.

B-8 - THIS INDENTURE of mortgage - 12 Aug 1741 - John Cooper of Lancaster Co., to
James Steel, Richard Peters, and Lynford Lardner all of the city of Philadelphia gentlemen.
John to secure payment of £50 14/ & 4d to John, Thomas, and Richard Penn Esqs.
proprietors, and in the consideration of the further sum of 5/ grants 240A. Land located in
Lancaster Co. on Pequea Creek, neighbors - Daniel Fierres, late of Abel Strettel, and

Palser Francis. Condition of repayment of £50 14/ & 4d is as follows - £11, 3/ & 7d on 12 Aug 1742, £10, 13/ on 12 Aug 1743, £10 2/ & 11d on 12 Aug 1744, £9 12/ & 7d on 12 Aug 1745, £9, 2/ & 3d residue on 12 Aug 1746. John Kinsey Esq. authorized to act in court of common pleas in the event of default. ... John Cooper ... Sealed and delivered in the presence of William Peters, and John Callahan ... Ack'd 24 Dec 1741 Thomas Cookson ... Rec'd 28 Dec 1741 Thomas Cookson ... Satisfaction in full 5 Nov 1745, Richard Peters, ... Witness - Thomas Cookson.

B-10 - THIS INDENTURE of mortgage - 12 Nov 1741 - George Mackarel of Lancaster Co., to James Steel, Richard Peters, and Lynford Lardner all of the city of Philadelphia gentlemen. George to secure payment of £20 due to John, Thomas, and Richard Penn Esqs. proprietors and in the consideration of the further sum of 5/ has granted 120A. Land located in Lancaster Co. on Pequea Creek, neighbors - John Thompson, Joseph Barnetts, and Alexander Davison. Condition of repayment of the sum of £20 is in the following manner - £5 4/ on 12 Nov 1742, £4 19/ & 2d on 12 Nov 1743, £4, 14/ & 5 d on 12 Nov 1744, £4 9/ & 7d on 12 Nov 1745, £4 4/ & 9d residue on 12 Nov 1746. John Kinsey Esq. authorized to act in the court of common pleas in the event of default. ... George (M) Mackael ... Sealed and delivered in the presence of James Agnew, and John Callahan ... Ack'd 24 Dec 1741 Thomas Cookson ... Rec'd 28 Dec 1741 Thomas Cookson.

B-13 - THIS INDENTURE of mortgage - 13 Oct 1741 - Henry Seller of Lancaster Co., to James Steel, Richard Peters, and Lynford Lardner all of the city of Philadelphia gentlemen. Henry to secure payment of £20 to John, Thomas, and Richard Penn Esqs. proprietors and in the consideration of 5/ has granted 2 tracts 150 3/4A. Tracts are located in Lancaster Co., first tract contains 132A, neighbor - Andreas Saltzgeber. Second tract contains 18 3/4A neighbors - Walter Newmn, David Evan, and George Prigell. Conditions of repayment of £20 is as follows - £5 4/ on 13 Oct 1742, £4, 19/ on 13 Oct 1743, £4, 14/ & 5d on 13 Oct 1744, £4, 9/ & 7d on 13 Oct 1745, £4 4/ & 10d residue on 13 Oct 1746. John Kinsey authorized to act in court of common pleas in the event of default. ... Henry Seller ... Sealed and delivered in the presence of William Peters and John Callahan ... Ack'd 24 Dec 1741 Thomas Cookson ... Rec'd 28 Dec 1741 Thomas Cookson ... Satisfaction in full 13 Oct 1743, Richard Peters ... Witness - Thomas Cookson.

B-16 - THIS INDENTURE - 5 Dec 1739 - John Page of Austin Fryers, London gentleman, William Allen of the city of Philadelphia, Esq., William Webb of Chester Co. Esq. and Samuel Powell Jr. of the city of Philadelphia merchant to Erasmas Buggameir of the Manor of Plumton Lancaster Co. yeoman, £86 10/ & 6d for 216A & 45 perches. One year indenture, Erasmas in actual possession. Rent of 1 red rose annually on 23 Jun. Land located in Plumton Manor, neighbors - intended to be granted to Frederick Sheffer. John, Thomas, Richard Penn did grant on 17 Sept 1735 to John Page 5,165A located on Tulpehocken Creek in Lancaster Co. Deed is recorded in Bk A, vol 7, pg 264. John to pay rent of 1 red rose annually on 24 Jun to Penns. John Page on 17 Feb 1736 appointed William Allen, William Webb and Samuel Powell Jr. as his attorneys. Letter of attorney is recorded in Bk D2, vol 2, pg 196. ... William Allen, William Webb, and Samuel Powell Jr. for John Page ... Sealed and delivered in the presence of Michael Sheffer and William Parsons ... Ack'd 29 Apr 1742 Conrad Weiser ... Rec'd 10 Jul 1743 Thomas Cookson.

B-20 - THIS INDENTURE - 4 Dec 1739 - John Page of Austin Fryers, London gentleman, William Allen of the city of Philadelphia Esq., William Webb of Chester Co. Esq. and Samuel Powell Jr. of the city of Philadelphia merchant to George Unrew of the Monor of Plumton Lancaster Co. yeoman, 5/ for 120A & 50 perches. Land located in Plumton Manor, 1 year indenture, neighbors - Land intended to be granted to John Furry, Christopher Keiser, Jacob Capff, Adam Lesh, Peter Sheffer, Michael Sheffer, Frederick Sherrer, and John Furry ... William Allen, William Webb, and Samuel Powell Jr. attorneys for John Page ... Sealed and delivered in the presence of Michael Sheffer and William Parsons ... No ack'd ... No rec'd.

B-21 - THIS INDENTURE - 5 Dec 1739 - John Page of Austin Fryers London gentleman, William Allen of the city of Philadelphia Esq., William Webb of Chester Co. Esq. and Samuel Powell Jr. of the city of Philadelphia merchant to George Unrew of Plumton Manor Lancaster Co. yeoman, £48 for 120A & 58 perches. George in actual possession. Land located in Plumton Manor, neighbors - intended to be granted to John Furry, Christopher Keiser, Cundred Long, Jacob Capff, Adam Lesh, Peter Sheffer, Michael Sheffer, Frederick Sheffer, and John Furry. John, Thomas, and Richard Penn Esqs. did by patent dated 17 Sept 1735 grant to John Page 5,165A on Tulpehocken Creek in Lancaster Co. Patent recorded 24 Jun ? Bk A, vol 7, pg 264. John appointed William Allen, William Webb, and Samuel Powell Jr. his attorneys on 17 Feb 1736 and recorded in Bk D2, vol 2, pg 196. ... William Allen, William Webb, and Samuel Powell Jr. for John Page ... Sealed and delivered in the presence of Michael Sheffer and William Parsons ... Ack'd 29 Apr 1742 Conrad Weiser ... Rec'd 11 Jul 1742 Thomas Cookson.

B-26 - THIS INDENTURE - 4 Dec 1739 - John Page of Austin Fryers, London gentleman, William Allen of the city of Philadelphia Esq., William Webb of Chester Co. Esq., and Samuel Powell Jr. of the city of Philadelphia merchant to Frederick Sheffer of Plumton Manor Lancaster Co., yeoman, 5/ for 275A in Plumton Manor. Neighbors - Land to be granted to Michael Sheffer, George Unrew, John Furry, Eramus Buggamire, Teter __. ... William Allen, William Webb, Samuel Powell Jr. attorneys for John Page ... Sealed and delivered in the presence of Michael Shaffer and William Parsons ... No ack'd ... No rec'd.

B-27 - THIS INDENTURE - 5 Dec 1739 - John Page of Austin Fryers, London gentleman, William Allen of the city of Philadelphia Esq., William Webb of Chester Co. Esq., and Samuel Powell Jr. of the city of Philadelphia merchant to Frederick Shaffer of Plumton Manor Lancaster Co. yeoman, £110 for 275A, in actual possession. Land located in Plumton Manor, neighbors - land intended to be granted to Michael Shaffer, George Unrew, and John Furry. Rent of 1 red rose every year on 20 Jun. John, Thomas, and Richard Penn proprietors did grant by patent dated 5 Sept 1735 to John Page a tract of 5,165A located on Tulpekocken Creek in Lancaster Co. Recorded in Bk A, vol 7, pg 264. Rent of 1 red rose 23 Jun. John appointed William Allen, William Webb, and Samuel Powell Jr. his attorneys 17 Feb 1736, recorded in Bk D2, vol 2, pg 196. ... William Allen, William Webb, Samuel Powell Jr. for John Page ... Sealed and delivered in the presence of Michael Sheffer and William Parsons ... Ack'd 5 Nov 1744 Conrad Weiser ... Rec'd 7 Nov 1744 Thomas Cookson.

B-32 - THIS INDENTURE - 5 Dec 1739 - John Page of Austin Fryers, London gentleman, William Allen of the city of Philadelphia Esq., William Webb of Chester Co. Esq. and Samuel Powell Jr. of the city of Philadelphia merchant to Michael Sheffer of Plumton Manor, £71 4/ for 178A, in actual possession. Land is located in Plumton Manor. Neighbors - land is intended to be granted to Godfrey Fiedler, Jacob Sheffer, Jacob Sheffer, Peter Sheffer, George Unrew, Frederick Sheffer, and Michael Miller. Rent of 1 red rose every year to John Page on 23 Jun. John, Thomas, and Richard Penn Esq. proprietors did by patent dated 17 Sept 1735 grant to John Page 5,165A located in Lancaster Co. on Tulpehocken Creek. Deed is recorded in Bk A, vol 7, pg 265. Payment of 1 red rose to the proprietors every year on 4 Jun. John granted power of attorney on 17 Feb 1736 to William Allen , William Webb, and Samuel Powell Jr. to sell land. Power of attorney recorded in Bk D2, vol 2, pg 196. ... William Allen, William Webb, Samuel Powel Jr. for John Page ... Sealed and delivered in the presence of Erasmus Buggermire and William Parsons ... Ack'd 29 Apr 1742 Conrad Weiser ... Rec'd 12 Jun 1742 Thomas Cookson.

B-37 - THIS INDENTURE - 5 Dec 1739 - John Page of Austin Fryers, London gentleman, William Allen of Philadelphia Esq., William Webb of Chester Co., Samuel Powell Jr. of the city of Philadelphia merchant to Conrad Weiser of Plumton Manor Lancaster Co. yeoman, £21 & 1/ for 52A 106 perches, in actual possession. Land located in Plumton Manor, neighbor - Anna Maria Gobelum. Land is part of a 5,165A tract granted to John Page on 17 Sept 1735 by John, Thomas, and Richard Penn Esqs., the proprietors. Deed recorded in Bk A, vol 7, pg 264. Rent of 1 red rose every year on 4 Jun. On 17 Feb 1736 John appointed William Allen, William Webb, and Samuel Powell Jr. his attorneys to act in his behalf in the sale of the land. Recorded in Bk D2, vol 2, pg 196. ... William Allen, William Webb, Samuel Powell Jr., for John Page ... Sealed and delivered in the presence of Michael Sheffer and William Parsons ... Ack'd 29 Apr 1742 James Sams ... Rec'd no date Edwin L. Reinhold.

B-41 - THIS INDENTURE - 14 Aug 1740 - James Hamilton of the city of Philadelphia to John Morris and Margaret his wife administratrix of Derick Updegraffe Esq. of Lancaster Co. James in consideration of the rents and service reserved to be paid and performed on the part of John Morris and Margaret his wife does grant a lot in Lancaster Township. Lot is located on King St., neighbor Sebastian Groffs, on the west side is Prince St. Rent of 7/ to be paid 1 May. Must erect a building on lot. ... James Hamilton ... Sealed and delivered in the presence of Thomas Yorke and James Mitchell ... Ack'd 9 Aug 1742 Thomas Cookson ... Rec'd no date Edmund L. Reinhold.

B-43 - THIS INDENTURE of mortgage - 20 Jul 1742 - John Morris of Lancaster Township, yeoman and Margaret his wife, Margaret was widow and administratrix of Derick Updegraef her husband dec'd, to Christopher Tringle of Lancaster Township potter, £195 10/ for lot in Lancaster Township. Lot is located on King and Prince St., neighbor - Sebastian Graf. Lot was granted to John and Margaret by James Hamilton of the city of

Philadelphia Esq. on 14 Aug 1740. ... John Morris and Margaret (~) Morris ... Sealed and delivered in the presence of Peter Young and Sebastian Graf ... Ack'd 21 Jul 1742 Thomas Cookson ... Rec'd 21 Jul 1742 Thomas Cookson.

B-46 - THIS INDENTURE of mortgage - 25 Jan 1742 - William Shephard of Lancaster Co., to Richard Peters of the city of Philadelphia gentleman £12 16/ for 131A. Land located in Lancaster Co., neighbors - John Cox, William Greers, and Joseph Hughes. William to secure payment of £12 16/ due to John, Thomas, and Richard Penn Esqs. and in consideration of the further sum of 5/ he grants 131A. Condition of repayment in the following manner - £3 18/ & 10d on 25 Jan 1743, £3 15/ & 2d on 25 Jan 1744, £3 11/ & 5d on 25 Jan 1745, £3 7/ & 9d residue on 25 Jan 1746. ... William Shephard ... Sealed and delivered in the presence of Samuel Carson and John Callahan ... Ack'd 26 Jan 1742 Thomas Cookson ... Rec'd 30 Jan 1742 Thomas Cookson.

B-49 - THIS INDENTURE of mortgage - 14 Jan 1742 - William McMeen of Lancaster Co. to Richard Peters and Lynford Lardner of the city of Philadelphia gentlemen, £40 7/ & 9d for 265A. Land located in Lancaster Co., neighbor - James Frimble. William to secure payment of £40 7/ & 9d due to John, Thomas and Richard Penn and for the further sum of 5/ grants 265A. Condition of repayment as follows - £10 & 3d on 14 Jan 1743, £9 10/ & 7d on 14 Jan 1744, £9 1/ & 7d on 14 Jan 1745, £8 11/ & 2d residue on 14 Jan 1746. ... William McMeen ... Sealed and delivered in the presence of William Peters and John Callahan ... Ack'd 26 Jan 1742 Thomas Cookson ... Rec'd 30 Jan 1742 Thomas Cookson.

B-52 - THIS INDENTURE of mortgage - 29 Dec 1742 - William Young of Lancaster Co., to Richard Peters and Lynford Lander both of the city of Philadelphia gentlemen, £32 for 190A. Land located in Lancaster Co., neighbors - George Stewart, George McCarrell, Joseph Barne, John McKelly, and John Rankin. William to secure payment of £32 due to John, Thomas, and Richard Penn and in the consideration of the further sum of 5/ grants 190A. Condition for repayment as follows - £9 10/ & 4d on 29 Dec 1743, £9 9d on 29 Dec 1744, 19/ 2d on 29 Dec 1745, 9/ 7d residue on 29 Dec 1746. ... William Young ... Sealed and delivered in the presence of William Peters and John Callahan ... Ack'd 26 Jan 1742 Thomas Cookson ... Rec'd 30 Jan 1742 Thomas Cookson.

B-55 - THIS INDENTURE of mortgage - 20 May 1743 - John Byers of Lancaster Co. to Richard Peters and Lynford Lardner both of the city of Philadelphia gentlemen, £50 for 236A. Land located in ? of Lancaster Co., neighbor - Jacob Medill, Stephen Cole, and Samuel Blyth. John to secure payment of £50 due to John, Thomas, and Richard Penn and in consideration of the further amount of 5/ does grant 236A. Condition of repayment as follows - £13 on 26 May 1744, £12 8/ on 26 May 1745, £11 16/ on 26 May 1746, £11 4/ on 26 May 1747, £10 12/ on 26 May 1748. ... John Byers ... Sealed and delivered in the presence of Traver Artis and John Callahan ... Ack'd 3 Jun 1743 Thomas Cookson ... Rec'd 7 Jun 1743 Thomas Cookson ... Mortgage satisfied no date.

B-58 - THIS INDENTURE of mortgage - 2 Jun 1743 - James McClenaghan of Lancaster Co. to Richard Peters and Lynford Landner both of the city of Philadelphia, gentlemen,

Sealed and delivered in the presence of Henry Kindy, and John Albright Keylher ...
Ack'd' 14 Jul 1743 Thomas Cookson ... Rec'd 14 Jul 1743 Thomas Cookson ... No
dower release.

B-97 - THIS INDENTURE of mortgage - 16 Nov 1742 - Andreas Wolf of Tulpehocken
Township Lancaster Co., tailor to Conrad Reif of Olery in Philadelphia Co. yeoman, £100
for 124A. Land is located on Tulpehocken Creek Lancaster Co. Neighbors - Andrea
Kreitzer, Caspar Wistar. Repayment of £115 as follows - £31 on 16 Nov 1743, 8 insuing,
£29 10/ on 16 Nov 1744, £28 on 16 Nov 1745, £26 10/ residue on 16 Nov 1746. ...
Andreas Wolf ... Sealed and delivered in the presence of John Bowman and Philapina
Rilawin ... Ack'd 2 Aug 1743 Thomas Cookson ... Rec'd 2 Aug 1743 Thomas Cookson.

B-100 - THIS INDENTURE - 22 Sept 1729 - James Logan of the city of Philadelphia
merchant and Sarah his wife to Gawin Miller of Kennet Township Chester Co., 5/ for
500A. Land located on Pequea Creek in Chester Co., neighbor - Rebecca Shaw ... James
Logan, Sarah Logan ... Sealed and delivered in the presence of Simon Hasby, and James
Johnson ... Ack'd none ... Rec'd none.

B-100 - THIS INDENTURE - 23 Sept 1729 - James Logan of the city of Philadelphia
merchant and Sarah his wife to Gawin Miller of Kennet Township Chester Co. yeoman,
£200 for 500A, 1 yr. indenture. Land located on Pequea Creek in Chester Co., neighbor -
Rebecca Shaw. This tract is one of 3 tracts which were granted to Israel Pemberton on 1
Oct 1711 and recorded in Bk A, vol 5, pg 232. Israel by indenture granted on 26 Sept
1723 the tract to James Logan. ... James Logan, Sarah Logan ... Sealed and delivered in
the presence of Simon Hasby and James Johnson ... Ack'd 29 Dec 1742 - William Webb
of Chester Co. ... Rec'd 15 Aug 1743 Thomas Cookson.

B-102 - THIS INDENTURE - 13 Jul 1743 - James Dinnen of Pennsboro Township
Lancaster Co., Indian trader to Edward Shippen of the city of Philadelphia merchant, £200
for 198A. Neighbors - Widow Pattens, John McFarland, and James Laughlins. Land was
granted to James Murrey on 6 Jan 1742. James by deed dated 12 Jul 1743 conveyed the
tract to James Dinnen. Payment due on 13 Jul 1744. ... James Dinnen ... Sealed and
delivered in the presence of Hugh Parker, and William Trent ... Ack'd 23 Jul 1743
Thomas Cookson ... Rec'd 23 Jul 1743 Thomas Cookson.

B-104 - THIS INDENTURE - 1 Jul 1743 - John Smoze of Leacock Township Lancaster
Co., yeoman to Michael Probtz of Leacock Township, tailor, £78 for 53 3/4A, enfeoff
release. Land located on the north side of Mill Creek, neighbors - Adam Miller. Where as
John, Thomas, and Richard Penn did by patent under Thomas Penn on 13 May 1735 did
grant to John Myley 150 3/4A in Leacock Township. John in turn granted by indenture on
19 Jun 1735 to Lewis Bennony 53 3/4A. Lewis by indenture dated 10 Jul 1736 granted
the 53 3/4A to Jacob Reesy. Jacob by indenture dated 1 May 1740 granted the tract to
James McConnel. James and Ann his wife granted on 7 Jul 1740 the land to John Smoze.
... John Smoze ... Sealed and delivered in the presence of Stephen Cessna and George
Smith ... Ack'd 19 Jul 1743 Thomas Cookson ... Rec'd 9 Aug 1743 Thomas Cookson..

B-107 - THIS INDENTURE of mortgage - 17 Mar 1743 - John Jones of Strasburg Township Lancaster Co. yeoman to Andrew Moore of Sadsbury Township in Chester Co., £80 for 166A. Land is located in Strasburg Township, neighbors - Thomas Story and Isaac Lefevers and John Fiere. Must pay in full by 3 May 1748. ... John Jones ... Sealed and delivered in the presence of Andrew Shaw and William Boyd ... Ack'd 8 Mar 1743 Samuel Jones ... Rec'd 15 Oct 1743 Thomas Cookson.

B-109 - THIS INDENTURE - 31 Aug 1743 - Thomas Spray of Darby Township Chester Co., husbandman and Mary his wife to Richard Peters of the city of Philadelphia gentleman, £60 for 209A. Land located in Pennsboro on the west side of Susquehanna River in Lancaster Co., neighbors - William Moretons, Thomas Fishers, and Mulikin. Land was granted to Thomas on 13 Aug 1743 and recorded in Bk A, vol 11, pg 217. ... Thomas (X) Spray, Mary (O) Spray ... Sealed and delivered in the presence of Joseph Crell and John Callahan ... Ack'd 25 Nov 1743/4 Conrad Weiser ... Rec'd 24 Jan 1743/4 Thomas Cookson.

B-111 - THIS INDENTURE - 1 Nov 1743 - William Bell of the city of Philadelphia merchant and Jane his wife to Richard Peters of the city of Philadelphia gentleman, £70 for 232A. Land located on a branch of Yellow Breeches Creek on the west side of the Susquehanna River in Lancaster Co. Neighbor - none mentioned. Land was granted to William Bell by patent 18 Aug 1742 and recorded in Bk A vol 12, pg 5. ... William Bell, Jane Bell ... Sealed and delivered in the presence of Josiah Wallis Jr. and John Callahan ... Ack'd 25 Nov 1743 Conrad Weiser ... Rec'd 24 Jan 1743/4.

B-112 - THIS INDENTURE - 15 Jul 1743 - William Logan of the city of Philadelphia merchant to Richard Peters of the city of Philadelphia gentleman. £150 for 874A. land is in his actual possession. First tract contains 433A and is located on Bermudian Creek within Manchester Township Lancaster Co., neighbor - Brice Blair. Second tract contains 441A and is also located on Bermundian Creek, neighbor - John Stars. The 874A was granted to William Logan by patent under the hand of George Thomas Esq. Lieutenant Governor on 9 Jul 1743. Recorded in Bk A, vol 11, pg 160. ... William Logan ... Sealed and delivered in the presence of Joseph Crell and John Callahan ... Ack'd 25 Nov 1743 Conrad Weiser ... Rec'd 10 Jan 1743/4 Thomas Cookson.

B-115 - THIS INDENTURE - 2 Jun 1743 - Peter Young of Lancaster Co. gentleman to Richard Peters of the city of Philadelphia gentleman £88 for 508A, land in his actual possession. Land is located in Manchester Township Lancaster Co.. neighbors - Hans Lynn, and Jacob Woland. Peter received land by patent under the hand of George Thomas Esq. Lieutenant Governor on 31 May 1743. ... Peter Young ... Sealed and delivered in the presence of William Peters and John Callahan ... Ack'd 25 Nov 1743 - Conrad Weiser ... Rec'd 16 Nov 1743 Thomas Cookson.

B-116 - THIS INDENTURE - 8 Nov 1743 - Edward Shippen of the city of Philadelphia merchant to Richard Peters of the city of Philadelphia gentleman, £40 for 180A. Land located in Bern Township Lancaster Co. on Schuylkill River, neighbors - Nicholas Soder, Samuel Wollaston, and James Kennison. Land was granted to Edward on 3 Nov 1743 and recorded in Bk A, vol 11, pg 150. ... Edward Shippen ... Sealed and delivered in the presence of Samuel Powell and John Callahan ... Ack'd 25 Nov 1743 Conrad Weiser ... Rec'd 26 Jan 1743/4 Thomas Cookson.

B-118 - THIS INDENTURE - 1 Nov 1743 - Edward Shippen of the city of Philadelphia merchant to Richard Peters of the city of Philadelphia gentleman, £70 for 165A. Land located on a branch of Conewago Creek on the west side of Susquehanna River in Lancaster Co. Neighbor - William Passamore. Land was granted to Edward on 18 Aug 1742. ... Edward Shippen ... Sealed and delivered in the presence of John Callahan and Edward Reiley ... Ack'd 26 Nov 1743 - Conrad Weiser ... Rec'd 26 Jan 1743/4 Thomas Cookson.

B-119 - THIS INDENTURE - 20 Sept 1743 - Mathias Young of Lancaster Co., yeoman and Margaret his wife to Richard Peters of the city of Philadelphia gentleman, £70 for 431A. Land is located in Manchester Township Lancaster Co., neighbor - Derrick Mumners. Land was granted to Mathias on 13 Aug 1742. ... Mathias Young, Margaret Young ... Sealed and delivered in the presence of Thomas Cookson and Francis Reynolds ... Ack'd and release of dower 20 Sept 1743 Thomas Cookson ... Rec'd 26 Jan 1743/4 Thomas Cookson.

B-121 - THIS INDENTURE - 28 Aug 1742 - Edward Shippen of the city of Philadelphia merchant to Richard Peters of the city of Philadelphia gentleman, £50 for 220A. Land is located on a branch of Bermundian Creek in Manchester Township Lancaster Co. Neighbors - Alexandar Underwood, and Robert Comers. The land was granted to Edward by patent dated 2 Aug 1742 and recorded in Bk A, vol 10, pg 462. ... Edward Shippen ... Sealed and delivered in the presence of Samuel Powell and John Callahan ... Ack'd 25 Nov 1743 Conrad Weiser ... Rec'd 26 Jan 1743 Thomas Cookson.

B-122 - THIS INDENTURE of mortgage - 20 Oct 1743 - Samuel Paterson of Lancaster Co. to Richard Peters and Lynford Lardner both of the city of Philadelphia gentlemen, £48 for 210A. Land is located in Lancaster Co. on the north side of Pequea Creek, neighbors - George Macarel, Joseph Barnett and Daniel Feogs. Samuel is bound unto Richard and Lynford in the amount of £48 due John, Thomas, and Richard Penn Esqs. Samuel to better secure payment and in consideration of the further amount of 5/ has granted 210A. Repayment as follows - £10 17/ 6d on 20 Oct 1744, £10 7/ 11d on 20 Oct 1745, £9 18/ 4d on 20 Oct 1746, £9 8/ 9d on 20 Oct 1747, £8 19/ 2d on 20 Oct 1748 £8 9/ 7d residue on 20 Oct 1748. ... Samuel Patterson ... Sealed and delivered in the presence of George Mackaroll, and John Callahan ... Ack'd 25 Nov 1743 Conrad Weiser ... Rec'd 26 Jan 1743/4 Thomas Cookson ... Full satisfaction Oct 1746, no signature.

B-125 - THIS INDENTURE - of mortgage - 18 Oct 1743 - Robert Wallace of Lancaster Co. to Richard Peters and Lynford Larders both of the city of Philadelphia gentleman, £31 15/ for 200A. Land located in Lancaster Co., neighbor - none mentioned. Robert to secure payment of £31 15/ due John, Thomas, and Richard Penn Esq. and in consideration of the further amount of 5/ does grant 200A. Condition or repayment as follows - £8 4/

11d on 18 Oct 1744, £7 17/ 4d on 18 Oct 1745, £4 9/ 9d on 18 Oct 1746, £7 2/ 2d on 18 Oct 1747, £6 14/ 7d residue on 18 Oct 1748. ... Robert Wallace ... Sealed and delivered in the presence of William Peters and John Callahan ... Ack'd 25 Nov 1743 Conrad Weiser ... Rec'd 26 Jan 1743/4 Thomas Cookson.

B-127 - THIS INDENTURE - of mortgage - 14 Sept 1743 - Casper Galt Felder and Henry Walder both of Lancaster Co., yeomen to William Parvons of the city of Philadelphia surveyor, £66 for 224A. Land located on Conewago Creek, neighbor - none mentioned. Casper and Henry are bound unto William in the amount of £66 10/. In order to secure the debt and in consideration of the further amount of 5/ grants 224A. Condition of repayment as follows - £26 10/ principle & £3 19/ interest on 20 Sept 1744, £20 principal & £2 18/ interest on 14 Sept 1745, £20 principal & £1 4/ interest on 14 Sept 1746. ... Casper Galt Felder, Henry (X) Walder ... Sealed and delivered in the presence of Nicholas Kraft and Isaac Willard ... Ack'd 13 Nov 1743 Conrad Wesier ... Rec'd 31 Jan 1743/4 Thomas Cookson ... Satisfaction in full 13 Aug 1746 Thomas Cookson.

B-129 - THIS INDENTURE - 21 Dec 1743 - Henry Carpenter of Lampeter Township Lancaster Co. yeoman to Salomea Wistar of the city of Philadelphia daughter of John Wistar by Salomea his wife and granddaughter of Hanry Carpenter, 5/ and for the natural love and affection he bears his granddaughter, 351A, enfeoff release. Land is located in Cocalico Township Lancaster Co., neighbor - none mentioned. Land is part of a tract of 700A granted by John, Thomas, and Richard Penn to Henry under the hand of Thomas Penn. Recorded in Bk A, vol 6, pg 300 on 22 May 1734. ... Henry (H) Carpenter ... Sealed and delivered in the presence of John Hair, Emanuel Hair, and Christian Carpenter ... Ack'd 26 Dec 1743 ... Rec'd 31 Jan 1744 Thomas Cookson.

B-132 - THIS INDENTURE of mortgage - 23 Aug 1743 - Adam Martin of Carnarvon Township Lancaster Co. to William Branson of the city of Philadelphia merchant, £116 8/ for 258A. Land is located in Carnarvon Township, neighbors - Robert Ellis, late of Matthias Atkinson. Adam is bound unto William in the amount of £116 8/. In order to better secure payment and consideration of the further amount of 5/ grants 258A. Condition of repayment as follows - £36 1/ 8d on 23 May 1744, £4 6/ 9d on 23 May 1745, £32 7/ 10d on 23 May 1746, £30 16/ 11d residue on 23 May 1747. Land has one mortgage dated 15 Apr 1742 made by Adam to John Kinsey to secure payment of £80 10/. ... Adam Martin ... Sealed and delivered in the presence of Samuel Flower, and George Martin ... Ack'd 8 Feb 1743 Thomas Cookson ... Rec'd _ Feb 1743/4 Thomas Cookson ... Full satisfaction 6 Feb 1750 William Branson.

B-134 - THIS INDENTURE - of mortgage - 1 Jan 1743 - Henry Wendal Zwettger of Lancaster Co. yeoman, and Anna Margaretta his wife to William Peters of the city of Philadelphia gentleman, £100 for 295A. Land is located on Mill Creek, neighbors - John Hoober, Martin Graffes, and Caspar Dellers. Tract was granted by patent 12 Nov 1741 and recorded in Bk A, vol 9, pg 474 to Caspar Stover, minister. Caspar and Catherine his wife convey the tract by lease and release to Wendal on 5 & 6 Jun 1742. ... Wendal Zwettger, Ann Margaret (X) Zwettger ... Sealed and delivered by Wendal in the presence of Edward Reily and John M. Knight ... Sealed and delivered by Anna Margaret in the presence of Thomas Cookson and George Smith ... Ack'd and release of dower 8 Feb 1743 Thomas Cookson ... Rec'd 8 Feb 1743 Thomas Cookson. ... Joseph Sims of the city of Philadelphia merchant and guardian of Sarah Woodrove assignee of William Peters the within named mortgagee in trust of the said Sarah who afterwards married with a certain Peter Tanner of the said __ and in the presence of a power of attorney to us directed from the said Peter Tanner __ the 19Apr 1744, we hereby ack'd full satisfaction ... Matthias Slough ... Rec'd 19 Apr 1744 Edward Shippen.

B-136 - THIS INDENTURE of mortgage - 16 Oct 1744 - John Foster to Richard Peters and Lynford Lardner of the city of Philadelphia gentlemen, £60 for 321A. Land is located in Paxtang Township, neighbor Joseph Kelso, Arthur Fosters, William Armstrong and Joseph Kelso. John in order secure payment of £60 due John, Thomas and Richard Penn and in consideration of the further amount of 5/ does grant 321A. Condition of repayment as follows - £15 11/ 8d on 16 Oct 1745, £14 7/ 4d on 16 Oct 1746, £14 3/ on 16 Oct 1747, £13 8/ on 16 Oct 1748, residue on 16 Oct 1749. ... John Foster ... Sealed and delivered in the presence of William Peters and John Callahan ... Ack'd 27 Oct 1744 Thomas Cookson ... Rec'd 28 Dec 1744 Thomas Cookson ... Full satisfaction 9 Nov 1748 Thomas Cookson.

B-138 - THIS INDENTURE - 26 Mar 1744 - George Gibson of Lancaster Borough inn-holder and Martha his wife to Archibald Little of Lancaster Borough, yeoman, 5/ for 127A. Land located on a branch of Pequea Creek in Lancaster Co., neighbors - William Richardson, Robert Hare, Thomas Johnstons, Archibald Douglas, and Archibald Little. Land was granted to George by patent under the hand of George Thomas Esq. Lieutenant. Governor on 17 Jun 1741 and recorded in Bk A, vol 11, pg 152. ... George Gibson, Martha Gibson ... Sealed and delivered in the presence of Thomas Cookson and James Gallbreath ... Ack'd none ... Rec'd Edwin Reinhold, no date.

B-139 - THIS INDENTURE - 27 Mar 1744 - George Gibson of Lancaster Borough inn-holder and Martha his wife to Archibald Little of Lancaster Borough yeoman, £127 for 127A, in his actual possession. Land located on a branch of Paquea Creek, neighbors - William Richardson, Robert Hare, Thomas Johnson, and Archibald Douglas. Land was granted to George on 17 Jun 1743 and is recorded in Bk A, vol 11, pg 152. ... George Gibson, Martha Gibson ... Sealed and delivered in the presence of Thomas Cookson and James Galbreath ... Ack'd and release of dower 27 Mar 1744 Thomas Cookson ... Rec'd 15 Jun 1745 Thomas Cookson.

B-141 - THIS INDENTURE of mortgage - 16 Jan 1750/1 - Henry Ernsperger of Conestoga Township Lancaster Co. to Philip Ellog of the city of Philadelphia, £100 for 99A. Land is located in Conestoga Township, neighbors - Adam Brownamans, and Philip Knight. Henry is bound unto Philip in the sum of £200. Condition for repayment of £100 by 16 Jan 1751/2. Henry to better secure and in consideration of the further amount of 2/ does grant 99A. Land was granted to Henry by the name of Henry Arnsberger on 2 May 1748 and recorded in Bk A, vol 13, pg 439. ... Henry Ernsperger ... Sealed and delivered in the presence of Jacob Rubb and Paul Isaac Vok ... Ack'd 11 Mar 1750 William Allen ... Rec'd 22 Mar 1750, no name.

B-143 - THIS INDENTURE of mortgage - 9 May 1744 - John Foutz of Lancaster Co. yeoman and Anne his wife to Patrick Carrigan of Lancaster Co., yeoman. £100 for 130A. Land is located in Strasburg Township, neighbors - Martin Miller, and Jacob Haine. Land was conveyed to John by Henry Haine and Christian his wife by lease and release on 6 & 7 May 1741. It is part of a tract of 3,380A surveyed to Amos Steele and by several conveyances conveyed to Henry Haine. ... John Foutz, Anne Foutz ... Sealed and delivered in the presence of Sabastian Graffe, and Michael Beyerle ... Ack'd and release of dower 9 May 1744 Thomas Cookson ... Rec'd 20 Jun 1744 no name.

B-145 - THIS INDENTURE of mortgage - 12 Apr 1744 - Andrew Culbertson of Lancaster Co. yeoman to Edward Shippen of the city of Philadelphia merchant £200 for 270A. Land is located in Hopewell Township Lancaster Co. neighbor - none named. Excluding 3 full 5ths of all royal mines. Andrew received land by patent dated 1 Jun 1749, recorded in Bk A, vol 11, pg 112. ... Andrew Culbertson ... Sealed and delivered in the presence of G. Crigh Parker and David Magan ... Ack'd 18 Apr 1744 John Reynolds ... Rec'd 29 Jun _ Thomas Cookson ... Full satisfaction received 1745/6 Edward Shippen.

B-147 - THIS INDENTURE - 24 Apr 1744 - John Wistar of the city of Philadelphia shopkeeper and Katherine wife to John Moser of Lancaster Co. yeoman, £200 for 167A. Land is located in Conestoga Manor Lancaster Co., neighbors - Jacob Kuntz, Abraham Stiner, and Michael Baughman. John received the land by patent dated 30 Jul 1741 and recorded in Bk A, vol 10, pg 334. ... John Wistar, Catherine Wistar ... Sealed and delivered in the presence of Conrad Swarts, J. Okely and Hans George Graffe ... Ack'd 3 May 1744 Emanuel Carpenter ... Rec'd 4 Aug 1744 Thomas Cookson..

B-149 - THIS INDENTURE of mortgage - 9 Mar 1743 - William Fulerton of Lancaster Co. to Richard Peters and Lynford Lardner both of the city of Philadelphia gentlemen, £45 for 218A. William to secure payment of £45 owed to John, Thomas, and Richard Penn Esq. and in consideration of the further sum of 5/ does grant 118A. Land is in two tracts, first contains 118A and is located on Pequea Creek in Lancaster Co., neighbors - formally Simon Woodrow now William Fullerton, William Ramsey and Humphrey Fullerton. Second contains 100A and is on Pequea Creek joining the other tract, neighbors - John Barnard, John Wells, William Fullerton formally surveyed to Robert Reed, Thomas Johnson and Stephen Cole. Condition of repayment as follows - £11 13/ 9d on 9 Mar 1744, £11 3/ on 9 Mar 1745, £10 12/ 3d on 9 Mar 1746, £10 1/ 6d on 9 Mar 1747, £9 10/ 9d residue on 9 Mar 1748. ... William Fullerton ... Sealed and delivered in the presence of William Peters and John Callahan ... Ack'd 10 Apr 1744 Thomas Cookson ... Rec'd 4 Aug 1744 Thomas Cookson.

B- 152 - THIS INDENTURE - 21 Dec 1743 - Daniel Carpenter of Earl Township Lancaster Co. yeoman and Magdalen his wife to Gabriel Carpenter of Lancaster Co. yeoman, brother of Daniel Carpenter 5/ for 110A, enfeoff. Daniel and Magdalen are moving. Land is located on Conastogoe Creek and is part of a 340A tract, neighbor - Henry Carpenter. Where as John, Thomas and Richard Penn Proprietors did by patent under the hand of Thomas Penn granted on 20 Mar 1733 to Henry Carpenter 1,550A.

Deed is recorded in Bk A, Vol 6, pg 290, on 10 May 1734. Henry and Salomea his wife did grant by indenture on 20 Sept 1737 to Daniel Carpenter 340A of the 1,550A tract. ... Daniel Carpenter, Magdalen Carpenter ... Sealed and delivered in the presence of Emanuel Hain ... Ack'd 26 Mar 1741 Conrad Weiser ... Rec'd 3 Apr 1744 Edwin L. Reinhold.

B-154 - THIS INDENTURE - 6 Mar 1743 - Thomas Musgrove of Lampeter Township Lancaster Co. yeoman to Abraham Musgrove of Lampeter Township yeoman, £40 for 225A. Land located in Lampeter Township, neighbors - Abraham Whitmore, Christopher Franicus, and Abraham Whitmore. Where as Tobias Collet, Daniel Quare, and Henry Gouldney of the city of London did by indenture of lease and release dated 13 & 14 Mar 1722 grant 600A to John Musgrove. John by lease and release dated 10 & 11 Oct 1740 granted to Thomas 450A part of the 600A tract. ... Thomas Musgrove ... Sealed and delivered in the presence of Samuel Patterson and Hannah Jones ... Ack'd 30 Apr 1743 Samuel Jones ... Rec'd 1 Aug 1744 Edwin L. Reinhold.

B-158 - THIS INDENTURE - 4 Jul 1744 - Henry Smith of Toles Lancaster Co., Indian trader to Edward Shippen of the city of Philadelphia merchant, £950 for 520A. Land is located on Swartara Creek Lancaster Co., neighbors - Rudolph Moyon, Thomas Fream and Richard Penn. Pay by 3 Jul 1745. ... Henry Smith ... Sealed and delivered in the presence of John Marsharall and William Trent ... Ack'd 7 Aug 1744 Samuel Jones ... Rec'd 28 Sept 1744 Thomas Cookson..

B-160 - THIS INDENTURE of mortgage - 15 May 1745 - David Tresler of Lancaster Borough, glazier and Susanna his wife to Caspar Wistar of the city of Philadelphia, brass button maker, £40 for 2 lots. The lots are located in Lancaster Borough on King St., neighbor - on east John Gurner, on west Mathias Young. Yearly rent of 7/. David purchased land from John and Maria Philippana Gurner on 14 May 1745. John received the lots by indenture from James Hamilton Esq. on 4 Jan 1740. ... David Tresler, Susanna Tresler ... Sealed and delivered in the presence of Edward Aworth and Thomas Cookson ... Ack'd 15 May 1745 Thomas Cookson ... Rec'd 15 May 1745 Thomas Cookson.

B-162 - THIS INDENTURE - 22 Feb 1742 - Thomas Doyle of Lancaster Borough, hatter and Elizabeth his wife to Philip Quigle of Lancaster Borough carpenter, £100 for 200A. Land is located in Manhaim Township, neighbors - John Moyers, Gaspar Wartman, Martin Moyer, Samuel Bothold and Michael Moyer. Granted to Thomas by patent from John, Thomas, and Richard Penn on 31 Jan 1738 and recorded in Bk A, vol 1 pg 177. ... Thomas Doyle, Elizabeth Doyle ... Sealed and delivered in the presence of Melchor Engle, and Lodwick Stayn ... Ack'd none ... Rec'd Edwin Reinhold, no date.

B-164 - THIS INDENTURE of mortgage - 3 Dec 1750 - John Oldoborger of Lancaster Borough yeoman, Mary Maudlin his wife to Michael Baughman of Manheim Township Lancaster Co., yeoman, £15 for 1 lot. Lot located in Lancaster Borough, neighbor - John Hornaborg. John bound to Michael in the sum of £30. Condition of payment of £15 by 3 Dec 1751. John and wife to better secure payment and in consideration of the further sum of 5/ does grant 1 lot John received lot from Adam Simon Kuhn on 14 Nov 1744. The lot is part of a portion of ground containing 50A that was granted to Adam on 20 Nov 1744 by John Molson and Frona his wife. ... John Oldeborger, Mary Maulin (X) Oldeborger ... Sealed and delivered in the presence of Thomas Cookson and Charles Morse ... Ack'd and release of dower 3 Dec 1750 Thomas Cookson ... Rec'd 23 Feb 1750 Edwin L. Reinhold.

B-166 - THIS INDENTURE - 15 Aug 1750 - George Oylor of Lancaster Borough Lancaster Co. yeoman, Rosina his wife to Abraham Whitmore of Lancaster Borough yeoman, £10 for lot in Lancaster Borough, neighbors - William Sowor and John Mufsor. Payment by 15 Aug 1751. ... George Gylor, Rosina Oylor ... Signed and delivered in the presence of Margaret Stout and David Stout ... Ack'd and release of dower 12 Aug 1750 Adam Simon Kuhn ... Rec'd 23 Feb 1750 Edwin Reinhold.

B-169 - THIS INDENTURE of mortgage - 18 Sept 1744 - Patrick McCarmish of Blockley Township in Philadelphia Co. and Ann his wife to Cornelia Bridges of the city of Philadelphia widow, £100 for 321A. Patrick is bound to Cornelia in the sum of £200. In order to secure better payment and in consideration of £5 grants 321A. Land located on Conodoguinet Creek in Hopewell Township Lancaster Co., neighbor - Robert Black. Patrick received land by patent from John, Thomas and Richard Penn on 12 Jan 1738 and recorded in Bk A, vol 1, pg 156. Condition of repayment of £100 as follows -£6 interest on 18 Sept 1745, £6 interest together with £100 on 18 Sept 1746. ... Patrick McCarmish, Ann McCormish ... Sealed and delivered in the presence of Joseph Stretch, Stephen Vidal, and John Reily ... Ack'd 22 Sept 1744 Thomas Cookson ... Rec'd 22 Sept 1744 no name. ... Satisfaction in full 21 May 1752, Cornelia Bridges.

B-171 - THIS INDENTURE of mortgage - 22 Sept 1744 - Mathias Sharemaker of Strasburg Township yeoman and Catherine his wife to Joseph King of the city of Philadelphia merchant, £75 for 200A. Land is located in Lancaster Co., neighbors - Woolrick Brakebill, John Eckman, Jacob Sturham, and Henry Shank. Mathias is bound to Joseph in the sum of £150. Condition of payment of £75 in one payment on 22 Sept 1745. Mathias to better secure payment and in consideration of the further amount of £5 grants 200A. ... Mathias (Ma) Sharemaker, Catherine (+) Sharemaker ... Sealed and delivered in the presence of Andrew Bartar and Edmond Anworth ... Ack'd and release of dower 22 Sept 1744 Thomas Cookson ... Rec'd 22 Sept 1744 Edwin L. Reinhold.

B-173 - THIS INDENTURE - 8 Feb 1739 - Conrad Weiser of Lancaster Co. yeoman and Anne Eve his wife to Mathias Warwick Township in Lancaster Co., yeoman. £62 for 234A, land in actual possession. Located on Great Spring Creek a branch of Tulpehocken Creek, neighbor - William Allen and George Hains. Conrad received land by patent on 4 Jan 1738 from John, Thomas and Richard Penn. Rent is 1/2 penny on 1 Mar. ... Conrad Weiser and Ann (+) Eve Weiser ... Ack'd 8 Nov 1744 Emanuel Carpenter ... Rec'd 30 Nov 1744 Thomas Cookson.

B-175 - THIS INDENTURE - 14 Jan 1740 - James Hamilton of the city of Philadelphia gentleman to Hannah Verherlst of Lancaster Co. widow of Corneluis Verherlst, lease of lot in Lancaster Township on Queen St. Neighbor - on south James Hamilton, Tatrick Craner. Rent of 7/. ... James Hamilton ... Sealed and delivered in the presence of Thomas Cookson and Samuel Gifford ... Rec'd 31 Jan 1744 Edwin L. Reinhold.

B-176 - TO ALL - 6 Jan 1740/1 - Hannah Verherlst administratrix of Corneluis Verherlst husband dec'd to John Hagerty of Lancaster Township, yeoman, £30 grants lot on Queen St. Neighbors - on south James Hamilton, Tatrick Craner. ... Hannah J. Verherlst ... Sealed and delivered in the presence of John Foulks and Thomas Cookson Ack'd none ... Rec'd 3 Jan 1744 Edwin L. Reinhold.

B-176 - THIS INDENTURE - 5 Sept 1744 - Robert Lee of Lancaster Borough yeoman and Ann his wife (administratrix of John Hagarty dec'd but now intermarried with Robert Lee) to Paul Whitesill of Lancaster Borough, £160 for 1/2 lot. Lot located on Queen St. James Hamilton by indenture on 14 Jan 1740 did grant to Hannah Verherlst all of a lot located in Lancaster Borough on Queen St. Hannah did on 26 Jan 1740 convey to John Hagarty the said lot. John died intestate leaving no issue, Ann was granted lot. ... Robert Lee, Ann (X) Lee ... Sealed and delivered in the presence of Edmund Aewoith, George Handy and Michael Fortinor ... Ack'd 22 Jan 1744 Thomas Cookson ... Rec'd 31 Jan 1744 Edwin L. Reinhold.

B-179 - THIS INDENTURE of mortgage - 28 Dec 1744 - Daniel Mendez da Castro of Lancaster Borough shopkeeper to Nathan Levy and David Frank both of the city of Philadelphia merchants, £102 for 1 lot. Lot located in Lancaster Township, neighbors - Conrad Swath, on east John Hart. Condition of payment entire sum of £102 on 8 Dec 1745. Lot was granted to Daniel by indenture on 10 Nov 1744 under the hand of James Hamilton. ... Daniel Menderda De Castro ... Sealed and delivered in the presence of Thomas Cookson and George Smith ... Ack'd none ... Rec'd 9 Apr 1745 no name.

B-181 - THIS INDENTURE of mortgage - 29 Apr 1745 - Daniel Mendez de Castro of Lancaster Borough shopkeeper to Nathan Levy and David Franks both of the city of Philadelphia merchants, £50 for 1 lot. Lot located in Lancaster Borough, neighbors - on north Conrad Swartz, John Hart on east, and James Hamilton on west. Lot was grant to Daniel on 10 Nov 1744. Lot is subject of an old mortgage dated 28 Dec 1744 of £102. Must pay sum of £50 by 28 Dec 1746. ... Daniel Mendez De Castro ... Sealed and delivered in the presence of Naplely Hart, Edmund Auworth ... Ack'd none ... Rec'd 6 Nov 1750 no name ... Full satisfaction 6 Nov 1750.

B-182 - THIS INDENTURE - 9 Oct 1739 - Hans Graff of Earl Township Lancaster Co. yeoman and Susanna his wife to Andrew Moseman and Christian Moseman of Earl Township, yeomen, £50 for 100A. enfeoff. Land is located on Conestoga Creek in Earl Township and is part of a larger tract patented to Hans on 18 Nov 1737 containing 1,419A. Recorded in Bk A, vol 8, pg 292. Rent 1/ per acre. ... Hans Graff, Susanna (S) Graff ... Sealed and delivered in the presence of Martin Graffe ... Ack'd 8 Oct 1739 Samuel Graff ... Rec'd 22 May 1745 Thomas Cookson.

B-184 - THIS INDENTURE - 26 Jul 1738 - Hans Graffe of Earl Township Lancaster Co. and Susanna his wife to Peter Graff (eldest son and heir of Hans and Susanna), for love and affection and £20 for 200A, enfeoff. Land located in Earl Township and is part of a larger tract of 1,419A granted to Hans on 18 Nov 1737. Recorded in Bk A, vol 8, pg 292. Neighbors - Henry Bear and Peter Good. Rent 1/ per year on 1 Mar for every acre. ... Hans Graff, Susanna (S) Graff ... Sealed and delivered in the presence of Andrew Moseman and Zack Butcher ... Ack'd 24 Nov 1740 Emanuel Carpenter ... Rec'd 22 May 1745 Thomas Cookson.

B-186 - THIS INDENTURE - 28 Apr 1740 - Hans Graff of Earl Township Lancaster Co. yeoman and Susanna his wife to Daniel Graff (son of Hans) of Earl Township yeoman, for love and affection and £20 grants 200A, enfeoff. Land located in Earl Township, neighbors - Mark Graff, Hans Graff, Andrew Moseman, and Daniel Graff. Land is part of a larger tract of 1,419A granted to Hans on 18 Nov 1737. Recorded in Bk A, vol 8, pg 292. ... Hans Graff, Susanna (S) Graff ... Sealed and delivered in the presence of Samuel Lightfoot, Benjamin Miller, Jacob (X) Lymmg, and Benjamin Lightfoot ... Ack'd none ... Rec'd 22 May 1745 Thomas Cookson.

B-188 - THIS INDENTURE - 14 Dec 1744 - Hans Moser of Lancaster Co. yeoman and Phrona his wife to Rev. M. Richard Locke and John Foulks, tanner of Lancaster Co., £20 for 1A, enfeoff. Land is located in Lancaster Borough, neighbors - James Hamilton Esq. on west, Adam Simon Kuhn on north. Land is part of larger tract containing 300A granted to Hans by John, Thomas and Richard Penn on 16 Nov 1737 under the hand of Thomas Penn and recorded in Bk A, vol 8, pg 314, 3 Jan 1737. ... Hans Moser, Frona (FM) Moser ... Signed sealed and delivered in the presence of Edmund Auworth, and Abraham Johnson ... Ack'd 16 Dec 1744 Thomas Cookson ... Rec'd 11 Apr 1745 Edwin L. Reinhold.

B-190 - THIS INDENTURE of mortgage - 15 Jan 1744/5 - Gabriel Davis of Carnarvon Township Lancaster Co. yeoman to John Chapman of East Nantmell Chester Co. founder, £150 for 78A. Land located in Carnarvon Township, neighbors - Moses Mucelewain, David Evans, and John Jenkins. ... Gabriel Davis ... Sealed and delivered in the presence of John Howel and Awbrey Roberts ... Ack'd 13 Mar 1745 Thomas Edwards ... Rec'd 6 May 1745 Thomas Cookson ... 8 Aug 1753, I John Gohain one of the executors of John Chapman dec'd do hereby ack'd to have received full satisfaction for his mortgage, John Gohain.

B-191 - THIS INDENTURE - 13 Mar 1741/2 - William Jones of Salisbury Township Lancaster Co., yeoman and Elizabeth his wife to Christopher Griffith of Salisbury Township yeoman, £30 for 50A, in his actual possession. Land is located in Salisbury Township, neighbors - John Griffith, William Jones, and Thomas Falkner. Tract is part of a larger tract of 200A granted by John, Thomas, and Richard Penn on 20 Jun 1718 to Ezekiel Harlen. Ezekiel by indenture dated 12 Feb 1718 granted the 200A to Morgan Jones. Jones by indenture on 16 Aug 1737 granted 50A to William Jones. ... William Jones, Elizabeth Jones ... Sealed and delivered in the presence of William Seymour, John

Taylor, Isaac Taylor, and John Jones ... Ack'd 13 Mar 1741/2 John Taylor ... Rec'd none.

B-193 - THIS INDENTURE - 16 Dec 1737 - John Griffith of Salisbury Township Lancaster Co. yeoman to Christopher Griffith of Salisbury Township yeoman (son of John), £140, natural love and affection for 50A, in actual possession. Land is located in Salisbury Township, neighbor - Thomas Falkners, Morgan Jones. The tract if part of a larger tract of 200A granted by John, Thomas, and Richard Penn on 20 Jun 1718 to Ezekiel Harlan, recorded in Bk A, vol 5, pg 348. Ezekiel and Ruth his wife by indenture granted 200A on 12 Feb 1718 to Morgan Jones. Morgan and Anna his wife granted to John Jones by lease and release on 8 Oct 1736. Jones in turn granted 50A to John Griffith. ... John (O) Griffith ... Sealed and delivered in the presence of Thomas Mark Hondorson, John Griffith Jr., and Thomas Griffith ... Ack'd none ... Rec'd 7 May 1745 Edwin L. Reinhold.

B-194 - THIS INDENUTRE - 14 May 1745 - John Taylor of Hempfield Township Lancaster Co., yeoman and Mary his wife to John Massar and Peter Leman both of Hempfield Township, yeomen, 5/ for 200A. Land located on Conastogoe Creek in Lancaster Co., late in Chester Co., neighbors - Henry Pards, and Michael Miller. ... John Taylor, Mary (O) Taylor ... Sealed and delivered in the presence of Henry Neafe and Joseph Pugh ... Ack'd none ... Rec'd no date Edward L. Reinhold.

B-197 - THIS INDENTURE - 15 May 1745 - John Taylor of Hempfield Township Lancaster Co. yeoman and eldest son and heir of John Taylor late of said town dec'd and Mary his wife, Peter Coot and Fronika his wife, late Fronika Taylor widow and administrator of John Taylor dec'd, Joseph Brown of Lancaster Co., yeoman and Barbara his wife, one of the daughters of John Taylor the elder, Fronika Taylor another of his daughters under age by Daniel Esleman of Lancaster Co. yeoman and guardian of Elizabeth Taylor another of his daughters under age by Ulrick Rhoodt of Lancaster Co., yeoman and her guardian and Mary Taylor another daughter of John Taylor the elder under age by Henry Bare her guardian to John Messer and Peter Leman both of Hempfield Township yeoman, whereas John Taylor died lately intestate seized of a tract of land containing 200A in Hempfield leaving issue of his son and 4 daughters, Barbara, Fronika, Elizabeth, Mary. Son gets double share and is charged with dower of thirds of the said Fronika his mother. Orphan's court held in Lancaster Co. on 9 May 1745, application was made by Peter Coot and Fronika his wife, Joseph Brown, and Barbara his wife, Fronika Taylor, Elizabeth Taylor and Mary Taylor for guardians to be chosen and appointed. Henry Neif, John Brewbaker, Christian Stoneman, and Jacob Browbaker were chosen to value the land. Land was valued at £477, divided is £69 10/ 1d a piece with £60 as dower rights. John Taylor, and Mary to John Massar and Peter Leman, £477 (£139 to John Taylor, £69 to Peter Coot and Fronika, £69 10/ to Joseph Brown and Barbara, £69 10/ to Daniel Essleman guardian of Fronika, £69 10/ to Ulrick Roodt guardian of Elizabeth, £69 10/ to Henry Bear guardian of Mary. Land is in actual possession of John and Peter and is located on a branch of Conestoga Creek now in Lancaster Co., neighbors - Henry Pares, Michael Miller. John received the land by patent granted on 20 Jul 1718 in his German name, Hans Snyder, and recorded in Bk A, vol 5, pg 336. ... Barbara (I)

Brown, Daniel Essleman, Ulrick (~) Roodt, Henry Bare, John Taylor, Mary (X) Taylor, Peter Coot, Fronika (11) Coot, Joseph (O) Brown ... Sealed and delivered in the presence of Henry Neif and Joseph Pugh ... Ack'd 15 May 1744 Thomas Cookson ... Rec'd 16 May 1745 Thomas Cookson.

B-201 - THIS INDENTURE - 4 Dec 1739 - John Page of Austin Fryer, London gentleman, William Allen of the city of Philadelphia Esq., William Webb of Chester Co. Esq., Samuel Powell Jr. of the city of Philadelphia merchant to Michael Miller of Plumton Manor Lancaster Co. yeoman and Marie Katharine his wife, 5/ for 141A. Land located in Plumton Manor, neighbors - intended to be granted to Godfrey Friedly and Michael Sheffer, Frederick Sheffer. ... William Allen, William Webb, Samuel Powell Jr., attorneys for John Page ... Sealed and delivered in the presence of Michael Sheffer and William Parson ... Ack'd none ... Rec'd none.

B-202 - THIS INDENTURE - 5 Dec 1739 - John Page of Austin Fryars, London gentleman, William Allen of the city of Philadelphia Esq., William Webb of Chester Co. Esq., Samuel Powell Jr. of the city of Philadelphia merchant to Michael Miller of Plumton Manor yeoman, and Marie Katharine his wife, £56 15/ for 141A in actual possession. Land located in Plumton Manor, neighbors - Godfrey Fridler, Michael Sheffer, Frederick Sheffer. Rent of 1 red rose on 23 Jun every year. Land is part of a larger tract of 5,165A granted to John Page by patent on 15 Sept 1735, located on Tulpehocken Creek. Rent of 1 red rose on 24 Jan every year. Deed is recorded in Bk A, vol 7, pg 264. John appointed William Allen, William Webb, and Samuel Powell Jr. as his attorneys to sell the land. ... William Allen, William Webb, Samuel Powell Jr. for John Page ... Sealed and delivered in the presence of Michael Sheffer, and William Parsons ... Ack'd 29 Apr 1742 Conrad Weiser ... Rec'd 17 May 1745 Edwin L. Reinhold..

B-206 - THIS INDENTURE - 13 Apr 1748 - Michael Miller of Tulpehocken Township Lancaster Co. yeoman and Mary Catherine his wife to John Sheffer of Tulpehocken, 5/ for 146A. Land is located in Plumton Manor, neighbors - Godfrey Friedler, Michael Sheffer, and Frederick Sheffer. ... Michael Miller, Maria Katherine Miller ... Sealed and delivered in the presence of none ... Ack'd none ... Rec'd Edwin L. Reinhold no date.

B-207 - THIS INDENTURE - 14 Apr 1742 - Michael Miller of Tulpehocken Lancaster Co. yeoman and Mary Catherine his wife to John Sheffer of Tulpehocken, smith £230 for 141A & 46 perches, land in actual possession. Land is located in Plumton Manor, neighbors - Godfrey Friedler, Michael Sheffer, Frederick Sheffer. Michael received land by a grant from John Page by his attorneys on 5 Dec 1739. ... Michael Miller, Marie Katherine Miller ... Sealed and delivered in the presence of none ... Ack'd 8 May 1742 Conrad Weiser ... Rec'd 16 May 1745 Edwin Reinhold..

B-209 - THIS INDENTURE - 4 Mar 1743 - Joseph Stone of Lancaster Co., yeoman and Phrona his wife to Benedict Eshleman of Lancaster Co., yeoman 5/ for 200A. Land located on Conestoga Creek, neighbor - Abraham Burkholder. ... Joseph (I) Stone, Frona

(F) Stone ... Sealed and delivered in the presence of Joseph Low, and George Smith ...
Rec'd Thomas Cookson no date ... Cert'd Edmund Reinhold no date.

B-210 - THIS INDENTURE - 5 Mar 1743 - Joseph Stone of Lancaster Co. yeoman, and
Phorna his wife to Benedict Eshleman of Lancaster Co. yeoman, £300 for 200A, in actual
possession. Where as Richard Hill, James Logan and Robert Ashton attorneys of Henry
Goldney, Josehua Gee, John Woods, and Thomas Oads surviving mortgagees under hand
by patent dated 21 Aug 1725 did grant to Francis Worley 500A. Land located on Pequea
Creek, and recorded in Bk A vol 6, pg _. Francis and Mary his wife did by lease and
release dated 22 & 23 Jul 1728 grant to Joseph Stone 200A, part of the 500A tract. ...
Joseph Stone, Frona (F) Stone ... Sealed and delivered in the presence of Joseph Low
and George Smith ... Ack'd 18 May 1745 Thomas Cookson ... Rec'd 18 May 1745 no
name.

B-212 - THIS INDENTURE - 4 Mar 1743 - Joseph Stone of Lancaster Co. yeoman and
Phrona his wife to Benedict Eshleman of Lancaster Co. yeoman, 5/ for 90A. Land located
in Lancaster Co., neighbor - John Swift ... Joseph Stone, Phrona (F) Stone ... Sealed
and delivered in the presence of Joshua Low and George Smith ... Ack'd none ... Edwin
Reinhold cert'd deed was recorded, no date.

B-213 - THIS INDENTURE - 5 Mar 1743/4 - Joseph Stone of Lancaster Co. yeoman and
Frona his wife to Benedict Eshleman of Lancaster Co., yeoman, £80 for 90A. Located on
a branch of the Susquehanna River in Lancaster Co., neighbors - John Swift. Where as
William Penn late proprietor did by lease and release dated 22 & 23 Mar 1681 grant to
Nicholas Moore, James Claybrook, Philip Ford, William Hart, Edwin Pierce, John
Lincock, Thomas Brafsey, Thomas Barker, and Edward Brooks 20,000A to be laid out in
lots near Philadelphia. Land was vested in Charles Read, Job Goodson, Evan Owen,
George Fitzwalter, and Joseph Pidgeon of the city of Philadelphia merchants. They did by
indenture convey to Francis Raeole (since dec'd) on 8 Jan 1724/5 400A. Land became
vested in his children - Francis, William, Joseph, Benjamin, (sons) Mary, Elizabeth,
Rebecca, (3 of his daughters) Abraham England and his wife Jane, the other daughter. By
their indenture of lease and release dated 19 & 20 Apr 1731 they did convey the 400A to
John Swift. By a warrant from the trustees, 100A of the 400A was laid out to John Swift
on a branch of Susquehanna River in Lancaster Co. John and Elizabeth his wife by lease
and release dated 25 & 26 Nov 1731 granted to Joseph Stone 90A being part of the 100A.
... Joseph Stone, Frona Stone ... Sealed and delivered in the presence of Joshua Low and
George Smith ... Ack'd 18 May 1745 Thomas Cookson ... Rec'd 18 May 1745 Thomas
Cookson ... Cert'd Edwin Reinhold no date.

B-217 - THIS INDENTURE - 6 Jul 1738 - Hans Graf of Earl Township Lancaster Co.,
yeoman and Susannah his wife to Samuel Graf their son, £20 love and affection for 219A,
enfeoff. Land is located in Earl Township, neighbors - Christopher Wingers, Mark Graf,
and Hans Redolph Negley. John, Thomas, and Richard Penn granted to Hans on 18 Nov
1737 1,419A, recorded in Bk A, vol 8, pg 292. Rent of 1/ per 100 acres by 1 Mar. ...
Hans Graff, Susanna (S) Graff ... Sealed and delivered in the presence of Andrews

61

Moseman, and Zach Butcher ... Ack'd 14 Nov 1740 Emanuel Carpenter ... Rec'd 22 May 1745 Thomas Cookson.

B-219 - THIS INDENTURE -26 Jul 1738 - Hans Graff of Earl Township Lancaster Co. yeoman and Susanna his wife to Mark Graf, one of the sons of Hans, £20 love and affection for 200A, enfeoff. Land is located in Earl Township, neighbor - Samuel Graff. John, Thomas, and Richard Penn conveyed on 18 Nov 1737 1,419A to Hans. Rent 1/ per 100 acres. Deed is recorded in Bk A, vol 8, pg 291. ... Hans Graff, Susanna (S) Graff ... Sealed and delivered in the presence of Andrew Moseman, Zack Butcher ... Ack'd 24 Nov 1740 Emanuel Carpenter ... Rec'd 22 May 1745 Thomas Cookson.

B-221 - THIS INDENTURE - 14 Mar 1722 - Tobias Collet of London, haberdasher, Daniel Quare of London, watchmaker, Henry Goldney of London, linen draper to John Henrick Stone of Strasburg in Chester Co., yeoman, £15 for 150A, enfeoff release, in actual possession. Land is located in Strasburg Township, neighbors - Colonel John Evans, Andrea Saldenrick. Land is part of a larger tract of 5,553A which was granted by William Penn under the hands of Richard Hill, Isaac Norris, James Logan on 25 Jun 1718 recorded in Bk A, vol 5 pg 306 to Tobias Collet, Daniel Quare, Henry Goldney, and the heirs of Michael Russell late of London dec'd. ... Tobias Collet, Daniel Quare, Henry Goldney ... Sealed and delivered in the presence of Sarah Dimsdale, John Estaugh, and Elizabeth Estaugh ... Ack'd 18 Nov 1723 Charles Read ... Rec'd 29 May 1745 Edwin L. Reinhold.

B-224 - THIS INDENTURE - 10 Oct 1724 - John Hendrick Stone of Strasburg Township Chester Co., yeoman to Peter Vanbebber Chester Co. yeoman, £95 for 150A, enfeoff. Land is located in Strasburg Township, neighbors - Colonel John Evans, Andrew Saldenrich. Land is part of 5,553A tract issued to Tobias Collet, Daniel Quare, Henry Goldney and heirs of Michael Russell dec'd all of London on 25 Jun 1718. Granted to John by lease and release on 13 & 14 Mar 1722. ... John Hendrick Stone ... Sealed and delivered in the presence of Dennis Cunrads, Peter Boyor, and Griffith Jones ... Ack'd 28 Feb 1738 Dick Johnson ... Rec'd 8 Jun 1745 no name ... Cert'd deed was recorded Edwin Reinhold.

B-226 - THIS INDENTURE - 18 May 1725 - Peter Vanbebber of Strasburg Township in Chester Co., yeoman and Ann his wife to Benjamin Whitmore of Strasburg Township, £80 for 150A, enfeoff. Land located in Strasburg Township, neighbor - Colonel John Evans. Peter received 250A on 10 Oct 1724 from John Hendrick Stone. ... Peter VanBebber, Ann (X) VanBebber ... Sealed and delivered in the presence of Francis Reynolds and Robert Macey ... Ack'd 28 Dec 1737 Samuel Blunston ... Rec'd 8 Jun 1745 no name ... Cert'd deed was recorded Edwin Reinhold.

B-228 - THIS INDENTURE - 28 Jan 1738 - Benjamin Wittmer the younger of Lancaster Co., yeoman and Mary his wife to Toris Boughwalder of Lancaster Co., yeoman, £55 for 56A, enfeoff release, in his actual possession. Land is part of a tract of 150A, neighbors - Colonel John Evans, Toris Boughalder, Benjamin Wittmor. By indenture dated 13 & 14 Mar 1722 from Tobias Collet, Daniel Quare, Henry Goldney all of London to John

Hendrick Stone of PA yeoman, was granted 150A in Chester Co. The land is part of a larger tract of 5,553A from William Penn under the hands of Richard Hill, Isaac Norris and James Logan dated 25 Jun 1718 and recorded in Bk A, vol 5, pg 306 and granted to Tobias Collet, Daniel Quare, Henry Goldney, and heirs of Michael Russell dec'd. The 5,553 is part of a larger tract of 60,000A which was granted by William Penn to Tobias, Daniel, Henry and heirs of Michael Russell on 12 Aug 1639 and recorded in Bk A, vol 2, pg 326. John H. Stone by deed dated 10 Oct 1724 did convey a tract of 150A to Peter Vanbebber. On 18 May 1725 Peter granted the 150A to Benjamin Wittmer the younger. Since the date of the last deed Michael Russell dec'd, his only son released his estate to Samuel Bonhain who released it to the purchasers under Tobias Collett, Daniel Quare, and Henry Goldney, recorded in Bk F, vol 10, pg 9. ... Benjamin Whitter, Mary (O) Whitter ... Sealed and delivered in the presence of John Whitmer and Jacob Whitmer ... Ack'd 2 Oct 1741 Samuel Jones ... Rec'd 8 Jun 1745 no name.

B-230 - THIS INDENTURE - 27 Jan 1738 - Toris Boughwalder of Lancaster Co. yeoman and Barbara his wife to Benjamin Wittmor the younger of Lancaster Co. yeoman, 5/ for 6A. Land is located in Lancaster Co., neighbors - Toris Boughwaldor, London Company ... Toris Boughwalder, Barbara (O) Boughwalder ... Sealed and delivered in the presence of Jacob Witmar, and John Witmar ... Ack'd none ... Cert'd deed was recorded Edwin Reinhold.

B-231 - THIS INDENTURE - 28 Jan 1738 - Toris Boughwalder of Lancaster Co., yeoman and Barbara his wife to Benjamin Wittmer the younger of Lancaster Co., yeoman, 6A. Land is located in Strasburg Township and is part of a 200A tract, neighbors -Toris Boughwalder, and the London Company. By indenture of lease and release dated 13 & 14 Mar 1722 made between Tobias Collet of London, haberdasher, Daniel Quare of London, watchmaker, Henry Goldney of London linen draper to Andreas Saldenrick of PA yeoman, did grant 200A of land on Conestoga Creek in Chester Co. but now in Lancaster Co. The land is part of a tract of 5,553A which William Penn by patent under the hands of his commissioners Richard Hill, Isaac Norris, James Logan on 25 Jun 1718 did grant to Tobais Collet, Daniel Quare, Henry Goldney, and the heirs of Michael Russell. Deed is recorded in Bk A, vol 5, pg 306. The 5,553A tract is part of a 60,000A tract that the proprietary granted to Tobias, Daniel, Henry and heirs of Michael Russell by indenture dated 12 Aug 1699 and recorded in Bk A, vol 2, pg 326. Andreas Saldenrich by deed of indenture dated 10 Dec 1729 granted 200A to Toris Boughwalder. Since the date of the last deed Michael Russell, weaver and only son and heir of Michael Russell dec'd released his estate to Samuel Bonham who released it to the purchasers under Tobias, Daniel, and Henry. Recorded in Bk F, vol 10, pg 956. ... Toris Boughwalder, Barbara (O) Boughwalder ... Sealed and delivered in the presence of Jacob Witmer, and John Witmer ... Ack'd 2 Oct 1741 Samuel Jones ... Rec'd 10 Jun 1745 no name ... Cert'd deed was recorded Edwin Reinhold.

B233 - THIS INDENTURE - 10 Mar 1743 - Benjamin Whitmore Jr. of Lancaster Co. yeoman and Mary his wife to John Bishung of Lancaster Co. yeoman, £10 for 6A, enfeoff. Land is part of a 200A tract and is located in Strasburg Township, neighbors - Toris Boughwalder and the London Company. William Penn, proprietary, did by patent under the hands of Richard Hill, Isaac Norris, and James Logan dated 25 Jun 1718 granted to Tobias Collett, Daniel Quare, Henry Goldney, and the heirs of Michael Russell dec'd 5,553A. Land is located in Strasburg Township Lancaster Co. They by lease and release dated 13 & 14 Mar 1722 granted to Andras Saldonrick 200A on Conestoga Creek, part of the 5,553A. Andreas did on 10 Dec 1729 grant 200A toToris Boughwalder. Michael Russell son Michael Russell released to Samuel Bonham who released to the purchasers under Tobis Collett, Daniel Quare, and Henry Goldney, his estate. Recorded in Bk F, vol 10, pg 956. Toris and Barbara by lease and release dated 27 & 28 Jan 1728 conveyed to Benjamin Whitmore 6A of the 200A. ... Benjamin Whitmer, Maria (O)Whitmer ... Sealed and delivered in the presence of James McClung and Theoph Hartman Jr. ... Ack'd 29 May 1745 Thomas Cookson ... Rec'd 10 Jun 1745 ... Cert'd deed was recorded Edwin L. Reinhold.

B-235 - THIS INDENTURE - 20 Dec 1744 - Benjamin Whitmore Jr. of Lancaster Co., yeoman and Mary his wife to John Bishung of Lancaster Co., yeoman, £235 for 103A, enfeoff. Land is located in Strasburg Township and is part of a 150A tract, neighbor - Toris Bouhwalder. William Penn granted under the hands of Richard Hill, Isaac Norris, and James Logan on 25 Jun 1718, 5,553A to Tobis Collett, Daniel Quare, Henry Goldney, and the heirs of Michael Russell dec'd. Land is located in Strasburg Township. They in turn granted by lease and release dated 13 & 14 Mar 1722 to John Hendrick Stone 150A, part of the 5,553A. John by indenture dated 10 Oct 1724 granted to Peter Vanbebber the 150A. Peter and Ann his wife by indenture dated 18 May 1725 granted to Benjamin Whitmore 150A. ... Benjamin Whitmore, Mary (O) Whitmore ... Sealed and delivered in the presence of James McClung and Throphilus Hartman Jr. ... Ack'd 29 May 1745 Thomas Cookson ... Rec'd 10 Jun 1745 no name ... Cert'd deed was recorded Edwin Reinhold.

B-238 - THIS INDENTURE of mortgage - 9 Feb 1744 - Daniel Carmichael of Lancaster Co. to Richard Peters and Lynford Lardner both of the city of Philadelphia gentlemen, £35 for 177 3/4A. Daniel to secure a payment of £35 due John, Thomas and Richard Penn and in consideration of the further amount of 5/ grants 177 3/4A. No location given, neighbor - Samuel Callwell. Condition of repayment as follows - £9 1/ 11d on 9 Feb 1745, £8 13/ 7d on 9 Feb 1746, £8 5/ 2d on 9 Feb 1747, £7 16/ 9d on 9 Feb 1748, £7 8/ 4d residue on 9 Feb 1749. ... Daniel (O)Carmichael ... Sealed and delivered in the presence of John Callahan and James Aiskell ... Ack'd 12 Apr 1745 Emanuel Carpenter ... Rec'd 11 Jun 1745 Thomas Cookson.

B-240 - THIS INDENTURE - 8 Dec 1744 - John Houston of Sadsbury Township Lancaster Co., miller to Evan Morgan of the city of Philadelphia merchant, £116 for 78A, enfeoff release. Land is located in Sadsbury Township, neighbor - William McClure. Land was granted to John by patent from John, Thomas, and Richard Penn on 28 Jan 1743/4. Deed is recorded in Bk A, vol 12, pg 42. ... John Houston ... Sealed and delivered in the presents of Samuel Bell and Robert Turner ... Ack'd 1 Jan 1744 Samuel Jones ... Rec'd 1 May 1745 Thomas Cookson..

B-242 - THIS INDENTURE of mortgage - 18 Oct 1744 - William Walter of Lancaster Co. to Richard Peter and Lynford Lardner both of the city of Philadelphia gentlemen, £48 15/ for 354A. William to secure payment of £48 15/ due John, Thomas and Richard Penn and in consideration of the further sum of 5/ grants 354A. Land is located in Pennsboro Township, neighbor - James Laws. Condition for repayment as follows - £12 13/ 4d on 18 Oct 1745, £12 1/ 8d on 18 Oct 1746, £11 10/ on 18 Oct 1747, £10 18/. 4d on 18 Oct 1748, £10 6/ 8d residue on 18 Oct 1749. ... William Walker ... Sealed and delivered in the presence of John (111) Harris, and John Callahan ... Ack'd 12 Oct 1744 Thomas Cookson ... Rec'd 1 Mar 1744/5 no name ... Cert'd deed was recorded Edwin Reinhold..

B-245 - THIS INDENTURE - 2 Apr 1744 - Richard Peters of the city of Philadelphia Esq. to David Wilson of Pennsboro Township Lancaster Co. yeoman, £50 for 198A. By warrant dated 4 Feb 1737 from the proprietors, was surveyed to James Betty a tract located on Yellow Breeches Creek in Pennsboro Township. James by deed dated 16 Jul 1743 sold the tract of 198A to Richard Peters. ... Richard Peters ... Sealed and delivered in the presence of James Galbreath, and John Callahan ... Ack'd 16 Jan 1744/5 Thomas Cookson ... Rec'd 11 Jan 1745 Thomas Cookson.

B-246 - TO ALL TO WHOM- no date - presents shall come, David Wilson of Pennsboro Township Lancaster Co. yeoman: by warrant from the proprietors dated 4 Jan 1737 was surveyed unto Francis Betty 266A. Tract was granted to David. Land is located in Pennsboro Township. On 5 Oct 1744 a warrant was issued for David Wilson for 250A adjoining the first tract, also a warrant for 260A adjoining a tract of 198A located on Yellow Breeches Creek in Pennsboro Township. The 198A has been sold to Richard Peters. David Wilson in consideration of £57 has signed over estate right and title and interest he has in the 3 above mentioned tracts. Altogether they equal 776A. ... David Wilson ... Sealed and delivered in the presence of James Gallbreath, and John Callaghan ... Ack'd 8 Jan 1744/5 Thomas Cookson ... Rec'd 11 Jun 1745 Thomas Cookson..

B-248- THIS INDENTURE of mortgage - 10 Jun 1745 - Peter Seites Jr. of Strasburg Township in Lancaster Co. yeoman and Ann his wife to John Wilkerson of the city of Philadelphia, brushmaker, £50 for 170A. Peter is bound to John in the sum of £100. Condition of repayment of £50 on 10 Jun 1746 in one entire payment. Peter and Ann in consideration of the debt and in consideration of the further sum of 5/ grants 170A. Land is located in Strasburg Township, neighbors - Martin Bear, Peter Seiks, and Henry Hains. ... Peter Seiks, Ann (^S) Seiks ... Sealed and delivered in the presence of Edmund Aiworth, and James Smith ... Ack'd 10 Jun 1745 Thomas Cookson ... Rec'd 10 Jun 1745 Thomas Cookson..

B-249 - THIS INDENTURE - 16 Jul 1743 - James Betty of PennsboroTownship Lancaster Co. yeoman to Richard Peters of the city of Philadelphia gentleman, £9 for 198A. Land is located in Yellow Breeches Creek in Pennsboro. Land was surveyed to James on 17 Apr 1738 by a warrant from the proprietors dated 4 Feb 1737. ... James Betty ... Sealed and delivered in the presence of John Callahan, and James Aiswell ... Ack'd 8 Jan 1745 Thomas Cookson ... Rec'd 12 Jun 1745.

B-251 - THIS INDENTURE - 16 Aug 1742 - Andrew Hamilton of the city of Philadelphia merchant and Mary his wife to Richard Peters of the city of Philadelphia gentleman, £60 for 300A. Land is located between little Conewago Creek on the west side of the Susquehanna River, neighbor - Baltzer Kneyers. Andrew received the land on 2 Aug 1742. Deed is recorded in Bk A, vol 10, pg 467. ... Andrew Hamilton, Mary Hamilton ... Sealed and delivered in the presence of Alexandar Graydon and Thomas Hatton ... Ack'd and release of dower 17 Jan 1744 Thomas Cookson ... Rec'd 12 Jun 1745 Thomas Cookson.

B-252 - THIS INDENTURE - 8 May 1744 - John Callen, alias Collins of Pennsboro Township yeoman to Richard Peters of the city of Philadelphia gentleman, £215 for 362A, in actual possession. Land is located on Susquehanna River in Pennsboro, neighbor - John Wells, James Armstrong. Land was granted to John by patent from John, Thomas and Richard Penn under the hand of Lt. Governor George Thomas Esq. and is recorded in Bk A, vol 11, pg 166 on 3 Mar 1742. ... John (I) Callen, alias Collins ... Sealed and delivered in the presence of Edward Shippen and Joseph Shippen ... Ack'd 8 Jan 1745 Thomas Cookson ... Rec'd 13 Jan 1745 Thomas Cookson.

B-254 - THIS INDENTURE - 13 May 1744 - William Richey of New Jersey yeoman and Eunice his wife to Richard Peters of the city of Philadelphia gentleman, £110 for 210A. Land is located on the east side of the Susquehanna River, neighbors - John Taylor, and Thomas Hicks. Land also has a mortgage of £57 on 15 Dec 1743 by William Richey. ... William Richey, Eunice Richey ... Sealed and delivered in the presence of John (X) Morrison, Bryan Leferty and John Callahan who is witness to William Richey ... Ack'd 8 Jan 1744/5 Thomas Cookson ... Rec'd 13 Jun 1745 no name ... Cert'd deed was recorded Edwin Reinhold.

B-256 - THIS INDENTURE - 5 Oct 1744 - David Wilson of Pennsboro Township Lancaster Co. yeoman to Richard Peters of the city of Philadelphia, 5/ for 198A. Land is located on Yellow Breeches Creek in Pennsboro, neighbors - none mentioned ... David Wilson ... Sealed and delivered in the presence of James Galbreath and John Callahan ... Ack'd none ... Rec'd none ... Cert'd deed was recorded Edwin Reinhold no date.

B-257 - THIS INDENTURE - 6 Oct 1744 - David Wilson of Pennsboro Township Lancaster Co. yeoman to Richard Peters of the city of Philadelphia Esq., £50 for 198A, in actual possession. Land is located on Yellow Breeches Creek in Pennsboro, neighbor - none mentioned. David received land by patent dated 13 May 1743. ... David Wilson ... Sealed and delivered in the presence of James Gallbreath and John Callahan ... Ack'd 8 Jan 1744 Thomas Cookson ... Rec'd 13 Jun 1745 Thomas Cookson.

B-258 - THIS INDENTURE - 24 Jul 1744 - Thomas Rennick of Paxtang Township Lancaster Co. yeoman to Richard Peters of the city of Philadelphia gentleman, £200 for 354A. Land is located in Paxtang Township, neighbors - William Richey, Thomas Mayes, Alexander Stanis and Samuel Parks. Includes an island opposite the tract in the Susquehanna River containing 28A. Tracts were surveyed on 20 Mar 1739 for Thomas, warrant dating 28 Mar 1738. ... Thomas Rennick ... Sealed and delivered in the presence of Edward Shippen, and John Callahan ... Ack'd 8 Jan 1744/5 Thomas Cookson ... Rec'd 13 Jun 1745 Thomas Cookson..

B-260 - THIS INDENTURE - 20 Nov 1744 - Joseph Chambers of Paxtang Township Lancaster Co. miller and Catherine his wife to Richard Peters of the city of Philadelphia £130 for 258A. Land is located in Paxtang Township on the Susquehanna River, neighbor -Thomas Gardiners, Robert Rennick, and William Rennick. Land was granted to Joseph by patent on 19 Nov 1744 in fee. ... Joseph Chambers, no signature for wife ... Sealed and delivered in the presence of Peter Worral, and John Callahan ... Ack'd 16 Jan 1745 Thomas Cookson ... Rec'd 14 Jun 1745 Thomas Cookson.

B-262 - THIS INDENTURE - 25 Dec 1744 - Septimus Robinson of the city of Philadelphia Esq. to Richard Peters of the city of Philadelphia, 5/ for 4 tracts containing altogether 956A. First tract contains 362A and is located in Cumru Township, neighbors - Thomas Nicholas, John Thomas, David Thomas, Francis Creeks, Leonard Mooma, and David Jones. Second tract contains 178A and is located in Cumru Township, neighbors - John Davis, David Evans, and David Thomas. Third tract contains 240A also located in Cumru Township, neighbors - Septimus Robinson and widow Davis. Fourth tract contains 176A, located in Cumru Township, neighbors Robert Ward, Anthony Morris, Peter Waggoner. ... Septimus Robinson ... Sealed and delivered in the presence of William Parson and Edward Sull ... Ack'd none ... Rec'd none ... Cert'd deed was recorded Edwin L. Reinhold.

B-263 - THIS INDENTURE - 26 Dec 1744 - Septimus Robinson of the city of Philadelphia Esq. to Richard Peters of the city of Philadelphia, £270 for 4 tracts equaling 956A, in actual possession. First tract contains 362A and located in Cumru Township Lancaster Co., neighbors - Thomas Nicholas, John Thomas, David Thomas, Francis Creeks, Leonard Mooma, and David Jones. Second tract contains 178A and is located in Cumru Township, neighbors - John Davis, David Evans, David Thomas. Third tract contains 240A is located in Cumru Township, neighbors - Septimus Robinson, and widow Davis. Fourth tract contains 176A and is also located in Cumru Township, neighbors - Robert Ward, Anthony Morris, Peter Waggoner. All the tracts were patented 6 Sept 1743. ... Septius Robinson ... Sealed and delivered in the presence of William Parson, and Edward Scull ... Ack'd 15 Jan 1744/5 Thomas Cookson ... Rec'd 15 Jun 1745 Thomas Cookson..

B-267 - THIS INDENTURE - 21 Dec 1744 - Emanual Carpenter of Lancaster Co. and Catherine his wife to Michael Weidler of Lancaster Co., yeoman. £15 for 15A enfeoff release. Land is located on the east side of Conestoga Creek, neighbor - none mentioned. Land is part of a 140A tract. Where as John, Thomas and Richard Penn by patent under the hand of Thomas Penn dated 12 Mar 1733 did grant to Henry Carpenter 1,550A. Land is located on branches of the Conestoga Creek in Lancaster Co. Rent due 1 Mar 1/ for every 100A. Deed is recorded in Bk A, vol 6, pg 290 on 10 May 1734. Henry and Salomea his wife by indenture dated 20 Sept 1737 granted to Daniel Carpenter 340A, part of the above tract. Daniel and Magdalin his wife did by indenture dated 21 Dec 1743 grant to Emanuel Carpenter 140A part of the 340A. ... Emanuel Carpenter, Catherine (C)

Carpenter ... Sealed and delivered in the presence of Sebastin Graff and George Lyne ... Ack'd 23 May 1745 Thomas Cookson ... Rec'd 17 Jun 1745 no name ... Cert'd deed was recorded Edwin L. Reinhold.

B-269 - THIS INDENTURE - 22 May 1745 - Emanuel Carpenter of Lancaster Co. Esq. and Catherine his wife to George Lyne of Lancaster Co., yeoman, £50 for 31A, enfeoff release. Land is part of a 100A tract granted to Emanuel. John, Thomas, and Richard Penn did by patent dated 17 May 1736 did grant to Mathias Snider 100A. Land is located in Lancaster Co. Mathias and Madalen his wife did by deed grant on 10 Oct 1740 the 100A to Emanuel Carpenter. ... Emanuel Carpenter, Catherine (C) Carpenter ... Sealed and delivered in the presence of Sebastin Graffe ... Ack'd 22 May 1745 Thomas Cookson ... Rec'd 17 Jun 1746 no name ... Cert'd deed was recorded Edwin Reinhold.

B-271 - THIS INDENTURE - 22 May 1745 - George Lyne of Lancaster Co. yeoman to Emanuel Carpenter of Lancaster Co. gentleman, £50 for 31A, enfeoff. Land is located in Leacock Township, neighbor - George Lyne. Land is part of a larger tract of 300A granted to George by John, Thomas and Richard Penn patent under the hand of Thomas Penn on 4 May 1736. Deed is recorded in Bk A, vol 9, pg 123, 29 Nov 1739. ... George Lyne ... Sealed and delivered in the presence of Sebastin Graff ... Ack'd 22 May 1745 Thomas Cookson ... Rec'd 17 Jun 1745 no name ... Cert'd deed was recorded Edwin Reinhold ... Sealed and delivered a second time by George Lyne 27 Dec 1764. ... Sealed and delivered in the presence of Isaac Yeates and Peter Hoofnagle ... George Lyne ... Ack'd 27 Dec 1764 Edward Shippen ... Rec'd 27 Dec 1764 Edward Shippen.

B-272 - THIS INDENTURE - 7 Mar 1744 - Adam Miller of York Township Lancaster Co. shopkeeper to James Johnson of Annapolis Maryland merchant, £40 for 2 lots. Lots located in the town of York, both on the west side Waters St., on the north side High St. ... Adam Miller ... Sealed and delivered in the presence of John Ranesay, and George Gibson ... Ack'd 7 Mar 1744/5 Thomas Cookson ... Rec'd 9 Mar 1745 no name ... Cert'd deed was recorded Edwin Reinhold.

B-273 - THIS INDENTURE - 7 Mar 1744 - Adam Miller of York Township Lancaster Co., shopkeeper to James Johnson of Annapolis Maryland merchant, £100 for house and lot. Located in York Township on west side Cadoras Creek, north side High St., now in occupation of Adam. Subject to mortgage to Samuel Sunston for securing payment of £48. ... Adam Miller ... Sealed and delivered in the presence of John Ramsay and George Gibson ... Ack'd 7 Mar 1744/5 Thomas Cookson ... Rec'd 9 Mar 1745 no name ... Cert'd deed was recorded Edwin Reinhold.

B-274 - KNOW ALL MEN - 7 Mar 1744/5 - Adam Miller of York Township Lancaster Co., shopkeeper does appoint James Johnson of Annapolis Maryland merchant his attorney to recover from all persons indebted to him. ... Adam Miller ... Sealed and delivered in the presence of John Ramsey and George Gibson ... Ack'd 7 Mar 1744/5 Thomas Cookson ... Rec'd 9 Mar 1745 no name ... Cert'd power of attorney was recorded Edwin L. Reinhold.

B-274 - KNOW ALL MEN - 8 Mar 1744 - James Johnson of Annapolis Maryland merchant appoints his friend George Swope of York Township Lancaster Co. shopkeeper his attorney to collect all sums due Adam Miller of York Township. ... James Johnson ... Sealed and delivered in the presence of George Gibson and John Ramsey ... Ack'd 8 Mar 1744/5 Thomas Cookson ... Rec'd 9 Mar 1745 no name ... Cert'd power of attorney was recorded Edwin Reinhold.

B-275 - THIS INDENTURE - 13 Jan 1744 - Sebastian Graff of Lancaster Borough Lancaster Co. gentleman and Eve his wife to Thomas Cookson of Lancaster Borough Esq., £40 for 204A, enfeoff. Land located in Manchester Township, neighbors - Joshua Kenworthy, Henry Weiseback, George Shell, Thomas Powell, and William Wyormans. Land was granted to Sebastin by patent from John, Thomas and Richard Penn under the hand of George Thomas Lt. Governor on 10 Jan 1744. Deed is recorded in Bk A, vol 12, pg 175. ... Sebastin Graffe, Eve Graffe ... Sealed and delivered in the presence of Edward Smout ... Ack'd and release of dower 13 Jan 1744/5 Edward Smout ... Rec'd 22 Jun 1745 no name ... Cert'd deed was recorded Benjamin Longenecker.

B-277 - 13 Jan 1744 - THIS INDENTURE - 13 Jan 1744 Sebastian Graffe of Lancaster Borough Lancaster Co. gentleman and Eve his wife to Thomas Cookson of Lancaster Borough, £40 for 206A, enfeoff. Land is located on Bermundian Creek in Manchester Township, neighbor - John Brennans. Land was granted to Sebastian by patent from John, Thomas, and Richard Penn under the hand of George Thomas Esq. Lieutenant Governor on 10 Jan 1744. Deed is recorded in Bk A, vol 12, pg 173. ... Sebastian Graffe, Eve Graffe ... Sealed and delivered in the presence of Edward Smout ... Ack'd and release of dower 13 Jan 1744/5 Edward Smout ... Rec'd 22 Jun 1745 no name ... Cert'd deed was recorded Benjamin Longenecker.

B-279 - THIS INDENTURE - 26 Jul 1745 - Joseph Dixon of New Garden Chester Co. yeoman and Sarah his wife to David Porter of Londonderry Township Chester Co. yeoman, £172 for 401 1/4A. Land is located on a branch of Marsh Creek on the west side of Susquehanna River on the road leading from Paxtang to Manheim, neighbor - none mentioned. Joseph received land by patent dated 20 Dec 1739 and recorded in Bk A, vol 11, pg 509. ... Joseph Dixon, Sarah Dixon ... Sealed and delivered in the presence of Nathaniel Porter, Samuel Morton and William Reed ... Ack'd and release of dower in Chester Co. 13 Jul 1745 William Webb ... Rec'd 22 Oct 1745 no name ... Cert'd deed was recorded Benjamin Longenecker.

B-281 - THIS INDENTURE - 1 May 1745 - Hatwell Verman of Lancaster Co., yeoman and Abigail his wife to William Hamilton of Lancaster Co., £200 for 200A, enfeoff. Land is located on Conestoga Creek in Lancaster Co. Neighbors - Joseph Branton, William Hamilton and Samuel Jones. Land is part of a larger tract of 601A granted to Hatwell by John, Thomas, and Richard Penn by patent dated 13 Feb 1734 and recorded in Bk A, vol 7, pg 76 on 15 Feb 1734. ... Hatwell Varman, Abigail Varman ... Sealed and delivered in the presence of Thomas Cookson and Tawos Jenith ... Ack'd and release of dower 1 Oct 1745 Thomas Cookson ... Rec'd 29 Oct 1745 no name ... Cert'd deed was recorded Benjamin Longenecker.

B-284 - ARTICLES OF AGREEMENT - 4 Nov 1745 - between Nicholas Bower of Lancaster Co. yeoman and Peter Bower of Lancaster Co., yeoman, one of Nicholas sons. Nicholas being advance in years commits the care of his plantation and stock over to son Peter by indenture in fee. He has also turned over all his cattle, horses, mares, colts, wagon, other misc. farm equipment. He rates the value to be £104 10/ which Peter has agreed to pay. Peter agrees to pay the sum of £66 12/ & 6d being the debts of Nicholas: Michael Theobald £15, Nicholas Bower £14 10/, Rev. McGegre £8, Dr. Begre 20/, Quit Rent of £3 2/ & 6d, and to release the sum of £25 due to him, Peter Bower. Peter also agrees to pay £37 17/ & 6d after the death of Nicholas upon an equal division of the same into eight parts amongst the brothers and sisters of Peter, sons and daughters of Nicholas. The sum of £4 14/ & 8d goes to each of them being of full age or when they come of age. Nicholas may enjoy full use of house where he now lives and Peter will deliver to him every year during his life 20 bushels of wheat, 5 bushels of rye, 1/2A of land to be plowed and sowed with flax seed, 5 lbs. of wool and fruit of 15 apple trees, 2 cows, and calves, and to feed, them. The calf only to be fed to benefit the butcher or sale, to cut and haul all his necessary pinewood. All children can take 1 sheep out of stock. Peter binds himself to Nicholas in the sum of £150. Before signing Peter agrees to provide a horse as often as he thinks proper. ... Peter Bower ... Sealed and delivered in the presence of Thomas Cookson and George Senk ... Ack'd 28 Jan 1745 Thomas Cookson ... Rec'd 28 Jan 1745 ... Cert'd article was recorded Benjamin Longenecker.

B-287 - KNOW ALL MEN - no date - that James Buckley late of Fallowfield Township in Chester Co., miller has released and forever quit claim unto James McFerson and George Caldwell of Drumore Township, Lancaster Co., yeomen all obligations, debts, etc. Particularly where they were held and firmly bound unto me in the sum of £20 dated 19 Mar 1736 with the condition under written for payment of £10 with interest on 16 Nov next. ... James Buckley ... Sealed and delivered in the presence of John Calwell, Samuel Simon and James Caldwell ... Cert'd release was recorded Benjamin Longernecker.

THIS INDENTURE - 31 Jul 1745 - Thomas Clark of Chester Co., yeoman and Rev. Adam Boyd of Chester Co., clerks and executors of the will of William Clark of Chester Co., yeoman dec'd to Jonathan Jones of Lancaster Co., yeoman. John, Thomas, and William Penn under the hand of George Thomas Esq. Governor granted on 22 May 1744 to Adam Boyd and William Clark 350A, recorded in Bk A, vol _, pg 360 on 18 Jul 1744. Land is located on Pequea Creek in Lancaster Co., neighbor - Joseph Jervis. In William's will dated 17 Sept 1732 he devised to his son William 200A, which is part of the above tract. The remaining 150A is to be divided equally among his 3 daughters, being Sarah. Esther, and Prisila. The executors by order of Orphans Court of Lancaster on 27 Mar 1744 made division of the tract. Thomas Clark and Rev. Adam Boyd in consideration of trust paid them, also in consideration of 5/ paid by Jonathan Jones grant 50A, endeoff. This being the share of Jonathan Jones. Neighbors - Abraham Neider, Joseph Jervice, and Prisila Clark. ... Thomas Clark, Adam Boyd ... Sealed and delivered in the presence of Patrick McLucess and James Whithill Jr. ... Jonathan Jones is husband to Esther Clark ... Ack'd 2 Aug 1745 James Whitehill ... Rec'd 14 Nov 1745 Thomas Clark.

B-289 - THIS INDENTURE - 1 Aug 1745 - Jonathan Jones of Lancaster Co. wheelwright and Esther his wife to Moses Mincher of Newcastle Co. on Delaware, waterman £73 for 50A enfeoff. Land is located on Pequea Creek, neighbors - Abraham Heides, Joseph Jervis, Prisilla Clark. The land was granted to Jonathan by Thomas Clark and Adam Boyd executors of the will of William Clark of Chester Co on 31 Jul 1745. It is the share of Esther Jones alias Clark daughter of William Clark now wife to Jonathan Jones. ... Jonathan Jones, Esther Jones ... Sealed and delivered in the presence of Patrick McLucass, James Whitehill Jr. ... Ack'd 2 Aug 1745 James Whitehill ... Rec'd 4 Nov. 1745 Thomas Cookson.

B-291 - THIS INDENTURE of mortgage - 18 Oct 1745 - Francis Johnson of Lancaster Co. merchant to Patrick Baird of the city of Philadelphia gentleman, £140 for 397A. Land is located on Conodoguinet Creek in Pennsboro Township, neighbors - none mentioned. Mortgage to be paid by 18 Oct 1746 in one entire sum. ... Francis Johnson ... Sealed and delivered in the presence of George Splomdt and John Ord ... Ack'd 18 Oct 1745 Thomas Greene ... Rec'd 18 Nov 1745 no name ... Cert'd deed was recorded Benjamin Longenecker.

B-293 - THIS INDENTURE of mortgage - 18 May 1745 - Jacob Beyerley of Lancaster Co., yeoman to Marcus Kuhl of the city of Philadelphia baker, £300 for 359A in 2 tracts. First tract contains 160A and is located in Earl Township Lancaster Co., neighbors - Jacob Sensing, Edward Owen, Rees Morgan, Jenkin Jenkins. Second tract is located in Earl Township adjoining the above tract containing 199A, neighbor - Henry Weaver. Full sum of £300 paid by 19 Mar 1746. ... Jacob Beverle ... Sealed and delivered in the presence of Jacob Riegar and James Smith ... Ack'd 18 Mar 1746 Thomas Cookson ... Rec'd none.

B-295 - THIS INDENTURE - 25 Sept 1745 - Thomas Penn, Margaretta Freame widow of Thomas Freame late of the city of Philadelphia dec'd, Richard Hickley of the city of Philadelphia merchant and Lynford Lardner, James Steel of the city of Philadelphia gentlemen to Abraham Stoner Jr. of Warwick Township Lancaster Co., yeoman, £105 for 236A, in actual possession. Land is located on a branch of Little Swartara Creek, neighbors - William Parfon and Thomas Freame. Tract is part of a 10,000A tract which Thomas received by patent dated 2 Oct 1743 recorded Bk A, vol 6, pg 195. Thomas, Margaretta and Richard by their power of attorney dated 8 Aug 1741, recorded Bk D2, vol 2, pg 313, appoint Lynford Lardner and James Steel as their attorneys. James Steel since departed. The will of Thomas Freame ca 22 Sept 1745 by a clause did give the executors the power to sell land and tenements, and to dispose of all lands including the above tract. ... Thomas Penn, Margaretta Freame, Richard Hockly, by Lynford Lardner ... Sealed and delivered in the presence of Lynford Lardner ... Ack'd no date Conrad Weiser and William Parfons ... Rec'd none ... Cert'd deed was recorded Edwin Reinhold no date.

B-297 - THIS INDENTURE - 9 Oct 1745 - Robert Patrick of Lancaster Co., yeoman and Rachel his wife to John Miller of Lancaster Co. yeoman, £106 for 93A enfeoff release. Land is located in Salisbury Township, neighbors - John Campbell, and Andrew Campbell. Robert received land by patent from John, Thomas and Richard Penn under the hand of

Thomas Penn on 9 Jun 1741, recorded in Bk A, vol 9, pg 426 on 21 Sept 1745. ...
Robert Patrick, Rachel (X) Patrick ... Sealed and delivered in the presence of Thomas
Cookson and George Sanderson ... Ack'd 9 Oct 1745 Thomas Cookson ... Rec'd no
date Edwin Reinhold.

B-298 - THIS INDENTURE of mortgage - 24 Dec 1745 - William Trent of Lancaster
Co., merchant and George Croghan of Lancaster Co., merchant to Abraham Mitchell of
the city of Philadelphia, hatter, £200 for 354A. Land is located on Conodoguinet Creek in
Pennsboro Township, neighbor - James Law. Conditions of repayment of £200 by 1 Oct
1746. ... William Trent, George Croghan ... Sealed and delivered in the presence of
William Blythe and David Magaw ... Ack'd 8 Dec 1745 Thomas Cookson ... Rec'd 28
Dec 1745 Thomas Cookson.

B-301 - THIS INDENTURE - 31 Dec 1745 - Abraham Neiff of Lancaster Co., yeoman
one of the sons of Hans Henry Neif of Lancaster Co., dec'd and Mary his wife to
Sebastian Graffe of Lancaster Co., merchant, £9 5/ & 8d for 2 2/3A, enfeoff release.
Land is located on Conestoga Creek in Strasburg Township now Lancaster Co., neighbor -
Sebastian Graffe. It is part of a 150A tract. Tobias Collet, Daniel Quare, Henry Goldney
did by indenture of lease and release dated 13 & 14 Mar 1722 grant to Hans 300A. Hans
has since granted 150A for the use of Benry Neiff his oldest son as his portion or share of
the estate. Hans has since died leaving issue of 2 sons Henry and Abraham and 2
daughters. His will gives his plantation and residue of the tract of 300A to Abraham
subject to the payment of certain sums of money to the daughters. Abraham has put up
security for the payment of all sums as were charged upon the plantation and has become
vested in absolute estate of inheritance. ... Abraham Neiff, Mary Neiff ... Sealed and
delivered in the presence of Thomas Cookson, Meloher Engel ... Ack'd 31 Dec 1745
Thomas Cookson ... Rec'd 27 Jan 1745 no name ... Cert'd deed was recorded Benjamin
Longenecker.

B- 303 - THIS INDENTURE - 8 Jan 1745 - Michael Crouse of Lancaster Co., yeoman to
Richard Peters of the city of Philadelphia gentleman, £90 for 435A in 2 tracts. The first is
located in Pennsboro Township and contains 155A. The second tract adjoins the first and
contains 280A, neighbor - John McClenahan. Michael, by warrant, was granted both
tracts on 1 Nov 1744. ... Michael Crouse ... Sealed and delivered in the presence of
James Smith ... Ack'd 25 Jan 1745/6 Thomas Cookson ... Rec'd 27 Jan 1746 no name
... Cert'd deed was recorded Edwin Reinhold.

B-304 - THIS INDENTURE - 8 Jan 1745 - Conrad Swartz of Lancaster Co. yeoman, to
Richard Peters of the city of Philadelphia gentleman, £20 for 285A. Land is located in
Hopewell Township Lancaster Co., neighbor - none mentioned. Conrad received the land
by warrant for 250A dated 1 Nov 1744. ... Conrad Swartz ... Sealed and delivered in
the presence of John Smith ... Ack'd none ... Rec'd 27 Jan 1745/6 no name ... Cert'd
deed was recorded Edwin Reinhold.

b- 305 - THIS INDENTURE - 10 Jan 1745 - Daniel Iwon of Lancaster Co., merchant to
Richard Peters of the city of Philadelphia gentleman, £__ for 600A, estimation. Land is

located on Little Conestoga on the west side of Susquehanna River, neighbor - none mentioned. Daniel received the land by warrant granted on 2 Nov 1744. ... Daniel Iwon ... Sealed and delivered in the presence of none ... Ack'd 25 Jan 1745/6 no name ... Rec'd 28 Jan 1745/6 no name ... Cert'd deed was record Benjamin Longenecker.

B-306 - THIS INDENTURE - 8 Jan 1745 - Casper Shaffonour of Lancaster Co. yeoman to Richard Peters of the city of Philadelphia gentleman, £15 for 161A. Land is located at the head of the Great Spring in Hopewell Township, neighbor - none mentioned. Casper received the land by warrant for 200A on 1 Nov 1744. ... Casper Shaffanour ... Sealed and delivered in the presence of James Smith ... Ack'd 25 Jan 1745/6 no name ... Rec'd 27 Jan 1745/6 no name ... Cert'd deed was recorded Edwin Reinhold.

B-307 - THIS INDENTURE of mortgage - 4 Feb 1745/6 - Jacob Bare of Lancaster Co., yeoman to Sebastian Graffe of Lancaster Borough gentleman, £250 for 137A. Land is located in Manheim Township, neighbors - John Davis, David Rudy, Isaac Bear, and Michael Widler. Must pay by 3 Feb next. ... Jacob Bare ... Sealed and delivered in the presence of George Graffe and Hans (HS) Sneblle ... The words grist mill, oyl mill, and saw mill, and several mills underlined ... Received of Sabastian £250, Jacob Bear ... Ack'd none ... Test - George Graffe ... Rec'd 21 Feb 1745/6 no name.

B- 309 - THIS INDENTURE - 10 Jan 1745/6 - James Galbreath of Lancaster Co. Esq. to Richard Peters of the city of Philadelphia Esq., £65 for 395A. Land located on Conodoguinet Creek in Hopewell Township, neighbors - John Finley, Thomas Alexander, David Osbara and John Kilpatrick. James receive the land by warrant for 400A in 1 Nov 1744. ... James Gallbreath ... Sealed and delivered in the presence of Adam Reed, and John Callahan ... Received full sum of £65, James Gallbreath ... Test - Adam Reed and John Callahan ... Ack'd none ... Rec'd 24 Feb 1745/6 Thomas Cookson.

B- 310 - THIS INDENTURE - 8 Dec 1735 - Susanah Patterson surviving and joint tenant of James Patterson late of Hempfield Township Lancaster Co., yeoman to Gordon Howard and James Michael both of Donegal Township yeomen. By proprietary warrant dated 23 Aug 1734 there was surveyed to James Logan of Stenton in Philadelphia Co., Esq. land located in Conestoga Manor containing 200A. By indenture dated 18 Nov 1734 and recorded in Bk A, vol 7, pg 5, James granted the tract to James Patterson and Susannah his wife. James by his last will, 3 Oct 1735, left the above tract of his son Thomas a minor of 3 yrs. Susannah in consideration of motherly love has given granted and enfeoffed to Gordon Howard and James Mitchell the above 200A in exchange for food, clothes, house, and schooling for Thomas her son, until he reaches the age of 21. ... Susannah (S) Patterson ... Sealed and delivered in the presence of John Emerson and Samuel Blunston ... Ack'd none ... Rec'd none ... Cert'd deed was recorded Edwin Reinhold.

B-312 - THIS INDENTURE of mortgage - 8 Feb 1745 - Jacob Bear the younger of Lancaster Co., miller to Peter Forney of Lancaster Co., yeoman, £175 for 137A. Land located in Manheim Township, neighbors - John Davis, David Rudy, John Long, Isaac

73

Bears, and Michael Weidlers. Subject to payment of £250 to Sebastian Graffe secured by a former mortgage dated 4 Feb 1745. ... Jacob Bare ... Sealed and delivered in the presence of George Honey and James Smith ... Ack'd 8 Feb 1745/6 Thomas Cookson ... Rec'd 6 Mar 1745/6 no name.

B-313 - THIS INDENTURE - 28 Sept 1745 - Robert Patrick Lancaster Co., yeoman and Rachel his wife to Abraham Neide of Lancaster Co. sadler, £113 10/ for 112A, enfeoff. The land is located in Salisbury Township, neighbors - Joseph Mays, Daniel Cookson, Joseph Jervis and William Clark dec'd. Land was granted to Robert by patent from John, Thomas, and Richard Penn under the hand of Thomas Penn on 9 Jun 1741, and recorded in Bk A, vol 9, pg 426 on 21 Sept 1741. ... Robert Patrick, Rachel (R) Patrick ... Sealed and delivered in the presence of Benjamin Blythe and James Whithill Jr. ... Ack'd 30 Sept 1745 James Whitehill ... Rec'd 6 Mar 1745 no name ... Cert'd deed was recorded Edwin Reinhold.

B-315 - THIS INDENTURE - 7 Nov 1745 - Edward Smout, John Postlethwaite, and William Bristow all of Lancaster Co., gentlemen to Lawrence Richardson of Lancaster Co., yeoman, £411 for 300A. An attachment was issued from court of Common Pleas against goods, lands, etc. of John Jones of Lancaster Co., yeoman. At suit, of James Morris, Nov 1744, the sheriff was to attach property. Edward Smout, John Postlethwaite and William Bristow were appointed auditors to settle creditors of John Jones and James Morris, a creditor. John indebted to James for £363 13/ & 3d, to Andrew Moore the sum of £55 7/ & 2d, Joseph Newlin £15 19/ & 3 farthings, besides the cost of the suit. Land was sold, purchased by Lawrence Richardson for £411. Land is located in Sadsbury Township and contains 300A. Land is in possession of Isaac Taylor. Plantation is called Gap. ... Edward Smout, John Postlethwaite, William Bristow ... Sealed and delivered in the presence of Robert Lee, Emanuel Arworth, and Joshue Low ... Ack'd 8 Nov 1745 Thomas Cookson ... Rec'd 14 Mar 1745/6 Thomas Cookson.

B-316 - THIS INDENTURE - 8 Apr 1746 - Michael Probtz of Lancaster Co., tailor and Margaret his wife to John Fierre of Lancaster Co., yeoman, £82 for 53 3/4A, enfeoff. A patent was granted by John, Thomas, and Richard Penn on 13 May 1735 to John Myley, a tract of 150 3/4A. Land is located in Leacock Township, neighbor - Adam Miller. John by indenture dated 19 Jun 1735 granted to Lewis Bennony 53 3/4A, of the above mentioned tract. Lewis by indenture dated 10 Jul 1736 granted the 53 3/4A to Jacob Reesy, Jacob granted on 1 May 1740 to James McConnell. James by indenture dated 7 Jan 1744 granted to John Smoze. John by indenture dated 1 Jul 1743 granted the tract to Michael Probtz. ... Michael (mifert) Probtz, Margaret (X) Probtz ... Sealed and delivered in the presence of Thomas Cookson and James Smith ... Ack'd 8 Apr 1746 no name ... Rec'd 17 Apr 1746 ... Cert'd deed was recorded Benjamin Longenecker.

B-318 - THIS INDENTURE - 3 Mar 1745/6 - Abraham Neide of Salisbury Township of Lancaster Co., sadler and Elizabeth his wife to Robert Miller of East Caln Township Chester Co., yeoman, £5 for 230A. Part of the tract, 30A stays as Abrahams. Land is located in Salisbury Township, neighbors - late of Daniel Cookson, now or late of Robert Patricks, now or late of William Clark. Term of 1 yr. was completed in July. ... Abraham

Neide, Elizabeth Neide ... Sealed and delivered in the presence of Charles Cookson and William Richardson ... Ack'd 4 Mar 1745/6 Edward Barwick ... Rec'd 14 May 1746 Thomas Cookson.

B-319 - THIS INDENTURE - 4 Mar 1745/6 - Abraham Neide of Salisbury Township, sadler and Elizabeth his wife to Robert Miller of East Caln Chester Co., yeoman, £220 for 230A. Samuel Smith, John Kinfey, Thomas Leck, John Watson, Thomas Chander, John Wright, all Trustees of the Loan Office by their indenture bearing the date of 10 Dec 1745 did grant to Abraham land containing 230A and located in Salisbury Township. Neighbors - late Daniel Cookson, now late of Robert Patrick, now or late of William Clark. ... Abraham Neide, Elizabeth Neide ... Sealed and delivered in the presence of Charles Cookson, and William Richardson ... Ack'd 4 Mar 1745/6 Edward Barwick ... Rec'd 15 May 1746 no name ... Cert'd deed was recorded Benjamin Longenecker.

B-321 - THIS INDENTURE - 8 Jan 1742 - William Baily of Lancaster Co., yeoman, and Keziah his wife to Richard Peters of the city of Philadelphia gentleman, £106 16/ & 9d for two tracts containing 386A. The first tract contains 266A and is located on the west side of Susquehanna River in Pennsboro Township, neighbors - William Cooper, Robert Mills. Second tract contains 120A and is located on Yellow Breeches Creek, neighbors - none mentioned. Land was granted to William and wife by patent dated 28 May 1745. ... William (X) Baily, Kesiah Baily ... Sealed and delivered by William Baily in the presence of William Peters and John Callahan, sealed and delivered by Kesiah Baily in the presence of George Smith and Thomas Cookson ... Ack'd none ... Rec'd 15 May 1746 ... Cert'd deed was recorded Benjamin Longenecker.

B-324 - THIS INDENTURE - 5 Nov 1744 - Peter Esleman of Lancaster Co., yeoman and Maudeline his wife to Jacob Miller and Jacob Sponsular of Lancaster Co., coopers, £140 for 150A. Land is located on Conestoga Creek, neighbors - Leonard Pendalls, and George Beards, £140 for 150A, enfeoff release. John, Thomas and Richard Penn did on 29 Nov 1739 by patent under the hand of Thomas, granted to Martin Myley a tract of 150A. Patent was recorded in Bk A, vol 1, pg 254 on 29 Nov 1739. Martin by indenture dated 4 May 1742 granted the 150A to Peter Esleman. ... Peter Esleman, Maudeline (+) Esleman ... Sealed and delivered by Peter in the presence of Thomas Cookson, sealed and delivered by Maudeline in the presence of George Smith ... ¬Ack'd 12 Nov 1744 Thomas Cookson ... Rec'd 27 May 1746 no name ... Cert'd deed was recorded Benjamin Longenecker.

B-325 - THIS INDENTURE - 29 May 1745 - Jacob Sponselar of Lancaster Co., cooper and Elizabeth his wife to Jacob Miller of Lancaster Co., cooper, £145 for 150A quit claim. Land is located on Conestoga Creek, neighbors - Leonard Pendal and George Bard. By patent from John, Thomas and Richard Penn under the hand of Thomas Penn dated 29 Nov 1739 was granted to Martin Myley a tract of 150A. Patent is recorded in Bk A, vol 1, pg 254 on 29 Nov 1739. Martin did by indenture dated 24 May 1742 grant the 150A to Peter Elselman. Peter and Maudeline his wife granted the tract to Jacob Miller and Jacob Sponseller on 5 Nov 1744. ... No signatures for Jacob and Elizabeth ... Sealed and delivered in the presence of none ... Ack'd 29 May 1745 Thomas Cookson ... Rec'd 30 May 1746 no name ... Cert'd deed was recorded Benjamin Longernecker.

B-327 - THIS INDENTURE - 10 Oct 1740 - John Musgrave of Lancaster Co., yeoman to Thomas Musgrave of Lampeter Township, son of aforesaid John, 5/ for 450A. Land is located in Lampeter Township, neighbors - Jacob Graff, Abraham Whitmore. Tract is in possession of Thomas. ... John Musgrave ... Sealed and delivered in the presence of Theophilus Owen, Benjamin Owen ... Ack'd 9 Oct 1746 Thomas Cookson ... Rec'd 30 May 1746 no name ... Cert'd deed was recorded Edwin Reinhold.

B-328 - THIS INDENTURE - 11 Oct 1740 - John Musgrave of Lancaster Co., yeoman to Thomas Musgrave of Lampeter Township, son of John. John did by indenture dated 10 Oct 1740, for love and affection grant 450A. Land is located in Lampeter Township, neighbors - late of Jacob Graff, Hans Brand, Abraham Whitmore. Thomas will pay mortgage on tract, he is in actual possession. The land is part of a 600A tract which was granted by lease and release to John on 13 & 14 Mar 1722 by Tobias Collet, Daniel Quare, Henry Gouldney of the city of London. ... John Musgrave ... Sealed and delivered in the presence of Theophilus Owen, Benjamin Owen ... Ack'd 30 Apr 1749 - Samuel Jones ... Rec'd 30 May 1746 ... Cert'd deed was recorded Benjamin Longenecker.

B-330 - THIS INDENTURE - 5 Dec 1739 - John Page of Austin Fryers London, gentleman, William Allen of the city of Philadelphia Esq., William Webb of Chester Co. Esq. and Samuel Powell Jr. of the city of Philadelphia merchant, to Christian Buffty of Plumton Manor Lancaster Co., yeoman, £96 16/ for 242A. Land is located on Tulpehocken Creek, neighbors - intended for Peter Freake, Peter Reed, Maria Cobelsin, and Jacob Sheffer. Rent of 1 red rose 23 Jun every year. John, Thomas, and Richard Penn granted to John Page by patent dated 17 Sept 1735, 5,165A. John named the tract Plumton Manor. Patent is recorded in Bk A, vol 7 pg 264. John pays rent of 1 red rose 24 Jun annually. John on 17 Feb 1736 appointed William Allen, William Webb, Samuel Powell Jr. as his attorneys to sell the land. Power of attorney is recorded in Bk D2, vol 2 pg 196. ... William Allen, William Webb, Samuel Powell Jr. for John Page ... Sealed and delivered in the presence of Michael Sheffer and William Parsons ... Ack'd 14 Apr 1746 Conrad Weiser ... Rec'd 3 Jun 1746 no name ... Cert'd deed was recorded Benjamin Longenecker.

B-333 - THIS INDENTURE of mortgage - 28 Apr 1746 - John Campbell of Pennsboro Township Lancaster Co., miller to Richard Peter of the city of Philadelphia Esq., £79 10/ for 100A. Land is located in Pennsboro on Yellow Breeches, west side of Susquehanna River, has a grist mill, neighbor - Charles Pippens. Must pay before 28 Apr 1747. ... John Campbell ... Sealed and delivered in the presence of John Robinson of Gilberts Manor Philadelphia Co. and John Callahan ... Ack'd 24 May 1746 Thomas Cookson ... Rec'd 25 Jun 1746 no name ... Cert'd deed was recorded Edwin Reinhold.

B-334 - KNOW ALL MEN - 21 May 1746 - I Henry Swancey of Lancaster Co., yeoman in consideration of £35 17/ paid by Richard Peters of the city of Philadelphia Esq., sold 3 tracts containing 550A, mortgage. The first tract contains 250A and is located on Stony Run on west side of Susquehanna River, this is where I now live. The tract was surveyed by virtue of a warrant dated 24 Dec 1742. The second tract contains 200A and is adjoining the above tract, it was surveyed by warrant on the same date. The third tract contains 100A and joins the first and second tracts, neighbors - none mentioned. Sum must be paid within the term of 2 years. ... Henry Swancy ... Sealed and delivered in the presence of Thomas Cookson and John Callahan ... Ack'd none ... Rec'd 25 Jun 1746 no name ... Cert'd deed was recorded Benjamin Longenecker.

B-334 - THIS INDENTURE of mortgage - 16 Apr 1746 - George Mackrel of Lancaster Co. yeoman, to Richard Peters and Lynford Lardner both of the city of Philadelphia, gentlemen, £46 for 203A. George to secure payment of £46 due John, Thomas, and Richard Penn and in consideration of the further sum of 5/ grants 203A. Land is located in Leacock Township, neighbors - John Varners, John Lyon, Joseph Evans, and Sebastian Royers. Condition of repayment as follows - £10 8/ & 6d on 16 Apr 1747, £9 19/ & 3d on 16 Apr 1748, £9 10/ & 1d on 16 Apr 1749, £9 10/ & 1d on 16 Apr 1750, £8 11/ & 8d on 16 Apr 1751, £8 2/ & 6d residue on 16 Apr 1752. ... George (M) Mackul ... Sealed and delivered in the presence of John Callahan of the city of Philadelphia, and James Aishell ... Ack'd 24 May 1746 Thomas Cookson ... Rec'd 26 Jun 1746 Thomas Cookson.

B-337 - THIS INDENTURE - 7 Nov 1745 - Moses Harlan of Monallen Township Lancaster Co., yeoman and Margaret his wife to Charles McClure and Francis McClure of Lancaster Co., gentleman, £115 for 300A, enfeoff release. Land is located on Conestoga Creek, neighbor - William Bells. Tract was granted to Moses by patent from John, Thomas, and Richard Penn under the hand of George Thomas Esq. Lt. Governor on 9 Oct 1745 and recorded in Bk A, vol 12, pg 351 on 10 Oct 1745. One half was granted to Charles and 1/2 granted to Francis. ... Moses Harlan, Margaret (+) Harlan ... Sealed and delivered in the presence of, the words Margaret his wife underlined, John Blackburn, David McCanaughy, and James Karr ... Ack'd 10 Aug 1745 Andrew Galbreth ... Rec'd 3 Jul 1746 no name ... Cert'd deed was recorded Benjamin Longenecker.

B-339 - THIS INDENTURE of mortgage - 15 Aug 1746 - Daniel Mendez de Castro of Lancaster Borough, merchant to Jacob Franks and Napthaly Hart Myers of New York city, merchant, £54 2/ for a Market Place. Tract located in Lancaster Borough, neighbors - James Hamilton, Conrad Swartz. Land was granted to Daniel Mendez under the hand of James Hamilton Esq. on 10 Nov 1744, subject to a payment of £102 and interest to Nathan Levy and David Franks. Land is secured by a former mortgage dated 28 Dec 1744 also subject of £50 to Nathan Levy and David Franks. Another mortgage dated 29 Apr 1745 of £54 2/ in 2 payments. The first payment on 1 Aug 1747, remaining on 1 Nov 1747. ... Daniel Mendez de Castro ... Sealed and delivered in the presence of Thomas Cookson and James Smith ... Ack'd 16 Aug 1746 Thomas Cookson ... Rec'd none ... Cert'd deed was recorded Benjamin Longenecker..

B-340 - THIS INDENTURE - 26 Jul 1746 - Christian Weltey of Lancaster Co., yeoman and Elizabeth his wife to Christian Hersey of Lancaster Co., yeoman, £47 for 67A, enfeoff. Land is located in Hempfield Township, neighbors - Andreas Hersey, Josia Scott. Land was granted to Christian by John, Thomas, and Richard Penn by patent under the

77

hand of George Thomas Esq. Lt. Governor on 13 May 1746 and recorded in Bk A, vol 13, pg 6 on 2 Jun 1746. ... Christian Welly, Elizabeth L. Welly ... Sealed and delivered in the presence of Thomas Cookson and Peter Worrall ... Ack'd 19 Aug 1746 Thomas Cookson ... Rec'd 19 Aug 1746 no name ... Cert'd deed was recorded Edwin Reinhold.

B-342 - THIS INDENTURE - 26 Aug 1746 Michael Crouse of Sancaton Township in Lancaster Co. and Elizabeth his wife to Richard Peters of the city of Philadelphia Esq. 5/ for 435A. Land is located on Conodoguinet Creek in Pennsboro, neighbor - John McClengahan. ... Michael Crouse ... Sealed and delivered in the presence of John Diemet, John Callahan ... Ack'd _ Sept 1746 Thomas Cookson ... Rec'd none ... Cert'd deed was recorded Edwin Reinhold.

B-342 - THIS INDENTURE - 27 Aug 1746 - Michael Crouse of Lancaster Township, inn-holder and Elizabeth his wife to Richard Peters of the city of Philadelphia Esq., £200 for 435A, in actual possession. Land is located on Conodoguinet Creek in Pennsboro Township, neighbor - John McClenaghan. Michael received patent for the land on 25 Aug 1746. ... Michael Crouse, no signature for Elizabeth ... Sealed and delivered in the presence of Captain John Diemer, and John Callahan ... Ack'd 21 Sept 1746 no name ... Rec'd none ... Cert'd deed was recorded Benjamin Longenecker.

B-344 - THIS INDENTURE - 10 Jun 1746 - Jacob Huber of Warwick Township Lancaster Co., yeoman and Elizabeth his wife to Henry Derkdorf of Warwick Township, yeoman, £292 10/ for 270A, in actual possession. Land is located in Warwick Township, neighbors - Peter Frauenbergers, Jacob Woolands, Jacob Weis, John Ernest, and John Stans. Jacob received the land by patent dated 7 May 1745 and recorded in Bk A, vol 13, pg 29. Jacob Huber, Elizabeth Huber ... Sealed and delivered in the presence of Martin Aighenburg and Christian Forney ... Ack'd 3 Oct 1746 Thomas Cookson ... Rec'd 7 Oct 1746 Thomas Cookson.

B-345 - THIS INDENTURE - 9 Jan 1744 - Samuel Bluntson of Hempfield Township Lancaster Co., yeoman to James Sample of Hempfield Township, blacksmith, £120 for 214A, in actual possession. Land is located in Derry Township Lancaster Co., neighbors - late of widow Laird, George Davis, and David McNaris. Samuel received the land by patent from John, Thomas, and Richard Penn on 6 May 1741. ... Samuel Blunston ... Sealed and delivered in the presence of Thomas Watson and Samuel Robinson ... Ack'd 1 Oct 1746 no name ... Rec'd 9 Oct 1746 no name ... Cert'd deed was recorded Benjamin Longenecker.

B-347 - THIS INDENTURE - 8 Jan 1745/6 - Samuel Blunston of Hempfield Township Lancaster Co., yeoman to James Sample of Hempfield Township, blacksmith, 5/ for 214A. Land is located in Derry Township, neighbors - widow Larid. ... Samuel Blunston ... Sealed and delivered in the presence of Samuel (8) Robinson and Thomas Watson ... Ack'd 1 Oct 1746 no name ... Rec'd 9 Oct 1746 ... Cert'd deed was rec'd Benjamin Longenecker.

B-348 - THIS INDENTURE - 9 Jun 1746 - Jacob Huber of Warwick Township, yeoman and Elizabeth his wife to Henry Denedorf of Warwick Township, yeoman, 5/ for 170A. Land is located in Warwick Township, neighbors - Peter Frovenberger, Jacob Woodland, Jacob Weis, John Emiss, John Harris. ... Jacob Huber, Elizabeth Huber ... Sealed and delivered in the presence of Martin Forney and Martin Argenburg ... Approved by Martin Argenburg before Ben? Smout 14 Oct 1746 ... Rec'd 10 Oct 1746 Thomas Cookson.

B-349 - THIS INDENTURE - 25 Oct 1746 - James Hamilton of the city of Philadelphia, gentleman to Andreas Beverly of Lancaster Township, for rents and services one lot. The lot is located in Lancaster borough on Queen St., neighbors - on north Philip Ramegh, south William Oaster. Rent of 14/ on 1 May. ... James Hamilton ... Sealed and delivered in the presence of Thomas Cookson ... Ack'd 22 Oct 1746 Thomas Cookson ... Rec'd 24 Nov 1746 Thomas Cookson.

B-350 - THIS INDENTURE - 12 Nov 1746 - Andreas Beverly of Lancaster Borough, inn-holder, Anna Katherine his wife to Philip Shryner of Manheim Township, yeoman, £130 for 1 lot. Lot located in Lancaster Borough on Queen St., neighbors - north Philip Ramegh, south William Ousler. By indenture dated 22 Oct 1746, James Hamilton of the city of Philadelphia, gentleman did grant to Andreas 1 lot in Lancaster Borough on Queen St. ... Andrea Beverly, Anna Catherine (AB) Beverly ... Sealed and delivered in the presence of Thomas Cookson and Sebastian Graffe ... Ack'd and release of dower 21 Nov 1746 Thomas Cookson ... Rec'd 26 Nov 1746 no name ... Cert'd deed was recorded Benjamin Longenecker.

B-352 - THIS INDENTURE - 28 Sept 1746 - John Hair of Lancaster Co., yeoman and Barbara his wife to Christian Longanaire of Lancaster Co., yeoman, £25 for 94A, enfeoff. Land is located in Rapho Township, neighbor - Jacob Riess, Henry Saunders, and John Bare. Land is part of a 290A tract granted to John by Michael Meyer and Barbara his wife by lease and release on 2 Apr 1736, recorded Bk A, pg 9, 12 Sept 1737. ... Hans Heer, Barbara (BH) Heer ... Sealed and delivered in the presence of Thomas Cookson, and James Smith ... Ack'd 28 Sept 1746 Thomas Cookson ... Rec'd 30 Apr 1747 no name ... Cert'd deed was recorded Benjamin Longenecker.

B-354 - THIS INDENTURE - 28 Jan 1750 - Michael Myer of Manheim Township, yeoman to James Hamilton of the city of Philadelphia Esq., 2/ for 200A. Land located in Manheim Township, neighbor - Henry Funk. ... Michael (MM) Myer ... Sealed and delivered in the presence of Lawrence Hoof and Charles Morse ... Ack'd 29 Jan 1750 Thomas Cookson ... Rec'd 11 Feb 1750 no name ... Cert'd deed was recorded Edwin Reinhold.

B-355 - THIS INDENTURE - 29 Jan 1750 - Michael Myer of Manheim Township Lancaster Co., yeoman and Elizabeth his wife to James Hamilton of the city of Philadelphia, Esq., £1,000 for 200A. Land is located in Mannheim Township, neighbor - Henry Funks. John Funk of Strasburg Township received by warrant dated 7 & 20 Sept 1749, from the commissioners Richard Hill, Isaac Norris, and James Logan, 200A. Deed recorded in Bk A, vol 6, pg 155 on 4 Feb 1731. By indenture dated 20 Feb 1724/5 John and Barbara did grant to Michael Myer the 200A. ... Michael (MM) Myer, Elizabeth (B) Myer ... Sealed and delivered in the presence of Charles Morse ... Received £1,000, Michael Myer ... Ack'd and release of dower 29 Jun 1750 Thomas Cookson ... Rec'd 11 Feb 1750 no name ... Cert'd deed was recorded Benjamin Longenecker.

B- 359 - THIS INDENTURE of mortgage - 3 Dec 1750 - John Snevely Jr. of Lancaster Co., yeoman to Joseph Sims of the city of Philadelphia, merchant and the guardian of Sarah Woodrop, infant under 21, £100 for 276A. John is bound to Joseph in the sum of £200. Condition for repayment of £100 by 2 Dec 1751. John to better secure payment and in consideration of the further sum of 5/ grants 276A. Tract is located on the west side of Conestoga Creek, neighbor - now or late of Joseph Funk. ... Joseph Snevely ... Sealed and delivered in the presence of Lewis Gordon and William Tea ... Received £100 on 3 Dec 1750, John Snevely ... Testee: Lewis Gordon ... Ack'd 5 Feb 1750 Thomas Cookson ... Rec'd 22 Feb 1750 no name ... Cert'd deed was recorded Benjamin Longenecker.

B-362 - THIS INDENTURE - 22 Oct 1746 - John Hart of Lancaster Borough, merchant to Thomas Doyle of Lancaster Borough, hatter, £100 for 1 lot, enfeoff. Pay before 22 Jun 1747. Lot located in Lancaster Borough on King St. north Queen St., neighbors - south Henry Bostler, east Joseph Jones. James Hamilton granted on 15 Jul 1745 to Moses Musgrove a lot in Lancaster Borough. Moses and Elizabeth his wife did on 24 Oct 1745 grant the lot to John Hart. ... John Hart ... Sealed and delivered in the presence of Thomas Cookson and James Smith ... Ack'd 27 Oct 1746 Thomas Cookson ... Rec'd 27 Nov 1746 ... Cert'd deed was recorded Benjamin Longenecker.

B-364 - THIS INDENTURE of mortgage - 1 Dec 1746 - Thomas Thornbrugh of Lancaster Borough, mason to Thomas Doyle of Lancaster Borough, hatter, £130 for 1/2 lot. Lot is located in Lancaster Borough on King St., east Water St., neighbors - west Garret Cavenagh, south King St. Yearly rent of 3/ 6d. Thomas Thornbrugh is bound unto Doyle by several indentures in the sum of £130. Thornbrugh to secure payment and in consideration of the further sum of 5/ grants 1/2 lot. Repayment in the following manner - £25 on 1 Dec 1747, £25 on 1 Dec 1748, £25 on 1 Dec 1749, £25 on 1 Dec 1750, £25 on 1 Dec 1751, £25 residue on 1 Dec 1752. ... Thomas Thornbrugh ... Sealed and delivered in the presence of Isaac Whitebach and George Smith ... Ack'd 27 Dec 1746 Thomas Cookson ... Rec'd 5 Jan 1746/7 ... Cert'd deed was recorded Benjamin Longenecker.

B-366 - THIS INDENTURE - 1 Jul 1746 - Francis McClure of Lancaster Co., and Charles McClure of Rapho, County Donegal of Ireland, gentleman to David McClure of Lancaster Co., gentleman, £180 for 300A, enfeoff. Land is located in Lancaster Co., neighbor - William Bell. By patent from John, Thomas, and Richard Penn under the hand of George Thomas Esq. Lt. Governor date 9 Oct 1745 did grant to Moses Harlan 330A. Land is located on Conestoga Creek, and recorded in Bk A, vol 2, pg 357. Moses and Margaret his wife by indenture dated 7 Nov 1745 granted to Charles McClure and Francis McClure the 300A. Charles by a letter of attorney dated 22 Mar 1746 did appoint Francis McClure and Andrew Sayers his attorneys to sell the land. ... Francis McClure, Charles

McClure, and Andrew Sayers ... Sealed and delivered in the presence of Jaret Graham and George Smith ... Ack'd 3 Dec 1746 James Whithill ... Rec'd 9 Jan 1746/7 ... Cert'd deed was recorded Benjamin Longenecker.

B-368 - THIS INDENTURE - 22 Mar 1745/6 - Know all Men - I Charles McClure of the Kingdom in the Parish of Rapho and the County of Donegal in the Kingdom of Ireland for divers and consideration appoint Francis McClure and Andrew Sayers of PA, gentleman my attorneys to sell 300A of land on Conestoga Creek, Chester Co. ... Charles McClure ... Witness - Will Porter, and Cuningham Porter ... Ack'd 13 Nov 1746 Charles Willing ... Rec'd 9 Jan 1746/7 no name ... Cert'd deed was recorded Benjamin Longenecker.

B-369 - THIS INDENTURE - 18 Sept 1746 - James Galbreth of Lancaster Co., gentleman and Elizabeth his wife to Richard Peters of the city of Philadelphia, gentleman, 5/ for 2 tracts containing 395A. First tract contains 153A and is located on Conodoguinet Creek in Hopewell Township, neighbors - John Kilpatrick, John Finley, Thomas Alexander, and David Osburns. Second tract contains 242A and is located in Paxton Township, neighbors - Robert Taylor, Adam Bratton, and Hugh Davys. ... James Galbreath, Elizabeth (g) Galbreath ... Sealed and delivered in the presence of Thomas Cookson and Michael Smosey ... Ack'd and release of dower 7 Nov 1746 Thomas Cookson ... Rec'd 11 Jan 1746/7 no name ... Cert'd deed was recorded Benjamin Longenecker.

B-370 - THIS INDENTURE - 19 Sept 1746 - James Galbeath of Derry Township Lancaster Co., gentleman and Elizabeth his wife to Richard Peters of the city of Philadelphia, £300 for 2 tracts containing 395A, in actual possession. First tract contains 153A and is located on Conodoguinet Creek in Hopewell Township, neighbors - John Kilpatrick, John Finleys, Thomas Alexander, and David Osburn. The second tract contains 242A and is located in Paxton Township, neighbors - Robert Taylor, Adam Bratton. James was granted the 2 tracts by patent on 17 Sept 1746. ... James Galbreath, Elizabeth (g) Galbreath ... Sealed and delivered in the presence of Thomas Cookson and Miles McLury ... Ack'd 7 Nov 1746 Thomas Cookson ... Rec'd 13 Jan 1746/7 no name ... Cert'd deed was recorded Benjamin Longenecker.

B-371 - THIS INDENTURE - 18 Sept 1746 - William Maxwell of Lancaster Co., gentleman and Susanna his wife to Richard Peters of the city of Philadelphia gentleman, 5/ for 370A. Land is located in Bethel Township, neighbors - widow David, Aaron Alexander, Thomas David and Philip Davis. ... William Maxwell, Susanna (S) Maxwell ... Sealed and delivered in the presence of John McCilland and Thomas Cookson ... Ack'd and release of dower 8 Nov 1746 Thomas Cookson ... Rec'd 16 Jan 1746/7 ... Cert'd deed was recorded Benjamin Longenecker.

B-372 - THIS INDENTURE - 19 Sept 1746 - William Maxwell Bethel Township Lancaster Co. Esq. and Susanna his wife to Richard Peters of the city of Philadelphia, gentleman, £135 for 370A, in actual possession. Land located in Bethel Township, neighbor - widow Davis, Aaron Alexander, Thomas Davids ... William Maxwell, Susanna (S) Maxwell ... Sealed and delivered in the presence of John McClillan and Thomas

Cookson ... Ack'd and release of dower 8 Nov 1746 Thomas Cookson ... Rec'd 16 Jan 1746/7 no name ... Cert'd deed was recorded Benjamin Longenecker.

B-374 - THIS INDENTURE - 6 Dec 1755 - Hugh Morrison of Bern Township Lancaster Co., yeoman and Mary his wife to Richard Peters of the city of Philadelphia, £80 for 180A, in actual possession. Land is located in Bern Township, neighbor - James Taylor. Hugh received this land by patent dated 5 Dec 1755. ... Hugh Morrinson, Mary (O) Morrison ... Sealed and delivered in the presence of Thomas (I) Sinken, Richard Hockley, Francis Parvin ... Ack'd 27 Feb 1745/6 Henry Harry ... Rec'd none ... Cert'd deed was recorded 1747 Benjamin Longenecker.

B-375 - THIS INDENTURE - 29 Jan 1747 - George Hoffman of Lancaster Township Esq. and Mary Madgelen his wife to Nathan Levy and David Frank of the city of Philadelphia, merchants, £266 13/ for 1 lot. Lot is located in Lancaster Township on King St., neighbors - east George Hoffman, west Andrew Beverly. Rent of 2/ 4d yearly. ... George Hoffman, Mary Magdalen (X inside a circle) Hoffman ... Sealed and delivered in the presence of David Stout and Peter Worrall ... Ack'd 29 Jun 1747 Peter Worrall ... Rec'd 29 Jun 1747 ... Cert'd deed was recorded Benjamin Longenecker.

B-382 - THIS INDENTURE - 20 Sept 1737 - Henry Carpenter of Lampeter Township, yeoman and Salomea his wife to Daniel Carpenter of Earl Township, yeoman, son of Henry and Salomea, 5/ and love and affection for 340A. Land is located in Earl Township, neighbors - Gabriel Carpenter, Emanuel Carpenter, Jacob Bear, and Michael Bear. Tract is part of 1,550A which was granted to Henry by patent under the hand of Thomas Penn on 12 Mar 1733. Land is located on Conestoga Creek and recorded in Bk A, vol 6, pg 290, on 10 May 1734. Rent of 1/ for every acre. ... Henry (H) Carpenter, Salomea Carpenter ... Sealed and delivered in the presence of Joseph Lowe and Thomas Cookson ... Ack'd 21 Feb 1737 Derrick Updegraef ... Rec'd 10 Jan 1746/7 no name ... Cert'd deed was recorded Benjamin Longenecker.

B-383 - THIS INDENTURE - 20 Sept 1737 - Henry Carpenter of Lampeter Township yeoman and Salomea his wife to Gabriel Carpenter of Earl Township, son of Henry and Salomea, 5/ and natural love, affection for 340A, enfeoff. This is the land Gabriel now lives on in Earl Township. Neighbors - Daniel Carpenter, Michael Bear, John Landus, Daniel Breman, and Henry Carpenter. Land is part of a tract of 1,550A which was granted to Henry Carpenter by John, Thomas, and Richard Penn. Land was granted under the hand of Thomas Penn on 12 Mar 1733, and recorded Bk A, vol 6, pg 290 on 12 May 1730. Emanuel and Daniel are other sons of Henry. ... Henry (H) Carpenter, Salomea (6 inside a circle) Carpenter ... Ack'd 21 Feb 1737 Derrick Updgraf ... Rec'd 20 Feb 1746/7 ... Cert'd deed was recorded Benjamin Longenecker.

B-385 - THIS INDENTURE - 20 Sept 1747 - Henry Carpenter of Lampeter Township, yeoman and Salomea his wife to Henry Carpenter of Earl Township yeoman, and son of Henry and Salomea, 5/ and love, affection, 320A, enfeoff. This is the land where Henry now lives. Tract is located on a branch of Conestoga Creek in Earl Township, neighbors - Roody Stoner, Emanuel Carpenter, Daniel Carpenter, Gabriel Carpenter, and Daniel

Berman. The land is part of a tract of 1,550A which was granted to Henry (father) by John, Thomas, and Richard Penn, 12 Mar 1733. Deed is recorded in Bk A, vol 6, pg 290, on 10 May 1734. ... Henry (HC) Carpenter, Salomea (6 in a circle) Carpenter ... Ack'd 21 Feb 1737 Derrick Updgraf ... Rec'd 24 Jan 1746/7 Thomas Cookson ... Cert'd deed was recorded Benjamin Longenecker.

B-387 - THIS INDENTURE - 10 Dec 1743 - Gabriel Carpenter of Earl Township yeoman and Apelona his wife to Henry Carpenter of Earl Township, yeoman and brother of Gabriel, 5/ for 21A. Land is located in Earl Township, neighbors - Garbriel Carpenter, Henry Carpenter. The tract is part of 340A which was granted to Gabriel by his father Henry and mother Salomea by lease and release dated 19 & 20 Sept 1737. The 340A is part of a larger tract of 1,550A granted to Henry (father) by John, Thomas, and Richard Penn on 12 Mar 1733 and recorded in Bk A, vol 6, pg 290 on 10 May 1734. ... Gabriel Zimmerman, Apelona (+) Carpenter ... Sealed and delivered in the presence of John Ludwig Klein, and Jurg Meille ... Ack'd 18 Jun 1744 Emanuel Carpenter ... Rec'd 24 Jan 1746/7 Thomas Cookson.

B-389 - THIS INDENTURE - 21 Dec 1743 - Daniel Carpenter of Earl Township yeoman and Magdaline his wife to Emanuel Carpenter, yeoman and brother of Daniel, 5/ for 140A, enfeoff. Land is located in Earl Township, neighbor - Henry Carpenter. Daniel is moving, land is part of a larger tract of 340A granted to Daniel by his father and mother, Henry and Salomea Carpenter on 20 Sept 1737. The 340A is part of a larger tract of 1,550A, granted to Henry by John, Thomas, and Richard Penn on 20 Mar 1735. Deed is recorded in Bk A, vol 6, pg 290 on 20 May 1734. ... Daniel Carpenter, Magdelin Zimmerman ... Sealed and delivered in the presence of Nicholas Lynn and Emanuel Bare ... Ack'd 26 Mar 1744 Conrad Weiser ... Rec'd 22 Jan 1746 Thomas Cookson.

B-391 - THIS INDENTURE - 21 Dec 1743 - Daniel Carpenter of Earl Township yeoman and Magdalina his wife to Henry Carpenter Jr. of Earl Township yeoman and brother to Daniel, 5/ for 90A, enfeoff. Tract is located on a branch of Conestoga Creek in Earl Township, neighbors - none mentioned. The 90A is part of a larger tract of 340A which was granted to Daniel by his father and mother, Henry and Salmoea Carpenter on 20 Sept 1737. The 340A is part of a 1,550A tract which was granted to Henry by John, Thomas, and Richard Penn on 12 Mar 1733 and recorded in Bk A, vol 6, pg 240 on 10 May 1734. ... Daniel Carpenter, Magdaline Carpenter ... Sealed and delivered in the presence of Nicholas Sey, and Emanuel Hair ... Ack'd 26 Mar 1744 Conrad Weiser ... Rec'd 23 Jan 1746/7 no name ... Cert'd deed was recorded Benjamin Longenecker.

B-393 - THIS INDENTURE of mortgage - 17 Jan 1740 - George Mendenhall of Leacock Township yeoman to Israel Penton of the city of Philadelphia, merchant, £250 for 2 tracts containing 298A. George is bound unto Israel in the sum of £500. George to better secure payment and in consideration of the further amount of 5/ grants 2 tracts containing 298A. The first tract contains 243A and is located in Leacock Township, neighbors - Philip Bausleman, John Vernon, John Veerner, Hattel Verner and Philip Houston. This tract was granted to George by Samuel Jones on 29 Mar 1744. The second tract contains 55A and is located in Leacock Township, neighbors - Hattel Verner, William Bamelton,

William Hamilton, and John Verner. George received this tract by indenture from Samuel Jones on 10 Apr 1744. Condition of repayment of £250 is a follows - £15 on 17 Jan 1747, £15 principle and £250 on 17 Jan 1748. ... George Mendenhall ... Sealed and delivered in the presence of Charles Brockden, James Wright, and Charles Pemberton ... Ack'd 17 Jan 1746 James Galbreath ... Rec'd 28 Jan 1746/7 no name ... Cert'd deed was recorded Benjamin Longenecker.

B-395 - THIS INDENTURE - 28 Nov 1746 - Jacob Neisley of Manheim Township yeoman and Mary his wife to Sebastian Graffe of Lancaster Borough yeoman, £6 for 25A enfeoff. Land is located in Manheim Township, neighbors - none mentioned. Tract is part of a larger tract of 101A granted to Jacob by John, Thomas, and Richard Penn under the hand of George Thomas Esq. Lt. Governor on 7 Oct 1730. ... Jacob Neisley, Mary (M) Neisley ... Sealed and delivered in the presence of Thomas Cookson, David Stout and Peter Grung ... Ack'd 28 Jan 1746/7 Thomas Cookson ... Rec'd 31 Jan 1746 no name ... Cert'd deed was recorded Benjamin Longenecker.

B-397 - GENERAL ASSEMBLY - no date - of the Province made in the fourth year of Lady Queen Anne, was entitled an act of better settling intestates estates, and provided the said Act of Assembly that no partition shall be made of ___ if the heir at law shall pay or secure to be paid to the younger children their respective shares of the value of such lands according to the judgment or valuing of 4 or more persons, indifferently to be chosen and agreed upon by the parties with in one year there upon the same shall be vested in him as fully and amply as he infant held the same in his life time, and where as the said tract of land has been valued by 4 different person and agreed upon by the parties as £300 and where as Christopher Trinkle, John Attebarger and John Miller parties to these present have entered into bonds with Jacob Loughman for payment of £240 for the youngest children - £60 to each of them at day and time to be mentioned. THIS INDENTURE of mortgage - Jacob Loughman of Conestoga Manor to Christopher Trinkle potter, John Aldebarger, joiner and John Miller blacksmith, all of Conestoga Manor, £120 for 150A. Land is located on Conestoga Creek, neighbors - Philip Rudyillys, Anthony Miller Jr. and Conrad Moyers. Jacob to better secure payment and in consideration of the further amount of 5/ grants 150A. Land was patented to Caspar Loughman on 18 Dec 1740. Caspar, a blacksmith, died intestate and left children, Jacob oldest son, Caspar, Dorothy wife of George Redenbough, Barbara and Frederick. ... Jacob Loughman ... Sealed and delivered in the presence of Thomas Cookson and David Stout ... Ack'd 24 Feb 1746/7 no name ... Rec'd 27 Feb 1746/7 no name ... Cert'd deed was recorded Benjamin Longenecker.

B-399 - THIS INDENTURE - 6 Nov 1746 - Philip Davis of Lancaster Co. to Richard Peters and Lynford Lardner of the city of Philadelphia gentlemen, £68 for 611A. Land is located on a branch of Conestoga Creek, neighbors - John Davy, Richard Sand, and James Harlan. Philip to secure payment of £68 6d due to John, Thomas, and Richard Penn and in consideration of the further amount of 5/ grants 611A. Condition of repayment as follows - £17 13/ & 7d on 6 Nov 1747, £16 17/ & 4d on 6 Nov 1748, £16 & 1/ on 6 Nov 1749, £15 4/ & 8d on 6 Nov 1750, £14 8/ & 4d on 6 Nov 1751. ... Philip Daves ... Sealed and delivered in the presence of Thomas Davinson of West Calon, Chester Co. and

John Callahan ... Ack'd 8 Nov 1746 Thomas Cookson ... Rec'd 7 Mar 1746/7 Thomas Cookson ... Cert'd deed was recorded Benjamin Longenecker.

B-401 - THIS INDENTURE - 9 Feb 1746/7 - Mary Prator of Earl Township Lancaster Co., widow of Anthony Prator late of Earl Township dec'd yeoman, to Anthony Elmaker of Earl Township yeoman, food, lodging, and clothing and care for the rest of Mary's life, for 189A. Land is located on a branch of Mill Creek. Anthony was granted 2 tracts by patent from John, Thomas, and Richard Penn on 10 Mar 1736 and 14 Jan 1739. First tract contains 151A and the second contains 218A. By Anthony's will he devised to Anthony Elmaker 189A but departed before it was completed, leaving no issue. Mary wanting to fulfill his will and in consideration of 5/ grants 189A, enfeoff. ... Mary (+) Prator ... Sealed and delivered in the presence of Andrew Caldwell and Baltzor Beasor ... Ack'd 14 Feb 1746 Edward Barwick ... Rec'd 7 Mar 1746/7 Thomas Cookson.

B-402 - THIS INDENTURE of mortgage - 9 Feb 1746/7 - John Connolly of Lancaster Co., gentleman to James Gillespie and John Hart of Lancaster Co., gentlemen, £646 12/ & 8d for 397A and 1 lot. The tract is located on little Conewago Creek, neighbor - Valentine Graffe. Lot is located in Lancaster Borough on Prince St. and on west Water St., neighbor - on south John Lowe. James Gillespie and John Hart for debt of John Connolly to James Wright and Gordon Howard guardians of James Ewing, William Ewing, Samuel Ewing and John Ewing, minors and orphans of Thomas Ewing dec'd in the penal sum of £1,293 5/ & 4d. Condition of repayment of £646 12/ & 8d before or on 8 Feb 1746/7. John Connolly to secure debt and in consideration of the further amount of 5/ grants 397A and 1 lot. ... John Connolly ... Sealed and delivered in the presence of Thomas Cookson and George Smith ... Ack'd 4 Mar 1746/7 Thomas Cookson ... Rec'd 11 Mar 1746/7 Thomas Cookson.

B-404 - THIS INDENTURE - 5 Nov 1746 - James Harriet Esq., high sheriff of Lancaster Co. to Thomas Cookson of Lancaster Borough, gentleman £520 for 600A. Land located the west side of Susquehanna River. Land was granted to Peter Chacter by John, Thomas, and Richard Penn by patent dated 2 Oct 1740. Sheriff ordered by the Court of Common Pleas on 5 Aug 1746 to sell the land of Peter Chactur for a debt of £647 13/ & 5d, which was recovered by Thomas Lawrence. Thomas was also granted 73/ 9d for damages. Sale was held 26 Aug 1745, Thomas Cookson was highest bidder. ... James Herriet ... Sealed and delivered in the presence of George Smith and James Smith ... Ack'd 7 Nov 1746 Thomas Cookson ... Rec'd 20 Mar 1746/7 no name ... Cert'd deed was recorded Benjamin Longenecker.

B-406 - THIS INDENTURE - 8 Nov 1746 - Thomas Cookson of Lancaster Borough, gentleman and Margaret his wife to Thomas Lawrence of the city of Philadelphia Esq., £520 for 600A, enfeoff. Land located on the west side of Susquehanna River in Paxton Manor, neighbor - none mentioned. Land was granted to Thomas by James Herriet Esq. sheriff by indenture dated 5 Nov 1746. ... Thomas Cookson, Margaret Cookson ... Sealed and delivered in the presence of Edward Smout, and Bob Thornbrugh ... Ack'd 7 Mar 1746/7 Edward Smout ... Rec'd 21 Mar 1746/7 ... Cert'd deed was recorded Benjamin Longenecker.

B-408 - THIS INDENTURE - 8 Jan 1746/7 - James Murray of Lancaster Co., house carpenter to Richard Peters of the city of Philadelphia, gentleman, 5/ for 472A. Land located in Hopewell Township, neighbor - none mentioned. ... James Murry ... James Aiskell, and John Callahan ... Ack'd none ... Rec'd none ... Cert'd deed was recorded Benjamin Longenecker.

THIS INDENTURE - 9 Jan 1746/7 - James Murray of Donegal Township Lancaster Co., house carpenter to Richard Peters of the city of Philadelphia, gentleman, £350 for 472A, in actual possession. Land located in Hopewell Township, neighbor - none mentioned. James received land by patent dated 7 Oct 1746 from the Proprietors. ... James Murray ... Sealed and delivered in the presence of James Aishell, and John Callaghan ... Ack'd none ... Rec'd none ... Cert'd deed was recorded Benjamin Longenecker.

B-411 - THIS INDENTURE - 13 Apr 1747 - Peter Worrall who intermarried with Sarah one of the nieces of Samuel Blunston late of Lancaster Co. first part, Thomas Pearson who intermarried with Hannah another niece of Samuel Blunston, second part, and Thomas Cookson and Peter Worrall guardians of Samuel Bethel a minor and legatee under the last will and testament of Samuel Blunston dec'd, third part. By account of James Wright, surviving executor of the will of Samuel, there is for payment of debts and specific legacies the sum of £1,730 15/ to be divided amongst heirs, according to directions, half to Samuel Bethel and the other half to be divided between Peter Worrell and Sarah his wife and Thomas Pearson and Hannah his wife. The sum of £1,736 is of debts secured by bonds and notes taken from James by Samuel Blunston and are assigned and transferred to Peter Worrall and Thomas Pearson and Thomas Cookson and Peter Worrall as guardians of Samuel Bethel. Peter Worrall, Thomas Pearson, Thomas Cookson have agreed that the £1,746 15/ should be equally born by all in proportion to their respective shares of the sum provided by the note or bond. ... Peter Worrell, Thomas Pearson, Thomas Cookson ... Sealed and delivered in the presence of David Stout and James Wright ... Ack'd 14 Apr 1747 Edward Smout ... Rec'd 14 Apr 1747 no name ... Cert'd deed was recorded Benjamin Longenecker.

B-412 - THIS INDENTURE - 10 Apr 1747 - Lawrence Richardson of Lancaster Co. and Mary his wife to Patrick Carrigan of Lancaster Co., yeoman, £330 for 221A. Location not given, neighbors - John Hildebrand, Simon King Christopher Sawer. Lawrence received land from patent from John, Thomas and Richard Penn under the hand of Thomas Penn on 6 Sept 1746. ... Lawrence Richardson, Mary Richardson ... Sealed and delivered in the presence of Edward Smout, and John Foulks ... Ack'd 10 Apr 1734 Edward Smount ... Rec'd 14 Apr 1747 ... Cert'd deed was recorded Benjamin Longenecker. Full satisfaction received 18 Mar 1756.

B-415 - THIS INDENTURE - 22 Apr 1747 - John Simon of Warwick Township Lancaster Co., yeoman to Joseph Parks of Chester Borough Chester Co., yeoman £100 for 135A, enfeoff. Land is located on a branch of Conestoga Creek in Warwick Township. neighbor - Jacob Beyerleys, Jacob Moyers, Christian Palmers. ... John Simon ... Sealed and delivered in the presence of Thomas Cummings and Henry Graham ... Ack'd 1747 no name ... Rec'd 8 Jun 1747 no name ... Cert'd deed was recorded Benjamin Longenecker ... By virtue of a warrant of attorney from Joseph Parker of Chester Co., recorded in Bk E, pg 69 received full satisfaction 18 Mar 1750, Edward Shippen

B-417 - THIS INDENTURE - 23 Apr 1746 - Lawrence Hoff of Lancaster Co., yeoman to Jacob Stoufer of Lancaster Co., yeoman, £320 for 141 1/2A, enfeoff. Location of land not given, has grist mill. Tract was granted to Lawrence by John, Thomas, and Richard Penn under the hand of George Thomas Esq. Lt. Governor on 27 May 1746, recorded in Bk A, vol 12, pg 417 on 20 May 1746. ... Lawrence Hoff ... Sealed and delivered in the presence of Peter Worrall and John Bowne ... Ack'd 23 Jun 1747 no name ... Rec'd 2 Jun 1747 no name ... Cert'd deed was recorded Benjamin Longenecker.

B-418 - THIS INDENTURE - 2 Mar 1743 - Daniel Feree of Strasburg Township, yeoman and Anna Maria his wife, Isaac Lefevre of Strasburg Township, yeoman and Catherine his wife to John Feree of Strasburg Township, yeoman, £40 for 383A. This is part of several tracts located in Strasburg Township, neighbors - John Jones, Philip Frerr. One tract contains 131A and one contains 191A. This land is for John during his natural life then to his heirs by his late wife Mary, daughter of John Musgrave. William Penn granted to Daniel Feree and Isaac Lefevre on 10 Sept 1722 a tract located on Little Beaver Creek, containing 2,000A. There was a considerable error discovered and the tract was resurveyed on 24 Jan 1733/4, found to contain 2,300A. New patent was issued for £21 on 29 Oct 1734, recorded in Bk A, vol __, pg 319 on 6 Nov 1735. Received with tract three full fifths of all royal mines. ... Daniel Faree, Anna Maria Fravee, Isaac Lefevre, Catherine Lefevre ... Sealed and delivered in the presence of Benjamin Whitmore, John Miller, and Jonathan Hearsley ... Ack'd 1 Jun 1747 Thomas Cookson ... Rec'd 9 Jun 1747 ... Cert'd deed war recorded Benjamin Longenecker.

B-421 - THIS INDENTURE - 17 Dec 1745 - Joseph Stoneman of Conestoga Township, yeoman and Francis his wife to John Cagey of Lancaster Co., yeoman, £300 for 151A. Land is located in Lancaster Co. and is part of a larger tract containing 250A, neighbors - none mentioned. The 250A was granted to Joseph Stoneman by Clelb Baker. ... Joseph (IS) Stoneman, Francis (F) Stoneman ... Sealed and delivered in the presence of David Jones Jr. and Isaac Saunders ... Ack'd and release of dower 17 Dec 1745 David Jones ... Rec'd 10 Jun 1747 ... Cert'd deed was recorded Benjamin Longenecker.

B-422 - THIS INDENTURE of mortgage - 1 Apr 1747 - John Scott of Pennsboro Township yeoman and Margaret his wife to Peacock Biggar of the city of Philadelphia, £32 5/ for 210A. Land is located on Conodoguinet Creek in Pennsboro Township. neighbors - none mentioned. John and Margaret to better secure a certain debt of £32 and in consideration of the further sum of 5/ grants 210A. ... John Scott, Margaret (X) Scott ... Sealed and delivered in the presence of John Reily and Robert Forde ... Ack'd and release of dower 1 Apr 1747 John Kinsey ... Rec'd 11 Jun 1747 no name ... Cert'd deed was recorded Benjamin Longenecker.

B-424 - THIS INDENTURE of mortgage - 1 Apr 1747 - Christopher Weitman of Cocalico Township, yeoman to John Ruble of Lancaster Co., yeoman £250 for 220A, enfeoff. Land is located in Cocalico Township, neighbors - Philip Stephen, George Hedges, Peter Hallam, Conrad Miller, William Boid, and Abraham Carn. Condition of repayment as follows - £50 on 17 Nov 1750, £200 in annual payments of £500 yearly until paid according to connotation of several obligations, 5 in number. ... Christopher Weitman ... Sealed and delivered in the presence of Thomas Cookson and James Smith ... Ack'd 1 Apr 1747 Thomas Cookson ... Rec'd 11 Jun 1747 no name ... Cert'd deed was recorded Benjamin Longenecker.

B-426 - THIS INDENTURE of mortgage - 11 May 1747 - John Leman of Lampeter Township, yeoman, one of the sons of Peter Leman, dec'd and Elizabeth his wife to Thomas Doyle of Lancaster Borough, hatter, £40 for 300A. Land is located in Strasburg Township, neighbor - Isaac Lefevre. Peter Leman died seized of 300A, in his will dated 9 Apr 1741 he left the 300A to John and Abe Leman. To be divided equally between them. Abe died intestate before he was 21 yrs. Peter received the land from Isaac Norris, James Loger, Thomas Griffith as attorneys for Joshua Gee, Thomas Oad and John Wood by patent dated 9 Dec 1728. ... John Leman, Elizabeth (X) Leman ... Sealed and delivered in the presence of Thomas Cookson, James Smith, and Daniel Borson ... Ack'd and release of dower 11 Jun 1747 Thomas Cookson ... Rec'd 11 Jun 1747 ... Cert'd deed was recorded Benjamin Longenecker.

B-428 - THIS INDENTURE - 26 May 1746 - Michael Baughman of Manheim Township, yeoman and Katherine his wife to Samuel Overhulls, of Lancaster Co., yeoman, 5/ for 207A. Land is located in Conestoga Manor, neighbors - late of John Bumgarner and Peter Rizer, Henry Kilheaver, late of Peter Kuger. ... Michael Baughman, Catherine (I) Baughman ... Sealed and delivered in the presence of Michael Goff, and Emanuel Carpenter ... Ack'd none ... Rec'd none ... Cert'd deed was recorded Benjamin Longenecker.

B-429 - THIS INDENTURE - 27 May 1746 Michael Baughman of Manheim Township and Katherine his wife to Samuel Overhulls of Lancaster Co., yeoman, £120 for 207A, enfeoff, in actual possession. Land is part of a tract of 500A, and is located in Conestoga Manor. Michael received the land by lease and release dated 31 Dec 1739 from Andrew Hamilton Esq. of the city of Philadelphia. It is part of a tract of 1,500A which Andrew received by patent dated 13 Dec 1735 from John, Thomas, and Richard Penn, under the hand of Thomas Penn. ... Michael Baughman, Catherine (I) Baughman ... Sealed and delivered in the presence of Michael Crouse and Daniel Mitinga ... Ack'd 7 May 1747 Emanuel Carpenter ... Rec'd 17 Jun 1747 no name ... Cert'd deed was recorded Benjamin Longenecker.

B-432 - THIS INDENTURE of mortgage - 25 Mar 1747 - Isabelle Hayes of Salisbury Township to Martha Cole of Chester Borough, Chester Co., widow of Stephen Cole dec'd and one of the executors of the will of Stephen Cole, Thomas Cummings of Chester Borough, cordwinder, and Rev. Richard Blackhouse of Chester Borough, the other executor, £130 for 208A, enfeoff. Land is located in Salisbury Township, neighbor - Thomas Johnson, William Hamilton, Robert Hoas, and James Keys. Condition of repayment as follows - £50 on or before 20 Nov 1748, £30 on or before 20 Nov 1749,

£50 residue on or before 20 Nov 1750. ... Isabella Hayes ... Sealed and delivered in the presence of John Holder, John Salkeld, John Baldwin and Henry Graham ... Ack'd 25 Jun 1747 James Whithill ... Rec'd 26 Jun 1747 no name ... Cert'd deed was recorded Benjamin Longenecker.

B-434 - THIS INDENTURE of mortgage - 25 Mar 1747 - William Hamilton of Salisbury Township, yeoman to Martha Cole of Chester Borough, widow of Stephen Cole dec'd and one of the executors of his will, Thomas Cummings of Chester Borough cordwainer, Rev. Richard Blackhouse of Chester Borough the other executor of Stephen Cole, £220 for 208A enfeoff. Land is located in Salisbury Township, neighbor - John Byers, William Fuller, Thomas Johnson, James Rees and James Keys. Condition of repayment as follows - £50 on 20 Nov 1747, £50 on 20 Nov 1748, £70 on 20 Nov 1749, £50 residue on 20 Nov 1750. ... William Hamilton ... Sealed and delivered in the presence of John Salkeld, John Colder, John Baldwin, and Henry Graham ... Ack'd 25 Jun 1747 James Whitehall ... Rec'd 27 Jun 1747 ... Edward Shippen with power of attorney, recorded in Bk G, pg 146, for Robert and Martha Russel of Chester Co., received full satisfaction from William Hamilton and Martha Cole, now Martha Russell. Thomas Cummings, Richard Blackhouse, executor of Stephen Cole received full satisfaction 27 Feb 1760, Edward Shippen.

B-437 - THIS INDENTURE - 17 Jun 1747 - John Funk of Lancaster Co., eldest son of Henry Funk late of Lancaster Co., yeoman dec'd to James Hamilton of the city of Philadelphia Esq., 5/ for 120A. Land is located in Strasburg Township, neighbors - Jacob Niesley, Peter Leman, John Mussar, and James Hamilton. ... John Funk ... Sealed and delivered in the presence of Jacob Niesley, Jost Musser, Jacob Schlaugh ... Ack'd 17 Jun 1747 Thomas Cookson ... Rec'd 27 Jun 1747 no name ... Cert'd deed was recorded Benjamin Longenecker.

B-438 - THIS INDENTURE - 18 Jun 1747 - John Funk of Lancaster Borough, yeoman, eldest son of Henry Funk, yeoman dec'd to James Hamilton Esq. of the city of Philadelphia, £500 for 120A, in actual possession. Land located in Strasburg Township, neighbors - Jacob Niesley, Peter Leman, John Musser, James Hamilton. By patent dated 13 Nov 1717 under the hands of Richard Hill, Isaac Norris, and James Logan was granted to Henry Funk in fee a tract in Strasburg Township containing 350A. Henry died intestate seized of 200A part of the 350A tract, before his death, by a instrument written in German he intended to transfer the 200A to his son Henry. Henry the father left other issue - John, Martin, Jacob, Samuel, Barbara now wife of Michael Myer Jr., Mary now wife of Jacob Nutt, Frona wife of Joseph Musserthey. By their indenture of release dated 18 Oct 1735, they released all their right and title to son Henry. Henry, the son died seized of 200A. His will dated 7 Oct 1736 gave 136A, part of the 200A, to eldest son John. John will pay other brothers, sisters, and widow. The father Henry was a alien and not naturalized at the time of his death and could not according to law take legal title to the land, 350A. John requested the proprietary to have 120A devised to him, by paying 5/ patent was granted on 28 Mar 1747, recorded in Bk A, vol 13, pg 192 on 29 May 1747. ... John Funk ... Ack'd 24 Jun 1747 Thomas Cookson ... Rec'd 29 Jun 1747 no name ... Cert'd deed was recorded Benjamin Longenecker.

B-441 - THIS INDENTURE - 3 Feb 1747 - Thomas Cookson of Lancaster Borough and Margaret his wife to Isaac Nunis Recus, and Joseph Simmons both of Lancaster Borough, merchants, £6 for 1/2A. Land is located in Lancaster Township, neighbor - Michael Meyer, and James Hamilton. The 1/2A is part of a lot granted to Thomas by James Hamilton by indenture dated 20 Jul 1743. ... Thomas Cookson, Margaret Cookson ... Sealed and delivered in the presence of David Stout, and Conrad Weiser ... Ack'd _ Jul 1742 no name ... Rec'd _ June 1747 no name ... Cert'd deed was recorded Benjamin Longenecker.

B-443 - THIS INDENTURE - 21 Nov 1737 - Peter Bumgardner of Lancaster Co., yeoman and Barbara his wife to John Dehuff of Lancaster Co., sadler, £273 4/ & 6d and the further sum of £62 15/ & 6d for 168A. Land is located on Little Conestoga Creek, neighbors - Hans Brubaker, Daniel Ashleman, and Jacob Brubaker. Land was granted to Peter by patent dated 24 Jun 1734 and recorded in Bk A, vol 6, pg 379. John owed mortgage to the trustees of the General Loan office of £62 15/ & 6d. ... Peter (PB) Bumgardner, Barbara (B) Bumgardner ... Sealed and delivered in the presence of Christian Stoneman, and Richard Harison ... Ack'd 5 Mar 1747 Derick Updegraef ... Rec'd 10 Jul 1747 no name ... Cert'd deed was recorded Benjamin Longenecker.

B-445 - THIS INDENTURE - 4 Jul 1746 - William Trent of the city of Philadelphia at present, gentleman to George Croghan of Lancaster Co., merchant, £150 for 1/2 of 354A, enfeoff. By indenture dated 7 Oct 1745 made or mentioned to be made between William Walker of Lancaster Co., yeoman and Elizabeth his wife to William Trent then of Lancaster Co., merchant and George Crogan of Lancaster Co., was granted a tract located on Conodoguinet Creek in Pennsboro Township, neighbor - James Laws. Tract contains 354A, 1/2 of which goes to William Trent and his heirs and 1/2 goes to George Crogan and his heirs. ... William Trent ... Sealed and delivered in the presence of Thomas Campbell, and Thomas Edwards ... Ack'd 3 Sept 1746 Septimus Robinson ... Rec'd 26 Jul 1747 no name ... Cert'd deed was recorded Benjamin Longenecker.

B-447 - THIS INDENTURE - 4 Jul 1746 - William Trent at present of the city of Philadelphia to George Crogan of city of Philadelphia, merchant, £70 for all his half of tract, enfeoff. By indenture dated 2 May __ between George Crogan and William Trent, George granted 1/2 of his share in land located in Pennsboro Township on Conodoguinet Creek, containing 171A. Neighbors - William Walker and James Silvers. ... William Trent ... Sealed and delivered in the presence of Thomas Campbell and Thomas Edwards ... Ack'd 3 Sept 1746 Septimus Robinson ... Rec'd 27 Jul 1747 ... Cert'd deed was recorded Benjamin Longenecker.

B-450 - THIS INDENTURE of mortgage - 10 Aug 1747 - David Bear of Leacock Township, yeoman to David Treslter of Lancaster Borough, gentleman, £100 for 232A. Land located in Leacock Township, neighbor - Henry Bear. John, Thomas, and Richard Penn granted to Abraham Bear under the hand of Governor George Thomas Esq. Lt. on 23 Apr 1742 a tract located in Leacock Township containing 441A. Deed is recorded in Bk A, vol 10, pg 306. Abraham and Frona his wife did by indenture dated 28 Jan 1747 grant the tract to David Bear. Repayment on or before 10 Aug 1748 entire sum. ... Davit bgv (David Bear) ... Sealed and delivered in the presence of George Graffe and George Smith ... Ack'd 10 Aug 1747 Thomas Cookson ... Rec'd 15 Aug 1747 ... Cert'd deed was recorded Benjamin Longenecker.

B-452 - THIS INDENTURE of mortgage - 22 Jul 1747 - David Trestler of Lancaster Borough, glazier and Susanna his wife to Casper Wister of the city of Philadelphia, brass button maker, 45/ for 1 of 2 lots, enfeoff. Lots are located in Lancaster Borough on King St., neighbor - on west Mathias Young. Pay entire amount on or before 22 Jul 1748. James Hamilton Esq. did by indenture dated 14 Jan 1744 grant to John Garner 2 lots, next to each other in Lancaster Borough. Each lot having a front on King St. John Garner and Maria Philippina his wife did by indenture dated 14 May 1745 grant to David Trestler the 2 lots. ... Joseph Davit Tuestler, Susanna Trestler ... Sealed and delivered in the presence of Sebastian Graffe, and George Smith ... Ack'd 11 Aug 1747 no name ... Rec'd 16 Aug 1747 no name ... Cert'd deed was recorded Benjamin Longenecker.

B-453 - THIS INDENTURE of mortgage - 13 May 1747 - David Fleming of Lancaster Borough, mason and Elizabeth his wife to James Webb of Lancaster Co., £31 11/ for 2 lots. Lots located in Lancaster Borough adjoining each other, with front on Prince St., neighbor - on west George Snyder. Pay by 2 Nov 1747. One lot was granted to George Adam Stees from James Hamilton on 15 Aug 1740. The other lot was granted to Gasper Loughman by indenture dated 22 Jun 1741. ... David Fleming, Elizabeth Fleming ... Sealed and delivered in the presence of Marcus Young, and George Smith ... Proved George Smith ... Ack'd ___ ___ 1747 no name ... Rec'd 15 Sept 1747 no name ... Full satisfaction received 7 May 1755, Edward Shippen.

B-455 - THIS INDENTURE - 13 Jun 1743 - James Logan of Pennsylvania, gentleman and his wife Sara to James Lowry of Donegal Township, trader, £160 for 210A. Land is located on Susquehanna River in Donegal Township, neighbors - David McCaldren, Samuel Smith, and John Galbreath. James received the tract by grant dated 25 Nov 1738 from Edward Shippen. Edward received the land by patent from John, Thomas, and Richard Penn on 29 Aug 1730. ... James Logan, Sara Logan ... Sealed and delivered in the presence of Thomas Armstrong, and Edward Shippen ... Ack'd 20 Aug 1747 Conrad Weiser ... Rec'd 11 Sept 1747 no name ... Cert'd deed was recorded Benjamin Longenecker.

B-456 - THIS INDENTURE - 1 Sept 1747 - Joseph Parke of Chester Co., yeoman and Agnus his wife to John Frazier of Lancaster Co., trader, £210 for 172A, enfeoff. Land located in on Susquehanna River in Paxtang, neighbors - Arthur Park, dec'd, Joseph Kelsy, and late of James Alorn. Joseph is son of Arthur who is dec'd. Arthur in his will dated 5 Jan 1739 left all right and title to his son Joseph. Arthur received the land from John, Thomas, and Richard Penn, under the hand of Thomas Penn on 21 Aug 1738, recorded in Bk A, vol 8, pg 94. ... Joseph Park, Agnus Park ... Sealed and delivered by Agnus in the presence of William Cook, and John Park ... Sealed and delivered by Joseph in the presence of George Smith and John Harris ... Ack'd 1 Sept 1747 Edward Smout ... Rec'd none ... Cert'd deed was recorded 14 Sept 1747 Benjamin Longenecker.

91

B-458 - THIS INDENTURE - 16 Sept 1747 - Lazarus Lowry of Lancaster Co., yeoman to John Lowry of Lancaster Co., yeoman and one of the sons of Lazarus, 5/ and love, affection for 288A. Land located in Donegal Township, neighbors - James Harris, James Mitchell, and David Byers. Lazarus received land by patent dated 6 Aug 1744 from John, Thomas, and Richard Penn to Lazarus and John Lowry. Deed is recorded in Bk A, vol 11, pg 514 on 23 Jul 1745. ... Lazarus Lowry ... Sealed and delivered in the presence of Thomas Cookson and George Gibson ... Ack'd 19 Sept 1747 Thomas Cookson ... Rec'd 3 Oct 1747 no name ... Cert'd deed was recorded Benjamin Longenecker.

B-460 - THIS INDENTURE - 13 Sept 1747 - Henry Bostler of Lancaster Co., yeoman and Anna Maria his wife to Francis Fortena and Michael Fortena both of Lancaster Township, yeoman, £200 for 10A. The land is located in Lancaster, neighbor Rody Meyer, James Hamilton Esq., and Peter Worral. Rent of 14/. ... Henry Bostler, Anna Maria Bostler ... Sealed and delivered in the presence of Peter Worrall, and David Stout ... Ack'd 13 Sept 1747 Peter Worrall ... Rec'd 6 Sept 1747 ... Cert'd deed was recorded Benjamin Longenecker.

B-461 - THIS INDENTURE of mortgage - 13 Nov 1747 - David Bare of Lancaster Co., yeoman and Sebastian Graffe of Lancaster Co., gentleman, £200 for 232A. Land is located in Leacock Township, neighbor - Henry Bare. This tract is part of a larger tract of 441A granted to Abraham Bare by patent from the Proprietary. Abraham and his wife Frena granted the land to David Bare. ... David Bare ... Sealed and delivered in the presence of Jacob Bare and George Smith ... Ack'd _ Nov 1747 Thomas Cookson ... Rec'd 2 Dec 1747 no name ... We Eva Graff, John Hopson, and Emanuel Carpenter executors of the will of Sebastian Graff dec'd, have received full satisfaction of this mortgage, 8 Dec 1763, Emanuel Carpenter, Eve Graff, and John Hopson, Edward Shippen.

B-463 - THIS INDENTURE of mortgage - 13 Oct 1747 - Moses White of Lancaster Co., yeoman to Richard Peters and Lynford Lardner both of the city of Philadelphia, gentlemen, £47 for 203 1/2A. Land located in Derry Township, neighbor - John Montgomery. Moses to secure payment of £47 owed to John, Thomas, and Richard Penn and in consideration of the further sum of 5/ grants 203 1/2A. Condition of repayment of £47 is as follows - £12 12/ & 6d on 13 Oct 1748, £11 13/ & 4d on 13 Oct 1749, £11 2/ on 13 Oct 1750, £10 10/ & 8d on 13 Oct 1751, 19/ & 4d residue on 13 Oct 1752. ... Moses White ... Sealed and delivered in the presence of William Morrison, and John Callahan ... Ack'd 2 Oct 1747 Thomas Cookson ... Rec'd 27 Nov 1747 no name ... Cert'd deed was recorded Benjamin Longenecker.

B-465 - THIS INDENTURE - 5 Nov 1747 - James Sterrat Esq. sheriff of Lancaster Co. to John Lite of Lancaster Co., yeoman, £200 for 200A. Land is located on the east side of Swartara Creek, neighbors - Adam Reed, and Robert Young. By a writ from the Court of Common Pleas in Lancaster, returnable on 4 Aug 1747, directed the sheriff to levy the goods of John Murray late of Lancaster Co., dec'd., being in the sheriff's bailiwick. (area of control) The sheriff is also to levy a debt of £100, which Oswld Peel recovered against John in court as 81/ 10d for damages, by the detention of the debt. John was seized with a tract of land in Hanover Township containing 200A. At the time of the delivery of the writ, his goods were in the hands of Mary Murray and John Dixon executors of John's will. John Lite was the highest bidder, £200. ... John Sterrat ... Sealed and delivered in the presence of John Rofs and James Wright ... Ack'd 3 Nov 1747 Thomas Cookson ... Rec'd __ Dec 1747 no name ... Cert'd deed was recorded Benjamin Longenecker.

B-467 - THIS INDENTURE - 3 Nov 1747 - Susanna Priest, widow of David Priest late of Pennsboro Township, yeoman dec'd intestate to William Priest, eldest son and heir at law of David (Susanna and William also administrators) to Richard Peters of the city of Philadelphia, gentleman, £100 for 1/2 of 212A. Land is located in Pennsboro Township at the mouth of Yellow Breeches Creek, neighbors - none mentioned. A warrant was granted by the Proprietary on 13 Nov 1744 to accept a survey made by Zackary Butcher on 2 Jul 1737. The survey was for David Preist for a tract in Pennsboro. David owes a considerable amount of money which his estate would not satisfy and leaving issue of 3 daughter, and a son, William. William petitioned Orphans Court and received a date of 1 Sept past for the sale of 1/2 of the tract. The tract was resurveyed by George Smith and sold to Richard Peters. ... Susanna (+) Priest, William Priest ... Sealed and delivered in the presence of Thomas Cookson and William Peters ... Ack'd 3 Nov 1747 Thomas Cookson ... Rec'd 3 Dec 1747 no name ... Cert'd deed was recorded Benjamin Longenecker.

B- 469 - THIS INDENTURE of mortgage - 16 Jan 1747 - Robert Henry of Lancaster Co., yeoman and Sara his wife to Mary Andrews of the city of Philadelphia spinster, £150 for 150A, enfeoff. Land is located on Conodoguinet Creek in Hopewell Township, neighbors - James Quiglesy, Joseph Woods, James Whitehill, and Samuel Colter. Tract was granted to Robert Henry by patent from the Proprietary on 14 Feb 1745, granted in fee. Must pay by 16 Jun 1747. ... Robert Henry, Sarah Henry ... Sealed and delivered by Robert Henry in the presence of William Pynell, and William Peters ... Sealed and delivered by Sarah Henry in the presence of John Hoge, Jonathan Hoge and David Hoge ... Ack'd none ... Rec'd none.

19 Oct 1747 - Robert Henry borrowed from Mary Andrews the further sum of £32 with the above tract acting as mortgage. Robert Bensy ... Sealed and delivered in the presence of William Peters and William Tea ... Ack'd 19 Nov 1747 John Hoge ... Rec'd __ Dec 1747 Thomas Cookson.

B- 472 - THIS INDENTURE - 1 Jan 1747/8 - Joseph Green of Salisbury Township, yeoman and Jane his wife to John Ellet of Salisbury Township, shopkeeper, £53 for 50A, enfeoff. Land is located on a branch of Pequea Creek, neighbors - none mentioned. The 50A is part of a larger tract of 250A which was granted to Thomas Green who was the father of Joseph. Thomas received land by patent from John, Thomas and Richard Penn on 8 Jun 1737. By Thomas's will dated 14 Nov 1741 he left 50A to Joseph. ... Joseph Green, Jane (O) Green ... Ack'd 1 Jan 1747/8 Thomas Cookson ... Rec'd 13 Jan 1747/8 no name ... Cert'd deed was recorded Benjamin Longenecker.

B-473 - 29 Dec 1747 - John Brubaker of Hempfield Township and Anne his wife to Daniel Ashleman of Hempfield Township, blacksmith, £9 14/ & 6d for 62 3/4A, enfeoff. Land is located in Hempfield Township, neighbors - Hans Adam Libhart, late of John Taylor, Daniel Eshleman, and Benjamin Horrsha. John received the land by patent from John, Thomas, and Richard Penn on 11 May 1747, recorded in Bk A, vol 13, pg 195 on 29 May 1747. ... John Brubaker, Anna (AB) Brubaker ... Sealed and delivered in the presence of George Sanderson and George Smith ... Ack'd 1 Jan 1747/8 Thomas Cookson ... Rec'd 13 Jan 1747/8 no name ... Cert'd deed was recorded Benjamin Longenecker.

B-475 - THIS INDENTURE - 10 Nov 1747 - Henry Leman of Robeson Township, yeoman to William Allen of the city of Philadelphia Esq., £70 for 154A. Land is located in Robeson Township, neighbor - Jacob Kreys. Henry is bound unto William in the amount of £140, in consideration of the debt and the further sum of 5/ grants 154A. Condition for repayment of £70 by 10 Nov 1748. ... Henry Leman ... Sealed and delivered in the presence of Alexandar Stuart and John Reily ... Ack'd 10 Nov 1747 Thomas Green ... Rec'd 13 Jan 1747 ... Cert'd deed was recorded Benjamin Longenecker.

B-476 - THIS INDENTURE of mortgage - 3 Dec 1747 - George Croghan of Lancaster Co., merchant to Jeremiah Warder of the city of Philadelphia, £500 for 2 tracts, together equal 475A. First tract contains 354A and is located in Pennsboro Township on Conodoguinet Creek, neighbor - James Law. Second tract contains 121A and is also located in Pennsboro Township on Conodoguinet Creek, neighbors - William Walkers, and James Slivers. Jeremiah is bound unto George in the sum of £1,000, in consideration of debt and the further sum of 5/ grants 354A. Condition of repayment in one entire payment by 1 Sept 1748. ... George Crogan ... Sealed and delivered in the presence of John Rody and Robert Forde ... Ack'd 9 Dec 1747 Thomas Cookson ... Rec'd 14 Jan 1747/8 no name ... Cert'd deed was recorded Benjamin Longenecker ... Full satisfaction received 27 Jun 1749, Thomas Cookson 29 Jun 1749.

B-478 - THIS INDENTURE - 24 Dec 1747 - John Davis of Manheim Township, fuller to Alexander Miller of Lancaster Co., yeoman, £31 for 42A. Land is located in Leacock Township and is part of a larger tract of 237A granted to John Davis by Jacob Bare and Barbara his wife on 27 Nov 1747. Neighbors - none mentioned. The 237A is part of a larger tract of 322A granted to Christopher Franciscus by Proprietary patent on 7 Mar 1733. Christopher and wife (no name) granted the tract to Jacob Bare by indenture dated 17 Nov 1739. ... John Davis ... Sealed and delivered none ... Ack'd 24 Dec 1747 Thomas Cookson ... Rec'd 19 Jan 1747/8 no name ... Cert'd deed was recorded Benjamin Longenecker.

B-480 - THIS INDENTURE - 1 Feb 1747 - James Sterrat, high sheriff to Mark Young of Lancaster Borough, shopkeeper, £83 for 1 lot. Lot is located in Lancaster Borough facing King St., neighbors - west Abraham Johnson, east Barbara Feil. Rent is 7/ due 1 May. James Hamilton Esq. by indenture dated 13 Aug 1740 granted to John Hagery 1 lot located in Lancaster Borough. John Bagerly seized of the lot died intestate without issue, leaving Anne, his widow, in possession of the lot. Anne intermarried to Robert Lee. Anne and Robert by indenture dated 14 Jun 1744 granted to Andreas Hersey, yeoman by way of mortgage for securing payment of £20. Andreas by assignment of this indenture of mortgage dated 4 May 1746 in consideration of the principle and interest due on mortgage assigned it to Conrad Swartz, George Graffe, Michael Crouse, Jacob Rieger, Paul Witsell and Barbara Yoisar. Robert and Anne made default in payment of £20, the estate became absolute to Conrad, George, Michael, Jacob, Paul and Barbara. Afterwards in May 1747 Conrad and Barbara went before the Court of Common Pleas in Lancaster and obtained a judgment against Robert Lee for £23 10/. They directed the sheriff to levy the premises. Lot was sold to Mark Young. ... James Sterrat ... Sealed and delivered in the presence of John Ross, and Peter Worrall ... Ack'd 2 Feb 1747 Thomas Cookson ... Rec'd 16 Feb 1747 ... Cert'd deed was recorded Benjamin Longenecker.

B-483 - THIS INDENTURE - 25 Feb 1747 - Andreas Silderick of Earl Township, yeoman to Doris Backwhaller of Lancaster Township, 10/ for 200A. Land is located in Lancaster Co., neighbor - Christian Landus, London Company, Col John Evans, formally Isaac Frederick. ... Andreas Silderick ... Sealed and delivered in the presence of Hans Landus and Hans Whitmore ... Ack'd none ... Rec'd none ... Cert'd deed was recorded Benjamin Longenecker.

B-483 - THIS INDENTURE - 25 Feb 1747 - Andreas Silderick of Earl Township, yeoman and Anna Maria his wife to Doris Buckwhaller of Lampeter Township, yeoman, £8 for 200A, in actual possession. Land is located in Lampeter Township, neighbors - formally Jacob Landus, formally John Evan, formally Isaac Frederick, formally Jacob Kendricks. Andreas received the land by indenture of lease and release dated 13 & 14 Mar 1722, from Tobias Collet, Daniel Quair, and Henry Goldney. ... Andreas Soldenick, Anna Mary Soldenick ... Sealed and delivered in the presence of Harvey Whitmore and Hans Landus ... Ack'd 27 Feb 1747 Emanuel Carpenter ... Rec'd 30 Mar 1748 ... Cert'd deed was recorded Benjamin Longenecker.

B-485 - THIS INDENTURE - 20 Mar 1747 - Herman Long of Hempfield Township, yeoman and Anna his wife to Henry Sanders, £37 for 70A. Land is located in Lebanon Township, neighbors - Henry Sanders, Herman Long, and Thomas Clark. Herman received the land from John, Thomas and Richard Penn by patent under the hands of Thomas Penn on 5 Jun 1740 and recorded in Bk A, vol 9, pg 216. ... Herman Long, Anna Long ... Sealed and delivered in the presence of Sebastian Graffe and George Smith ... Ack'd 12 Mar 1747 Thomas Cookson ... Rec'd 31 May 1748 no name ... Cert'd deed was recorded Benjamin Longenecker..

B-487 - THIS INDENTURE - 24 Mar 1747 - George Gibson of Lancaster Co., inn-holder and Martha his wife to Richard Peters of the city of Philadelphia Esq. 5/ for 232A. Land is located in Pennsboro Township, neighbor - John Mitchell ... George Gibson, Martha Gibson ... Sealed and delivered in the presence of Lynford Landners and Edmund Physick ... Ack'd none ... Rec'd none ... Cert'd deed was recorded Benjamin Longenecker.

B-488 - THIS INDENTURE - 25 Mar 1748 - George Gibson of Lancaster Co., inn-holder and Martha his wife to Richard Peters of the city of Philadelphia Esq., £150 for 230A, in actual possession. Land is located on Conodoguinet Creek in Pennsboro Township, neighbor - John Mitchell. George received the land by patent from John, Thomas and Richard Penn on 19 Mar 1748. ... George Gibson, Martha Gibson ... Sealed and delivered in the presence of Lynnford Lander and Edmund Physick ... Ack'd 31 Mar 1748 Thomas Cookson ... Rec'd 1 Apr 1748 no name ... Cert'd deed was recorded Benjamin Longenecker.

B-489 - THIS INDENTURE of mortgage - 15 Jan 1747 - Henry Clark of Warrington Township, yeoman to Mary Plumsted of the city of Philadelphia, widow, £50 for 125A. Lance is located in Warrington Township, neighbor - Thomas Davidson. Henry is bound unto Mary in the sum of £100, to better secure repayment and in consideration of the further amount of 5/ grants 125A. Condition of repayment by 15 Jan 1748. ... Henry Clark ... Sealed and delivered none ... Ack'd 15 Jan 1747/8 John Kinsey ... Rec'd 2 Apr 1748 ... Edward Shippen by power of attorney directed to William Allen on 1 Oct 1761 and recorded Bk G, pg __ certify full satisfaction of mortgage 29 Aug 1762 William Allen.

B-490 - TO WHOM - no date - these present comes Israel Pemberton Jr. of the city of Philadelphia, merchant - Greetings - John Pauli as guardian of Ulrick and Christian, the two sons of the late John Giligen, miller, who was brother of Christian Giligen formally of the Republic of Bern in Switzerland and who died on passage to Pennsylvania. John died intestate and Christian Nydegger and John Wysenback both in the name of their wives, Elizabeth and Anna Zahad, also Ulrick Zahad, are the children of Anne Giligen and Christian Zahn and Durs Stockley as father and guardian of his own children by his wife Elizabeth Giligan who with Christian, John, Ulrick, Elizabeth, Anne, and Barbara Stockly are all of the kindred of Christian Giligen. They did by power of attorney dated in Bern 15 Feb last past appoint Israel Pemberton to be their attorney to receive their shares of personal estate of Christian Giligens dec'd amounting to about £540. Hans Zimmerman of Cocalico was administrator of Christian Giligen, he is now released. Ulrick Zahn guardian of the six children. ... Isreal Pemberton Jr., John Pauli guardian of Ulrick and Christian Giligen, Christian Nydegger and John Wysenback for their wives Elizabeth and Anne Zahad, Ulrick Zahad, Durs Stockley father and guardian of his 6 children Christian, John, Ulrick, Elizabeth, Anne, and Barbara ... Sealed and delivered in the presence of Israel Pemberton, John Pemberton, and William Peters 21 Oct 1747 ... Ack'd 1747 no name ... Rec'd 1748 no name ... Cert'd instrument was recorded Benjamin Longenecker.

B-492 - THIS INDENTURE - 21 Sept 1747 - Bastian Reyes of Warwick Township, yeoman and Agnus his wife to Peter Beckes, Wendel Laber, Jacob Heggy, and Tillman Sheets, £2 for 2 1/2A. Land is located in Warwick Township, neighbors - surveyed to Peter Kober now in possession of Mathias Wains. Bastian and Agnus are moving. This tract also includes the Dutch Reform church burying ground. It is part of a 286A tract which was granted by patent to Mathias Ryer in fee from the Proprietary on 26 Jan 1743 and recorded in Bk A, vol 12, pg 40. ... Bastian Reyes (German), Agnus Reyes ... Sealed and delivered in the presence of George Witman, Hendrick Rei___ (German) ...

Ack'd 3 Oct 1747 Conrad Weisner ... Rec'd 4 Apr 1748 no name ... Cert'd deed was recorded Benjamin Longenecker.

B-493 - TO ALL PEOPLE - 21 Sept 1747 - Peter Becker, Wendal Laber, Jacob Haggy and Tillman Sheets, by indenture made on 21 Sept 1747 between Bastian Reyer of Warwick Township, yeoman and Angies his wife and us all of Warwick Township, yeoman did grant and release land in Warwick Township containing a tract which on the north side is surveyed to Dieter Rober now in possession of Mathias Uland and on the east southwest by other land of Bastian Reyor containing 2 1/2A including the German Reformed Church and burying ground. It is part of a 286A tract granted by the Proprietary by patent on 26 Jan 1743 to Bastin Reyer in fee. Deed is recorded in Bk A, vol 12, Pg 40. The 2 1/2A was granted to members of the Dutch Reformed Church in Warwick Township. ... Jacob Heggy, Wendel Laber, Peter Becker, Tillman Sheets (all in German) ... Sealed and delivered none ... Ack'd 1 Feb 1747 Conrad Weiser ... Rec'd 6 Apr 1748 ... Cert'd instrument was recorded Benjamin Longenecker.

B-495 - THIS INDENTURE of mortgage - 28 Jan 1747 - Martin Mannsburgor of Manchester Township, miller to John Connolly of Hempfield Township, gentleman, £790 for 397A, enfeoffed release. Land is located on Little Conewago Creek on west side of Susquehanna River, neighbors - Valentine Graf, Andrew Hamilton dec'd, and Daniel McLoughery. Repayment as follows - £100 1 Nov 1748, £100 1 Nov 1749, £130 1 Nov 1750, £124 1 Nov 1751, £118 1 Nov 1752, £120 1 Nov 1753, £106 residue 1 Nov 1754. ... Martin Mannsburgor ... Sealed and delivered in the presence of Thomas Cookson, and George Smith ... Ack'd 28 Jan 1747/8 Thomas Cookson ... Rec'd 12 Apr 1748 no name ... Cert'd deed was recorded Benjamin Longenecker.

B-497 - THIS INDENTURE - 1 Dec 1747 - Felix Landus and Mary his wife of Lebanon Township to Jacob Donner of Lampeter Township, yeoman 5/ for 200A. Land is located in Lampeter Township, neighbor - John Bundely. ... Felix Landus, Mary (M) Landus ... Sealed and delivered in the presence of George Smith and Hans Musser (German) ... Ack'd 22 Jan 1747/8 Thomas Cookson ... Rec'd 14 Apr 1748 ... Cert'd deed was recorded Benjamin Longenecker.

B-498 - THIS INDENTURE - 2 Dec 1747 - Felix Landus of Lebanon Township, yeoman and Mary his wife to Jacob Donner of Lampeter Township, yeoman, £600 for 200A, in actual possession. Land is located in Lampeter Township, neighbor - John Bundeley. The tract is part of a 400A tract that Felix received from his father Felix who is dec'd and mother Rosanna by indenture of lease and release dated 25 & 26 Mar 1737. Felix the father received the land by patent of lease and release dated 19 & 20 Feb 1718 and recorded in Bk F, vol 4, pg 800 from Tobias Collet, Daniel Quare, and Henry Goldney of London. The 400A is part of a tract of 5,550, which Tobias, Daniel, Henry, and the heirs of Michael Russell received from the late William Penn on 25 Jun __ and recorded in Bk A, vol 5, pg 306. ... Felix Landus, Mary (M) Landus ... Sealed and delivered in the presence of George Smith and Hans Musses (German) ... Ack'd 22 Jan 1747 Thomas Cookson ... Rec'd 14 Apr 1748 no name ... Cert'd deed was recorded Benjamin Longenecker.

B-501 - THIS INDENTURE - 15 Mar 1747/8 - Michael Baughman of Lancaster Co. and Catherine wife to Christian Baughman of Lancaster Co., yeoman and one of the sons of Michael and Catherine, 5/ and love, affection for 2 tracts equaling 249A. The first tract contains 239A and is located in Manor Township, neighbor Jacob Brubaker, Abraham Bares. Second tract contains 10A and is located in Monor Township, neighbor - land Michael Baughman intends to grant to his daughter Elizabeth. Clause - provided that if Christian should marry and his wife should survive him she shall have all of the 2 tracts to enjoy and maintain their children all her natural life. These tracts are part of a larger tract containing 689A granted to Michael by the Proprietary by patent on 20 Feb 1738 and recorded in Bk A, vol 1, pg 180. ... Michael Baughman, Katherine (KB) Baughman ... Sealed and delivered in the presents of Hans Zimmerman and Andrew Miller ... Ack'd none ... Rec'd 12 May 1748 no name ... Cert'd deed was recorded Benjamin Longenecker.

B-503 - THIS INDENTURE - 15 Mar 1747/8 - Michael Baughman of Lancaster Co., yeoman and Catherine his wife to Elizabeth Baughman of Lancaster Co., spinster and one of the daughters of Michael and Catherine, love, affection and 5/ for 240A. Land is located in Manor Township, neighbor Abraham Stoner. Tract is part of a larger tract containing 689A granted to Michael by John, Thomas, and Richard Penn under the hand of Thomas Penn on 20 Feb 1738 and recorded in Bk A, vol 1, pg 180. ... Michael Baughman, Katherine (KB) Baughman ... Sealed and delivered in the presence of Hans Zimmerman and Andrew Miller ... Ack'd none ... Rec'd 12 May 1748 no name ... Cert'd deed was recorded Benjamin Longenecker.

B-505 - THIS INDENTURE - 10 Jan 1745 - James Galbreath of Lancaster Co., Esq. and Elizabeth his wife to Richard Peters of the city of Philadelphia Esq., £180 for 309A, in actual possession. Land is located on Susquehanna River in Paxtang Township, neighbors - Thomas Renicks, and Alexandra Stephens. James received the land by Proprietary patent dated 24 May 1745 in fee. ... James Galbreath, Elizabeth (e) Galbreath ... Sealed and delivered in the presence of Adam Reed and William Baxter ... Ack'd none ... Rec'd 16 Mar 1748 no name ... Cert'd deed was recorded Benjamin Longenecker.

B-506 - THIS INDENTURE - 11 Mar 1747/8 - Michael Baughman of Manheim Township, yeoman and Katherine his wife to Michael Baughman the younger and Ulrick Burkhart both of Manheim Township, yeomen, 5/ for 259A. The land is located in Lebanon Township, neighbors - Michael Baughman, Martin Myley, Balzar Oar. For the love and affection Michael and Katherine bear for their daughter Anne who lately intermarried with Peter Witmore of Lancaster Co., yeoman and in consideration of 5/ paid by Michael Baughman the younger and Ulrick Buckhart, enfeoff release, grant to them upon special trust 2 tracts. The tracts join each other, the first contains 192A and the second contains 67A. For the special purpose of use for Peter Witmore and Anna his wife during their natural lives, and after the land should go to Anna's children to share and share alike. ... Michael Baughman, Katherine (K) Baughman ... Sealed and delivered in the presence of Thomas Cookson and Conrad Schevant ... Ack'd 11 Mar 1747/8 ... Rec'd 17 May 1748 no name ... Cert'd deed was recorded Benjamin Longenecker.

B-508 - THIS INDENTURE - 11 Mar 1747/8 - Michael Baughman of Lancaster Co. and Katherine his wife to Joest Kingry, yeoman, £37 1/ for 239A, enfeoff. The land is located in Lebanon Township, neighbors - Michael Baughman, Jacob Memmas, Michael Kingry. The tract is part of a larger tract of 420A granted to Michael by patent from John, Thomas, and Richard Penn under the hand of George Thomas Esq. Lt. Governor on 31 Mar 1746. Deed is recorded in Bk A, vol 13, pg 66 on 8 Aug 1746. ... Michael Baughman, Katherine (K) Baughman ... Sealed and delivered in the presence of Thomas Cookson and Conrad Schwartz ... Ack'd 11 Mar 1747/8 no name ... Rec'd 17 Mar 1748 no name ... Cert'd deed was recorded Benjamin Longenecker.

B-510 - THIS INDENTURE - 11 Mar 1747/8 - Michael Baughman of Manheim Township yeoman, and Katherine his wife to Michael Kingry of Lebanon Township, yeoman, £28 1/ for 181A, enfeoff. Land is located in Lebanon Township, neighbors - Yost Kingry, Jacob Memmas, George Miller, Richard Rampton. The tract is part of a larger tract of 520A which was granted to Michael by patent from John, Thomas, and Richard Penn under the hand of George Thomas Esq. late Lt. Governor on 31 Mar 1746. Deed is recorded in Bk A, vol 13, pg 66 on 8 Aug 1746. ... Michael Baughman, Katherine (K) Baughman ... Sealed and delivered in the presence of Thomas Cookson and Conrad Schwart ... Ack'd 11 Mar 1748 no name ... Rec'd 18 Mar 1748 no name ... Cert'd deed was recorded Benjamin Longenecker.

B-512 - THIS INDENTURE - 17 Mar 1747/8 - Michael Baughman of Lancaster Co., yeoman and Katherine his wife to Michael Whitmore and Ulrick Buckhart of Lancaster Co., yeomen, 5/ for 237A. For the natural love and affection Michael and Katherine bear for their daughter Barbara who lately intermarried Jacob Stoner of Lancaster Co. yeoman, and in consideration of the sum of 5/ paid by Michael and Ulrick they grant in special trust 237A. Location not shown, neighbor - Michael Baughman Jr. The tract is part of a larger tract of 342A and a tract of 199A. These were granted to Michael by the Proprietary by patent dated 28 Feb 1738 and 28 Apr 1741. They are recorded in Bk A, vol 9, pg ?. The tracts are for the use of Jacob Stoner and Barbara, then to pass to their heirs. ... Michael Baughman, Katherine (KB) Baughman ... Sealed and delivered in the presence of Hans Zimmerman and Andrew Miller ... Ack'd 17 Mar 1748 no name ... Rec'd 18 May 1748 no name ... Cert'd deed was recorded Benjamin Longenecker.

B-514 - THIS INDENTURE - 18 Mar 1747/8 - Michael Baughman of Lancaster Co., yeoman and Katherine his wife to Michael Baughman the younger of Lancaster Co., yeoman and Magdalene his wife, 5/ and love, affection for 233A, enfeoff. Land is located in Lancaster Co., neighbor - Jacob Stoner. Part of the tract was granted to Michael by the Proprietary by patent on 28 Feb 1738. ... Michael Baughman, Katherine (KB) Baughman ... Sealed and delivered in the presence of Hans Zimmerman and Andrew Miller ... Ack'd 18 Mar 1747/8 no name ... Rec'd 19 May 1748 ... Cert'd deed was recorded Benjamin Longenecker.

B-517 - THIS INDENTURE - 23 Mar 1747 - Joseph Williams of Lancaster Borough, mason and Jane his wife to Jacob Lite of Lancaster Co., yeoman, £75 for 125A. Land is located on a branch of Conestoga Creek, neighbor - Thomas Morgan, Joseph Silas, Robert Ellis. Subject to a payment of £39 for a mortgage at the Loan Office by 8 Jun 1742. ... Joseph Williamson, Jane Williamson ... Sealed and delivered in the presence of Thomas Cookson and Margaret Nelson ... Ack'd 23 Mar 1748 no name ... Rec'd 19 Mar 1748 ... Cert'd deed was recorded Benjamin Longenecker, recorder.

B-519 - THIS INDENTURE - 5 Aug 1747 - James Lennox of Earl Township, yeoman and Ruth his wife to Jacob Liecht of Carnavon Township, yeoman, £140 for 2 tracts containing 234A. The tracts are located in Earl Township, first contains 180A, neighbors - John Gungle, Conrad Foys, Philip Swegers, and Evan David. The second tract contains 54A, neighbors Thomas William, Jacob Summy, Hanie widower. James received the land from John, Thomas, and Richard Penn in 1746. Patent is recorded in Bk A, vol 12, pg 504. James by indenture dated 11 Jun 1746 mortgaged the premises unto John Kinsey to secure a payment of £60. Jacob Liecht has undertaken the payment. ... James Lennox, Ruth Lennox ... Sealed and delivered in the presence of Andrew Gahn and Paul (e) Gahn ... Ack'd 10 Aug 1747 Thomas Edwards ... Rec'd 19 May 1748 ... Cert'd deed was recorded Benjamin Longenecker.

B-521 - THIS INDENTURE - 24 Jun 1747 - John Earl of Warrington Township, cordwainer to James Lenox of Earltown Township, yeoman, £200 for 235 1/2A, enfeoff. Land is located on Beaver Creek on the west side of the Susquehanna River, neighbors - none mentioned. John received the land from John, Thomas and Richard Penn on 18 Jun 1743, recorded in Bk A, vol 11, pg 41 on 4 Jul 1743. ... John Earl ... Signed, sealed, and delivered in the presence of Samuel Underwood, and John Wright ... Ack'd none ... Rec'd 2 Jan 1748 ... Cert'd deed was recorded Benjamin Longenecker.

B-523 - THIS INDENTURE - 24 May 1748 - John Mendenall of Earl Township, yeoman to Moses Mendenall, son of John, of Earl Township, yeoman, £42 10/ for 2 tracts, enfeoff release. First tract contains 44A and is located in Earl Township, neighbors - Evan Edwards, Henry Griger, in actual possession. The second tract contains 104A and is located in Earl Township, neighbors Christian Hildebrand, John Mendenall, Evan Edwards. William Penn by deed dated 3 & 4 May 1682 granted unto James Craven of the city of Limrick, merchant, 1,000A. James by will dated 4 Feb 1694 devised land to Richard Craven his son. Richard by deed dated 11 & 12 Jul 1728 granted the tract of Benjamin Craven of Dublin, merchant. Benjamin by deed dated 10 & 11 Mar 1728 granted the land to James Miller of New Garden, Chester Co. James by deed dated 29 & 30 Oct 1730 granted 500A of the 1,000A tract to John Mendenall. The 500A was surveyed by warrant dated 16 Apr 1743. John, Thomas, and Richard Penn by patent under the hand of Anthony Palmer Esq. the present Commissioner dated 17 May 1748 and recorded in Bk A, vol 13, pg 348 granted the 500A unto John Mendenall. ... John Mendenall ... Sealed and delivered in the presence of William Elliot, Jacob Hildebrand, and Christian Hildebrand ... Ack'd 26 May 1748 Thomas Edwards ... Rec'd 11 Jun 1748 ... Lancaster 26 Jan 1761, by virtue of a power of attorney to me directed and ack'd that James Pemberton has received full satisfaction of this mortgage from William , Hamilton ... Witness - John Hopson ... 26 Jan 1761 Edward Shippen. This acknowledgment was written on this deed but is obviously meant for another deed.

B-525 - THIS INDENTURE of mortgage - 21 May 1748 - John Varner of Leacock Township, inn-holder to William Allen of the city of Philadelphia Esq., £100 for 310A. Land is located on a branch of Mill Creek, neighbors - Philip Fierre, John Fierre, John Line, Samuel Jones, Jacob Bear. John is bound unto William in the sum of £200, condition of repayment of £100 on 21 May 1749, in one entire payment. John to better secure payment and in consideration of the further amount of 5/ grants 310A. John received this tract from John, Thomas, and Richard Penn by patent dated 16 Jun 1741 and recorded in Bk A, vol, 10, pg 253, in fee. ... John Varner ... Sealed and delivered in the presence of Alexandar Stuart, and John Reily ... Ack'd 21 May 1748 William Till Esq. ... Rec'd 17 Jun 1748 no name ... Cert'd deed was recorded Benjamin Longenecker.

B-527 - THIS INDENTURE - 17 May 1748 - Hans Zimmerman alias John Carpenter of Cocalico Township, yeoman to Israel Pemberton of the city of Philadelphia, merchant, £400 for 900A. Land is located in Cocalico Township, neighbors - Woolrick Carpenter, Peter Brickers. Hans is bound to Israel in the sum of £800, condition of repayment of £400 is £24 on 17 May 1749, £24 on 17 May 1750 £24 & £400 on 17 May 1751. Hans to better secure payment and in consideration of the further sum of 5/ grants 900A. ... Hans Zimmerman ... Sealed and delivered in the presence of Joseph Galloway and Arthur Forster ... Ack'd 17 May 1748 John Kinsey Esq. ... Rec'd 17 Jun 1748 no name ... By virtue of a power of attorney to me directed on 1 Aug 1755 under the hands of James Pemberton and John Pemberton executors of the will of Israel Pemberton dec'd, recorded in Bk d, pg 286, I ack'd full satisfaction of this mortgage on behalf of James and John Pemberton, 13 Jun 1757 John Kinsey ... Ack'd 13 Jun 1751 Edward Shippen.

B-529 - THIS INDENTURE of mortgage - 1 Dec 1747 - John Jones of Strasburg Township, yeoman to Andrew Moore of Salisbury Township Chester Co., miller, £150 for 195A. Land is located in Strasburg Township, neighbor - Thomas Story, Isaac Lefevers, John Feree. Pay by 17 May 1751, £155. ... John Jones ... Sealed and delivered in the presence of William Boyd, and William Moor Smith ... Ack'd 25 May 1748 - James Whithill ... Rec'd 20 Jun 1748 no name ... Cert'd deed was recorded Edwin L. Reinhold.

B-531 - THIS INDENTURE - 15 Jun 1748 - Lazarus Lowry of Donegal Township, yeoman to Dennis Soluhan of Donegal Township, trader, £150 for 150A, enfeoff. Land is located in Donegal Township, neighbors - James Logan, Thomas Mitchell, and John Lowry. Land is part of a larger tract of 411A which was granted to Lazarus by Proprietary patent in Oct 1747 under the hand of the Honorable Anthony Palmer, President of the Council. ... Lazarus Lowry ... Sealed and delivered in the presence of Nathanial Little and George Smith ... Ack'd 20 Jun 1748 Thomas Cookson ... Rec'd 20 Jun 1748 no name ... Cert'd deed was recorded Benjamin Longenecker.

B-535 - THIS INDENTURE - 31 Jan 1739/40 - Aaron Musgrave of West Sadsbury, yeoman and Elizabeth his wife to Joseph White of West Sadsbury, yeoman, £106 for 200A. Land is located in West Sadsbury, neighbors - none mentioned. Land is part of a 340A tract granted by Proprietary patent on 13 Nov 1738 to Aaron Musgrave in fee. ...

no signature ... Ack'd none ... Rec'd none ... Cert'd deed was recorded Benjamin Longenecker.

Problem with page numbering, there are 2 page 535 on separate pages.

B-535 - THIS INDENTURE of mortgage - 1 Jul 1748 - Jacob Beyerle yeoman to Joseph Spangenberg of Bethlehem Township in Bucks Co., clerk, Charles Brockden of the city of Philadelphia gentleman, Timothy Horsefield of Brookland Township in Kings Co. Nassau Island, of NY, butcher, £500 for 359A, in 2 tracts. The first tract contains 160A and is located in Earl Township, neighbors - Henry Weaver, Jacob Sensing, Edward Owen, Rees Morgan, and Jenkin Jenkins. Second tract contains 199A and is located in Earl Township, neighbor - Henry Weaver. Contained in the tracts is a grist mill, oil mill, and saw mill. Jacob Beyerle is bound to Joseph, Charles, and Timothy in the sum of £1,000. Condition for repayment of £500, entire amount on 1 July 1749. Jacob to better secure payment and in consideration of the further amount of 5/ grants 2 tracts. Joseph, Charles and Timothy are guardians of Thomas, Isaac, James, and May Noble, infants under age and children of Thomas Noble late of the city of NY, merchant dec'd. ... Jacob Beyerle ... Sealed and delivered in the presence of Marcus Kahl, ___ Lemon, and John Bannester ... Ack'd 1 Jul 1748 Thomas Cookson ... Rec'd 1 Jul 1748 ... Cert'd deed was recorded Benjamin Longenecker.

B-536 - THIS INDENTURE of mortgage - 18 Dec 1747 - Michael Haverstick of Lancaster Co. yeoman to William Coleman and James Pemberton of the city of Philadelphia merchants, and executors of the will of Samuel Powell the younger late of the city of Philadelphia, merchant dec'd, £200 for 150A. The land is located in Lancaster Co., neighbors - on south John Bare, on east Abraham Plater, on west Jacob Esseman, on north Tobias Stone. Michael received the land from John Bare and Elizabeth his wife by indenture dated 29 Nov 1747. Condition for repayment as follows - £12 on 18 Dec 1748, £12 on 18 Dec 1749, £12 on 18 Dec 1750, £212 on 18 Dec 1751. ... Michael Haverstick ... Sealed and delivered in the presence of John Galloway, and Arthur Forster ... Ack'd 18 Dec 1747 John Kinsey ... Rec'd 12 Jun 1748 Thomas Cookson ... Nicholas Waln attorney at law appears as attorney for Joseph Potts and Sarah his wife, to whom this mortgage was assigned, Sarah being the daughter of Samuel Powell and the person to whom the mortgage money belongs. Ack'd full satisfaction received on this mortgage ... Nicholas Waln ... Ack'd 11 Dec 1769 Edward Shippen.

B-538 - THIS INDENTURE - 15 Dec 1747 - John Scott of Pensborough Township, yeoman and Margaret his wife to George Crogan of Lancaster Co., merchant, £220 for 210A, enfeoff. Land located in Pennsboro Township on north side of ConodoguinetCreek, neighbors - none mentioned. John received the land from Robert Buchanan and Jane his wife on 3 Aug 1743. Robert received the tract from John, Thomas, and Richard Penn by patent under the hand of George Thomas Esq. Lt. Governor on 23 Aug 1742. ... John Scott, Margaret (+) Scott ... Sealed and delivered in the presence of William Hoge Jr., Thomas Paine, and Johnathan Hoge ... Received from George Crogan £220, John Scott ... Ack'd 1 Mar 1747/8 John Hoge ... Rec'd none ... Cert'd deed was recorded Benjamin Longenecker 1 Mar 1748/8.

B-541 - THIS INDENTURE of mortgage - 2 Aug 1748 -John Balthazor Pidzor of Earl Township, distiller and Dorothy his wife to Henry Von Aker of the city of Philadelphia, shopkeeper, £100 for 128A. Land is located in Earl Township, neighbor - Evan Davis, John Mackalwain, and Michael Rank. John is bound unto Henry in the sum of £200, condition of repayment of £100 on 2 Aug 1749. John and Dorothy to secure payment and in consideration of the further sum of 5/ grant 128A. ... John Balthazor Pidzor ... Sealed and delivered in the presence of James (X) Hicky, and Elizabeth (6) Swihm. ... Ack'd 6 Aug 1748 Thomas Cookson ... Rec'd 16 Aug 1748 no name ... Cert'd deed was recorded Benjamin Longenecker.

B-543 - THIS INDENTURE - 10 Aug 1748 - Moses Mendenhale of Earl Township, yeoman and Mary his wife to Henry Von Aker of the city of Philadelphia, shopkeeper, £60 for 148A. Land is located in Earl Township, first tract contains 104A, neighbors - Christian Hildebrand, John Mendenhale. Second tract contains 44A neighbors - Even Edward, and Henry Geiger. Moses is bound unto Henry in the sum of £120. Condition of repayment of £60 by 10 Aug 1749. Moses to secure better payment and in consideration of the further sum of 5/ grants 44 1/2A. ... Moses Mendenhale, Mary Mendenhale ... Sealed and delivered in the presence of John Walter and Hannah Holston ... Ack'd and release of dower 12 Aug 1748 Thomas Cookson ... Rec'd 14 Aug 1748 Thomas Cookson.

B-545 - THIS INDENTURE - 15 Dec 1747 - John Scott of Pennsboro Township, yeoman and Margaret his wife to George Crogan of Lancaster Co., merchant, £220 for 210A. Land located in Pennsboro Township, neighbors - none mentioned. John received the land from Robert Buchanan and his wife Jane by indenture on 3 Aug 1743. Robert received the land by patent from John, Thomas and Richard Penn under the hand of George Thomas Esq. late Lt. Governor on 23 Aug 1742. ... John Scott, Margaret (+) Scott ... Sealed and delivered in the presence of William Hoge Jr., Thomas Paine, and Jonathan Hoge ... Rec'd of George Crogan £220, John Scott ... Ack'd 1 Mar 1747/8 John Hoge ... Rec'd 22 Sept 1748 no name ... Cert'd deed was recorded Benjamin Longenecker.

The above deed was recorded twice on page 538 and 545.

B-547 - THIS INDENTURE - 7 Sept 1748 - Hiam Soloman Bunn of Lancaster Borough, shopkeeper to Joseph Simons of Lancaster Borough, yeoman. £45 for 1 lot. Lot located in Lancaster Borough on Queen St. facing Penns Square, neighbor - Samuel Bethel dec'd., east Isaac Nanus Recus, and Dennis Connelly. James Hamilton of the city of Philadelphia on 19 Aug 1742 did lease to Thomas Campbell of the city of Philadelphia, merchant for 21 years the above lot. Thomas by deed dated 10 May 1744 assigned the lot to John Connally, now dec'd. George Smith, Thomas Doyle, and John Hart are executors of the will of John Connally, and by virtue of the power and authority given them by his will did by deed grant the lot to Hiram Solomon Bunn for 15 years from 19 Aug 1747. ... Hiam Solomon Bunn ... Sealed and delivered in the presence of Joseph Solomon, Peter

Worrall, and David Stout ... Ack'd 16 Sept 1748 Thomas Cookson ... Rec'd 23 Sept 1748 ... Cert'd deed was recorded Benjamin Longenecker.

B-548 - THIS INDENTURE - 29 Mar 1748 - Mandaline Graffe of Heidelburg Township, widow of George Graffe dec'd to George Graffe and Catherine his wife, Sebastian Graffe, Hans Graffe, Leonard Holstine and Barbara his wife, Frederick Kapp and Eva Maria his wife, Martin Kapp and Margaret his wife, George Emert and Eva Marie his wife, and Andrew Groffe, all next of kin to George Graffe dec'd., 5/ for 400A in 2 tracts joining each other. Land is located in Heidelberg Township, neighbors - none mentioned. George died without issue, but wife Mandaline, he left all of his possessions to her. Disputes and differences arose between Mandaline and the next of kin. George and others have agreed to release claim to the estate in return of 1/2 of the 400A. ... Mandaline Graffe ... Sealed and delivered in the presence of Emanuel Carpenter, and Thomas Cookson ... Ack'd 29 Mar 1748 Conrad Weiser ... Rec'd 27 Sept 1748 ... Cert'd deed was recorded Benjamin Longenecker.

B-551 - THIS INDENTURE - 23 May 1748 - John Leman of Lancaster Co., yeoman and Elizabeth his wife to Fredrick Sagert of Lancaster Co. yeoman, £70 for 35A, enfeoff release. Land is located in Lampeter Township, neighbors - Christian Neave, Henry Herclerods, John Leman, Daniel Leman, and Isaac Lefevre. The tract is part of a larger tract containing 500A and granted to Peter Leman by patent under the hands of Isaac Norris, James Logan, and Thomas Griffith late commissioners on 19 Dec 1728. Patent is recorded in Bk A, vol 6, pg 173. Peter Leman father of John died, and by virtue of his will dated 29 Apr 1741 and by indenture of bargain and sale from the surviving devisees was grant 300A tract, making 500A. ... John Leman, Elizabeth (X) Leman ... Sealed and delivered in the presence of Isaac Leman and George Smith ... Ack'd none ... Rec'd 23 May 1748 no name ... Cert'd deed was recorded Benjamin Longenecker.

B-552 - THIS INDENTURE - 23 May 1748 - John Leman of Lampeter Township, yeoman and Elizabeth his wife to Christian Neave of Lancaster Co., yeoman, £50 for 25A, enfeoff release. Land is located in Lampeter Township, neighbors - Christian Neave, Henry Herclerods, Frederick Sagert, Isaac Lafevre. The tract is part of a 300A tract which John received from the will of his father Peter and by indenture from the surviving heirs. Peter received the land by patent under the hands of Isaac Norris, James Logan, and Thomas Griffith, on 19 Dec 1728, recorded in Bk A, vol 6, pg 173. ... John Leman, Elizabeth (X) Leman ... Sealed and delivered in the presence of Isaac Leman, and George Smith ... Ack'd 23 May 1748 Thomas Cookson ... Rec'd 23 May 1748 Thomas Cookson.

B-554 - THIS INDENTURE - 23 May 1748 - John Leman of Lampeter Township, yeoman and Elizabeth his wife to Henry Herclerode of Lancaster Co., yeoman, £80 for 40A, enfeoff release. Land is located in Lampeter Township, neighbors - Michael Danegar, John Lemans, Frederick Sagert, and Christian Neave. The tract is part of a 300A tract which John received from the will of his father, Peter, dated 29 Apr 1741, and by indenture from the surviving heirs. Peter received the tract by patent under the hands of Isaac Norris, James Logan, and Thomas Griffith on 13 Dec 1728 and recorded in Bk A, vol 6, pg 173. ... John Leman, Elizabeth (X) Leman ... Sealed and delivered in the presence of Isaac Leman, and George Smith ... Ack'd none ... Rec'd 23 May 1748 ... Cert'd deed was recorded Benjamin Longenecker.

B-568 - KNOW ALL MEN - 4 May 1747 - I Samuel Hunter administrator of the goods of Mary Middleton late of Lancaster Co. dec'd, have ordained and appointed George Gibson of Lancaster Borough, inn-holder my attorney. I am moving. ... Samuel Hunter ... Sealed and delivered in the presence of George Smith and Samuel Dovoney ... Ack'd none ... Rec'd 9 Nov 1748 no name ... Cert'd deed was recorded Benjamin Longenecker.

B-568 - THIS INDENTURE of mortgage - 20 May 1748 - Tobias Boeckell of Heidelburg Township, yeoman to Joseph Spanenberg of Bethlehem Township Bucks Co., clerk, Charles Brogden of the city of Philadelphia, gentleman, Timothy Horsefield of Brookland Township Nassau Island NY, butcher, (guardians for Thomas, Isaac, James and Mary Noble, infants and surviving children of Thomas Noble late of NY, merchant dec'd) £20 for 50A. Land is located in Heidelburg Township, neighbor - Jacob Groidor. Tobias is bound unto Joseph, Charles, and Timothy in the sum of £40, condition for repayment of £20 by 20 May 1749. Tobias to better secure payment and in consideration of the further sum of 5/ grants 50A. Land was granted to Tobias by patent from the Proprietary on 13 May 1748. ... Tobias Boeckell ... Sealed and delivered Owen Rise and John Hopson ... Ack'd 10 Nov 1748 Edward Smout ... Rec'd 10 Nov 1748 no name ... Cert'd deed was recorded Benjamin Longenecker.

B-570 - THIS INDENTURE of mortgage - 9 Sept 1748 - Jacob Hoober of Warwick Township, yeoman to William Coleman and James Pemberton both of the city of Philadelphia, merchants and executors of the will of Samuel Powell Jr. late of the city of Philadelphia, merchant dec'd., £250 for 269A. Land located in Warwick Township, neighbors - John Kingry, Christian Bammberyor. Jacob is bound to William and James in the sum of £500 condition for repayment of £250 by 9 Sept 1749, being the monies of the children of Samuel Powell Jr. dec'd. Jacob to better secure payment and in consideration of the further amount of 5/ grants 269A. ... Jacob Hoober ... Sealed and delivered in the presence of Arthur Forster and C.B. ... Ack'd 10 Sept 1748 Thomas Greene ... Rec'd 15 Nov 1748 no name ... In the presence of a power of attorney to me directed from James Pemberton to surviving mortgagee written, named, dated 16 May 1770 and recorded at Lancaster in Bk P, pg 102. I acknowledge full satisfaction of the mortgage for James Pemberton, 24 Nov 1770 James Whitehill attorney ... Ack'd before me same day and year, Edward Shippen.

B-571 - THIS INDENTURE of mortgage - Joseph Thomas of Lancaster Borough, yeoman and Mary his wife to Patrick Carridgan of Lancaster Co., gentleman, £50 for 1 lot. Lot is located in Lancaster Borough on Kings St., neighbor - now or late of Gambriel Imble. Lot was granted by James Hamilton Esq. to Andrew Miller by indenture dated 14 Jan 1740 and by several conveyances to Joseph. Pay by or before 20 may 1749 in one entire payment. Joseph has borrowed sum of £50 from Patrick, pay on or before, 20 May 1748. ... Joseph Thomas, Mary Thomas ... Sealed and delivered in the presence of

Thomas (TG) Gale and George Smith ... Ack'd 19 Nov 1748 Thomas Cookson ... Rec'd none ... Cert'd deed was recorded Benjamin Longenecker.

B-572 - THIS INDENTURE - 3 Dec 1748 - George Croghan of Lancaster Co., Indian trader to Mary Plumsted of the city of Philadelphia widow, £300 for 2 tracts. The first tract contains 210A and is located in Pennsboro Township on Conodoguinet Creek, neighbors - none mentioned. Second tract contains 172 1/2A and is located in Paxton Township, neighbors - late of Arthur Parks dec'd, Joseph Kelsy, and James Alcorn. George received land by grant from John Frazier on 22 Jul 1748. John received land from Joseph Park and wife Agnes on 1 Sept 1747, who received by will from Arthur Park late of Chester Co., yeoman and Joseph's father. Arthur received land by Proprietary patent on 21 Aug 1738. ... George Croghan ... Sealed and delivered in the presence of William Plumsted and William Peters ... I ack'd I have received £300, George Croghan ... Present - William Plumsted, and William Peters ... Ack'd 3 Dec 1748 Thomas Cookson ... Rec'd 7 Dec 1748 Thomas Cookson ... Cert'd deed was recorded Benjamin Longenecker.

B- 574 - THIS INDENTURE - 10 Dec 1743 - Henry Carpenter of Lampeter Township, yeoman to Daniel Carpenter of Lampeter Township, son of Henry, 5/ and love, affection for 242A, in 2 tracts. First tract contains 212A and is located in Lampeter Township, neighbors - Henry Harris, Benjamin Bowman, and Ulrick Hanson. Second tract joins the first and contains 30A and is the same tract Henry granted to son Christopher. Henry received the land by lease and release dated 20 & 21 Feb 1737 from Christopher Franciscus and wife Margaret, recorded in Bk F, vol 9, pg 409 on 9 Mar 1738. The 212A which Henry received is part of a larger tract containing 530A which Christopher received on 28 Oct 1701 under the name of Stophall Franciscus. It was a Proprietary patent under the hands of Edward Shippen, Griffith Owen, and Thomas Story and recorded in Bk A, vol 4, pg 239. ... Henry (HC) Carpenter ... Sealed and delivered in the presence of - Words granting 30A and adjoining to tract of 212 first underlined - John Hair, Thomas Meyer, Daniel LeFevre ... Ack'd 10 Dec 1743 Emanuel Carpenter ... Rec'd 9 Dec 1748 ... Cert'd deed was recorded Benjamin Longenecker.

B-575 - THIS INDENTURE - 29 Nov 1744 - Henry Carpenter of Lampeter Township, yeoman to Jacob Carpenter of Lampeter Township, son of Henry, 5/ and love, affection for 270A. Land is located in Lampeter Township, neighbors - Henry Harris Sr., Henry Harris Jr., Daniel Carpenter, John Weaver, and David Lawrence. The 270A is part of a larger tract of 318A which Henry received from Christopher Franciscus on 2 Jun 1712 under the name of Henry Zimmerman. The 318A is part of a larger tract of 530A granted to Christopher under the name of Stophall Franciscus on 8 & 12 Oct 1701 by Proprietary patent under the hands of Edward Shippen, Griffith Owen and Thomas Story. Patent is recorded in Bk A, vol 4, pg 233. ... Henry (HC) Carpenter ... Sealed and delivered in the presence of Daniel Zimmerman, Hendrick Zimmerman, and Daniel Ferre ... Ack'd 1 Dec 1744 Emanuel Carpenter ... Rec'd 1 Dec 1748 no name ... Cert'd deed was recorded Benjamin Longenecker.

B-577 - THIS INDENTURE - 4 July 1741 - Caleb Baker of Conestoga Township, gunsmith and Martha his wife to Jacob Good of Conestoga Township, yeoman, £225 for 250A. Land is located on Pequea Creek on the Susquehanna River, neighbors - David Jones, late of Robert Baker dec'd. The 250A is part of a larger tract of 500A. The whole tract was first surveyed to John French of New Castle on Delaware River, gentleman, who with his wife Eve did by indenture dated 15 Jun 1720 grant the 500A to Joseph Rodman of the city of Philadelphia, merchant. Joseph by his will devised land to Sarah his wife and her heirs. Sarah by indenture dated 14 Apr 1724 granted land to Robert Baker the father of Caleb. Robert died intestate. Orphans Court ordered the personal goods be sold to satisfy his debts. By indenture dated 6 Feb 1738/9 land was granted to John Cunningham of Lancaster Co., yeoman, who by indenture dated 7 Feb 1738 granted to Caleb Baker. Patent was granted by John, Thomas, and Richard Penn on 23 Oct 1739 for 500A and recorded in Bk A, vol 10, pg 267. ... Caleb Baker, Martha Baker ... Sealed and delivered by Caleb Baker , C. Brockdon, and John Ord ... Sealed and delivered by Martha Baker Maww Yatt, John Jones ... Received of Jacob Good £275, Caleb Baker, Martha Baker ... Witness - Olson Landus ... Ack'd 15 Jul 1741 David Jones ... Rec'd none ... Cert'd deed was recorded Benjamin Longenecker.

B-579 - THIS INDENTURE - 28 Nov 1748 - Margaret Good widow of Peter Good of Lancaster Co., yeoman dec'd, Jacob Good eldest son of said dec'd, Michael Prennaman and Anne his wife daughter of dec'd, Christian Shank and Barbara his wife another daughter of dec'd, John Stover and Margaret his wife daughter of dec'd, Elizabeth Good and Mary Good daughter of Peter Good youngest son of dec'd to John Good of Lancaster Co., yeoman another son of Peter dec'd., 5/ for 165A. Land is located on the east side of Pequea Creek, neighbors - Samuel Roger, now or late of William Middleton. Peter directed before his death verbally, in front of several witness, how he wanted his land to be divided among his heirs. It was confirmed by his will dated 6 Oct 1745, John is to have the 165A. This is the same tract that Caspar Wiser and wife Catherine granted by indenture dated 27 Apr 1738 to Peter Good the father in fee. ... Margaret (M) Good, Jacob (I), mark has another line thru the center of the I, Good, Michael Prennaman, Anna (O) Prennaman, Christian Shank, Barbara (X) Shank, John Stover, Margaret (w) Stover, Elizabeth (X) Good, Mary (m) Good ... Ack'd 10 May 1748 Thomas Cookson ... Rec'd 10 Dec 1748 no name ... Cert'd deed was recorded Benjamin Longenecker.

B-580 - THIS INDENTURE - 13 Nov 1748 - Margaret Good widow of Peter Good of Lancaster Co., yeoman dec'd, Jacob Good eldest son of dec'd, John Good another son of dec'd, Michael Prennaman and Anna his wife daughter of dec'd, John Shaffer and Margaret his wife and daughter of dec'd, Elizabeth Good and Mary Good daughters of dec'd's younger son Peter, to Christian Shank who intermarried with Barbara daughter of dec'd., 5/ for 203A. Land located on east side of Pequea Creek, neighbors - William Sharrat, John Good, Samuel Boyers. Before his death Peter directed verbally in front of witness how he wanted his land divided among his heirs. Later he wrote his wishes in German, it being his will. Will was proved on 6 Oct 1745. Peter wanted Christian Shank and Barbara to have 203A, which is part of a 250A tract that was granted to Peter by James Hamilton of the city of Philadelphia on 5 May 1739. ... Margaret (M) Good, Jacob (I) mark has line thru the center, Good, John Good, Michael Prennaman, Anna (O)

107

Prennaman, John Shaffer, Margaret Shaffer, Elizabeth (X) Good, Mary (m) Good ...
Sealed and delivered in the presence of Samuel Bonde, George Smith ... Ack'd 10 Dec
1750 Thomas Cookson ... Rec'd 10 Dec 1748 no name ... Cert'd deed was recorded
Benjamin Longenecker ... Deed delivered to Jacob Good 20 Dec 1750.

B-582 - THIS INDENTURE - 29 Nov 1748 - Margaret Good widow of Peter Good late
of Lancaster Co., yeoman dec'd, Jacob Good eldest son, Michael Prennaman and Anna his
wife and daughter of dec'd, Christian Shank and Barbara his wife and daughter of dec'd,
John Stover and Margaret his wife and daughter of dec'd, Elizabeth and Mary Good
daughters of Peter younger son of dec'd to John Good of Lancaster Co., yeoman and son
of dec'd, 5/ for 50A. Tract located on east side of Pequea Creek, neighbors - none
mentioned. Peter Good the father died seized of 250A. Before his death he stated
verbally in front of several witness how he wanted his land divided among his heirs. Later
he wrote his will in German stating the same, John was to have 50A. The other heirs in
consideration of 5/ paid by John grant their shares in the 50A. Land was granted to Peter
by James Hamilton on 5 May 1739 in fee. ... Margaret (M) Good, Jacob (I) mark has line
thru the center, Good, Michael Prennaman, Anna (O) Prennaman, Barbara (X) Shank,
Christian Shank, John Stover, Margaret (M) Stover, Elizabeth (X) Good, Mary (X) Good
... Sealed and delivered in the presence of Samuel Bond, and George Smith ... Ack'd 10
Dec 1748 Thomas Cookson ... Rec'd 10 Dec 1748 no name ... Cert'd deed was
recorded Edwin L. Reinhold.

B-583 - THIS INDENTURE - 26 Mar 1740 - Martin Funk of Lancaster Co., yeoman and
Susanna his wife and daughter of Jacob Sowdor late of Lancaster Co., dec'd to John Rorer
of Lampeter Township, £200 for 300A. Henry Graff and Susanna wife by deed dated 16
May 1719 granted to Jacob Sowder 300A located in Lancaster Co., neighbors - John
Randolph, London Co., William Hughes, and Isaac Lefevers. Henry received the land
from William Penn on 16 Jun 1718 and recorded in Bk A vol 5, pg 316. In Jacob's will
written in high Dutch, he stated he wanted the land valued and that his daughters Mary
Sowder now wife of John Sowdor, and Susanna Sowdor now wife of Martin Funk should
have £100 of the estate. His wife Anna was to have £80 and use of the Plantation for 3 yrs
then the plantation was to go to the daughters. Will dated 8 Mar 1733. After 3 years John
Rorer and Martin Funk took possession of the land on 25 Mar 1740. ... Martin Funk,
Susannah (X) Funk ... Sealed and delivered in the presence of Emanuel Carpenter, and
Samuel Blunston ... Ack'd and release of dower 8 May 1748 Conrad Weiser ... Rec'd 20
Dec 1748 ... Cert'd deed was recorded Benjamin Longenecker.

B-584 - THIS INDENTURE - 29 Jun 1747 - Mary Daugherty of Lancaster Township
widow to Mary Lollard of Lancaster Township widow, £40 for east 1/2 of lot. Lot is
located in Lancaster Borough on King St., neighbors - east Mary Daugherty, west Michael
Graf. Lot was first granted to Corneluis Verhulst by James Hamilton on 20 May 1735.
Corneluis and Johanna assigned deed to Michael Byorley on __ Apr 1738. Michael and
Catherine his wife assigned to Mary Daugherty on __ Jul 1743. After death of Mary
Lollard 1/2 lot is to go to her daughter Ann Lollard for life. ... Mary Daugherty ...
Sealed and delivered in the presence of David Stout, and Benjamin Price ... Ack'd 28
Aug 1747 Thomas Cookson (first ack'd crossed out) ... Ack'd 1 Dec 1754 Thomas

Cookson ... Rec'd 24 Dec 1751 no name ... Cert'd deed was recorded Benjamin Longenecker.

B-586 - THIS INDENTURE - 24 Jun 1747 - Mary Daugherty of Lancaster Township widow to Mary Lollard of Lancaster Township widow, £200 for 2 lots. First lot is located in Lancaster Township on King St., with east side on Duke St. Second lot faces Duke St. Lots were granted to Mary Daugherty by James Hamilton by indenture dated 13 Aug 1740. ... Mary Daugherty ... Sealed and delivered in the presence of Benjamin Price and David Stout ... Ack'd 2 Dec 1751 Thomas Cookson ... Rec'd 2 Dec 1751 no name ... Cert'd deed was recorded Edwin Reinhold ... Cert'd deed was recorded Benjamin Longenecker.

B-587 - THIS INDENTURE - 24 Jun 1747 - Mary Daugherty of Lancaster Township widow to Mary Lollard of Lancaster Township widow, £50 for 1 lot. Lot is located in Lancaster Township on Moon St., neighbors - north Jacob Schlough, south Peter Berts. ... Mary Daugherty ... Sealed and delivered in the presence of Benjamin Price and David Stout ... Ack'd 2 Dec 1751 ... Rec'd 24 Dec 1751 no name ... Cert'd deed was recorded Edwin L. Reinhold.

B-588 - THID INDENTURE of mortgage - 23 Apr 1748 - Jacob Bear of Manheim Township, miller and Barbara his wife to Sebastian Graffe of Lancaster Borough, gentleman, £150 for 157A. Land is located in Manheim Township and contains a grist, oyl, and saw mill, neighbors - John Davis, David Rudy, Isaac Bear, Michael Weider. Pay by 23 Apr 1749. ... Jacob Bear, Barbara Bear ... Sealed and delivered by Jacob Bear in the presence of Marcus Young, and George Smith ... Sealed and delivered by Barbara Bear in the presence of John Davis and George Smith ... Ack'd 21 Jun 1748 Thomas Cookson ... Rec'd 21 Jun 1748 no name ... Satisfaction in full from Sebastian Graffe 8 Jan 1750 Thomas Cookson.

B-589 - THIS INDENTURE of mortgage - 27 Dec 1748 - Michael Haborstick alias Havorstick of Conestoga Township, weaver to Samuel Emlin of the city of Philadelphia, shopkeeper, £300 for 150A. Land is located on Conestoga Creek, neighbors - Philip Rudicilly, Anthony Miller Jr., and Conrad Myers. Michael is bound to Samuel Emlin in the sum of £600, condition of repayment of £300 by 27 Dec 1749. To better secure payment and in consideration of the further sum of 5/ grants 150A. This is the same 150A which John, Thomas and Richard Penn by indenture dated 12 Dec 1740, recorded in Bk A, Vol 10, pg 187 granted to Caspar Loughman. Caspar dying intestate leaving issue of Jacob Loughman eldest son, Dorothy wife of George Ridenbigh, Barbara wife of Jacob Rubley, Frederick Loughman. Jacob took tract and paid the other heirs for their shares. ... Michael Haborstick ... Sealed and delivered in the presence of C. Brockden, and Robert Loors ... Ack'd 27 Dec 1748 John Kinsey ... Rec'd 3 Jan 1748 ... By power of attorney to me from Samuel Emlin this mortgage 21 Apr 1767, recorded B M, pg 167 satisfaction in full 22 Jun 1767, Mathias Slough ... Ack'd before me on same day and year, Edward Shippen.

B-591 - THIS INDENTURE - 8 Nov 1748 - Edward Crawford and Elizabeth his wife, James Wilson and Martha his wife, Abraham Lowry and Sarah his wife, Mary Sterret spinster all of Lancaster Co., to James Sterret and Joseph Sterret of Lancaster Co, yeomen, 10/ for 604A enfeoff release. Land located in Rapho Township, neighbors - none mentioned. Elizabeth, Martha, Sarah, Mary, James, and Joseph all children of John Sterret late of Lancaster Co. dec'd. James and Joseph have paid 10/ to other children for their shares in their fathers estate, 604A, in 2 tracts. ... Martha (M) Wilson, James Wilson, Abraham Lowry, Sarah Lowry, Mary Sterret, Edward Crawford, Elizabeth (X) Crawford. ... Sealed and delivered by Abraham and Sarah his wife in the presence of Benjamin Swope, Leonard (HL) Barnet ... Sealed and delivered by Mart Sterret in the presence of Alexandra Work, and Andrew Work ... Sealed and delivered by James Wilson and Martha his wife and Edward Crawford and Elizabeth his wife in the presence of Jane Smith and Sidney Smith ... Ack'd and release of dower of Mary Sterret 13 Nov 1748 Peter Worrall ... Ack'd and release of dower for Elizabeth Crawford 4 Nov 1748, Samuel Smith ... Ack'd and release of dower for Sarah Lowry 16 Nov 1748, George Swope Esq. ... Ack'd and release of dower for Martha Wilson 29 Dec 1748 James Gilbreath ... Rec'd 4 Jan 1748 ... Cert'd deed was recorded Benjamin Longenecker.

B-593 - THIS INDENTURE - 20 Jan 1748 - Daniel Lefevre of Pequea, yeoman to John Hare of Pequea, yeoman. John has grist mill near land of Daniel on Pequea Creek. By damning the water necessary for mill, it has overflowed the river into Daniel's land. John has agreed to pay rent. In consideration of land located on both sides of Pequea Creek, paying every year on 11 Jan £3 10/. ... Daniel Lefevre, John Hare ... Sealed and delivered in the presence of Robert Thomas and Thomas Cookson ... Ack'd 20 Jan 1748 Thomas Cookson ... Rec'd 13 Jan 1748 ... Cert'd instrument was recorded Edwin Reinhold.

B-595 - THIS INDENTURE - 18 Jan 1748 - Emanuel Herman of Lampeter Township, yeoman and Mary his wife to Daniel Herman the younger of Lampeter Township, yeoman. Daniel Herman the elder grants 107A in exchange for 100A. Excepting 4A out of the 107A which was granted to John Hare. Land is located in Lampeter Township, neighbors - Daniel Herman, late of Emanuel Hare, and Daniel ?. The tract is part of a tract of 150A granted among other lands to Emanuel Herman the older on 15 Feb 1739.

Daniel Herman the older of Lampeter Township, yeoman and Mary his wife to Emanuel Herman, 100A in exchange for 107A, excepting 4A. Land is located in Lampeter Township, neighbors - Peter Bollar, and John Evans. The 100A is part of a larger tract of 300A granted to Daniel Herman the elder on 18 Oct 1747. ... Emanuel Herman, Mary Herman, and Daniel Herman ... Sealed and delivered - none ... Ack'd 21 Jan 1748 Thomas Cookson ... Cert'd deed was recorded Benjamin Longenecker.

B-597 - THIS INDENTURE - 18 Jan 1748 - Emanuel Herman of Lampeter Township, yeoman and Mary his wife to John Hare of Lampeter Township, yeoman, £12 12/ for 4A. Land is located in Lampeter Township on the east side of Pequea Creek, neighbors - none mentioned. The tract is part of a larger tract of 107A granted by Emanuel Herman and Mary his wife to Daniel Herman the younger. ... Emanuel Herman, Mary Herman ... Sealed and delivered none ... Ack'd 21 Jan 1748 Thomas Cookson ... Rec'd 21 Jan 1748 ... Cert'd deed was recorded Benjamin Longenecker.

B-598 - THIS INDENTURE - 15 Feb 1739 - Daniel Herman of Lampeter Township, yeoman and his wife Mary to Emanuel Herman of Lampeter Township, yeoman and son of Daniel and Mary, £67 for 3 tracts equaling 300A, enfeoff. Land is located in Lampeter Township. First tract contains 100A, neighbors - John Hesse, late of Peter Bellor, Daniel Herman and William Evans. Second tract contains 50A, neighbors - late of Daniel Herman and William Evans. Third tract contains 150A, neighbors - Daniel Herman and William Evans. By patent under Richard Hill, Isaac Norris, and James Logan granted to John Evans of the city of London, a tract in Strasbury containing 100A on 16 Dec 1716 and recorded in Bk A, pg 203. John granted on 5 Mar 1716 to John Moore of the city of Philadelphia, gentleman the100A tract. It is recorded in Bk E 7, vol 10, pg 374. Moore by lease and release dated 3 & 4 Sept 1730 granted the tract to William Evans. William by indenture of lease and release dated 24 & 25 Dec 1731 granted the tract Daniel Herman. William Evans then by lease and release dated 30 & 31 Jan 1731 granted 300A, part of a 1,000A to James Webb. James Webb by lease and release dated 16 & 17 Jul 1735 granted 50A of the 300A to Daniel Herman. William Penn by patent under the hands of Richard Hill, Isaac Norris and James Logan conveyed on 13 Dec 1717, 450A to Daniel Herman. The land is located in Lampeter Township. Rent is £12 per 100A on 1 Mar. Deed is recorded in patent Bk A, vol 5, pg 273. Daniel and Mary Herman for £67 paid by Emanuel Herman. ... Daniel (DH) Herman ... Sealed and delivered in the presence of Jonas LeRon, and Hans Carpenter ... Ack'd 14 Jun 1740 Emanuel Carpenter ... Rec'd 26 Jan 1748 ... Cert'd deed was recorded Benjamin Longenecker.

B-603 - THIS INDENTURE - 4 Apr 1748 - Isaac Lefevre of Strasburg Township, yeoman and Catherine his wife to Daniel Lefevre of Strasburg Township, yeoman, 5/ for 300A. Land is located in Strasburg Township, neighbors - Philip Ferree, Joseph English and Daniel Ferree. ... Isaac Lefevre, Katherine Lefevre ... Sealed and delivered in the presence of Daniel Ferree, Jacob Ferree, and Thomas Harter ... Ack'd none ... Rec'd 26 Jan 1748 ... Cert'd deed was recorded Benjamin Longenecker.

B-604 - THIS INDENTURE - 5 Apr 1748 - Isaac Lefevre of Strasburg Township, yeoman and Katherine his wife to Daniel Lefevre of Strasburg Township, yeoman 5/ and love, affection for 300A, enfeoff, in actual possession. Land is located in Strasburg Township, neighbors - Philip Ferree, Joseph English, Daniel Ferree. Isaac received land by patent under the hands of Richard Hill, Isaac Norris, and James Logan on 12 Nov 1716 and recorded in Bk A, vol 5, pg 190 on 3 Jan 1715. ... Isaac Lefevre, Katherine (K) Lefevre ... Sealed and delivered in the presence of Daniel Ferree, Jacob Ferree, and Thomas Herton ... Ack'd 19 Apr 1748 no name ... Rec'd 27 Jan 1748 ... Cert'd deed was recorded Benjamin Longenecker.

B-606 - THIS INDENTURE - 10 Jan 1748 - William Webster Sr. of East Marlborough Township in Chester Co. and Elizabeth his wife to William Webster the younger of East Marlborough Township, and son of William Sr., £95 and love, affection for 275A, in 2 tracts. Land is located in Salisbury Township on a branch of Octoraro Creek. George Thomas Esq. Lt. Governor granted by patent dated 23 Dec 1746 to William Webster 2 tracts. The first tract contains 234A, second contains 41A, recorded in Bk A, vol 14, pg

101. ... William Webster, Elizabeth (X) Webster ... Sealed and delivered in the presence of Moses Pyle, John Swayne, and F. Woodward ... Ack'd in Chester Co. 6 Feb 1748/9 William Webb ... Rec'd 10 Feb 1748/9 no name ... Cert'd deed was recorded Benjamin Longenecker.

B- 609 - THIS INDENTURE - 9 Jan 1748/9 - William Webster of East Malbrough in Chester Co., sadler and Elizabeth his wife to William Webster younger of East Malbrough, sadler and son of William, 5/ for 275A. Land is located in Salisbury Township on a branch of Octoraro Creek, neighbors - Richard Moor, James Chamberlain, James Whitehall, George Duffells, John Fleming. ... William Webster Sr., Elizabeth Webster ... Sealed and delivered in the presence of Moses Pyle, John Swayne, and Woodward ... Ack'd none ... Rec'd 10 Feb 1748 ... Cert'd deed was recorded Benjamin Longenecker.

B-610 - THIS INDENTURE - 10 Jul 1747 - James Lowry of Lancaster Co., trader and Susanna his wife, late Susanna Patterson daughter of James Patterson dec'd, Rebecca Patterson of Lancaster Co., spinster and mother of the daughter of the dec'd to John Connolly of Lancaster Co, yeoman, £200 for their shares in James Patterson's estate, 2/3 each amounting to 200A. Tract is located in Conestoga Manor, neighbors - none mentioned. John, Thomas and Richard Penn by patent dated 21 Nov 1730 under the hand of Thomas Penn granted to James Patterson and Susanna his wife a tract containing 200A. Recorded in Bk A, vol 7, pg 5. In James will he left to his son Thomas, then a minor of 3 years old all the above tract. Will is dated 3 Oct 1735. Susanna by deed dated 18 Dec 1735 for motherly love and affection granted the tract to Gordon Howard and James Mitchell of Lancaster Co., yeomen. Condition of indenture is that Susanna can live and use the land for 18 years and she will provide for Thomas food, schooling, etc. If she should die then they will provide for the infant children for the remainder of the term. If Thomas should die before the end of term then the undivided interest is to be vested in James Lowry and Susanna his wife, and Rebecca Patterson and the heirs of Sarah, late wife of Benjamin Chambers, all heirs of James and Susanna. Thomas has since died. ... James Lowry, Susanna Lowry, Rebecca Patterson ... Sealed and delivered in the presence of Thomas Cookson and George Sanderson ... Received 10 Jul 1747 of John Connolly £200, James Lowry, Rebecca Patterson ... Teste - Thomas Cookson ... Rec'd 24 Feb 1748/9 no name ... Cert'd deed was recorded Benjamin Longenecker.

B-612 - THIS INDENTURE - 20 May 1748 - Susanna Connolly of Lancaster Co., widow, George Smith, John Hart, and Thomas Doyle all of Lancaster Borough, gentlemen to Gordon Howard of Lancaster Co., yeoman, £450 for 200A, enfeoff release. Tract is located in Conestoga Manor, neighbors - none mentioned. John, Thomas, and Richard Penn by patent dated 21 Nov 1730 under the hand of Thomas Penn granted to James Patterson dec'd and his wife Susanna a tract containing 200A. Patent is recorded in Bk A, vol 7, pg 5. James by his will devised the tract to his son Thomas who at the time was a minor of 3 years old. Will is dated 3 Oct 1735. Susanna did by deed of trust grant to Gordon Howard and James Mitchell of Lancaster Co., yeomen, to hold for the infant children. Condition is that she may reside on the land for 18 years. If Thomas should die before the end of the term, which he has, the undivided interest became vested in Susanna wife of James Lowry and Rebecca Patterson, and the heirs of Sarah late wife of Benjamin

Chambers. The heirs did by deed of trust dated 9 Jul 1747 release to John Connolly of Lancaster Co., yeoman since dec'd all of their shares, 2/3 each. John Connolly by his will appointed Susanna, George Smith, John Hart, Thomas Doyle the executors of his will. They are to sell land. ... Susanna Connolly, George Smith, John Hart, Thomas Doyle ... Sealed and delivered in the presence of Conrad Weiser, and James Gillespie ... Ack'd 17 Feb 1748/9 Thomas Cookson ... Rec'd 25 Feb 1748/9 no name ... Cert'd deed was recorded Benjamin Longenecker.

B-614 - THIS INDENTURE - 12 May 1748 - Gordon Howard of Lancaster Co., yeoman to Susanna Connolly of Lancaster Co., widow, £450 for 2/3 of 200A tract. Land is located in Conestoga Manor, neighbors - none mentioned. Susanna, George Smith, John Hart, and Thomas Doyle are executors of the will of John Connolly late of Lancaster Co., yeoman. By his will, 2/3 part of a tract of 200A was devised to Gordon Howard. Gordon received the land in trust for Susanna Connolly and her heirs and the sum of £450. The money is Susanna, Gordon for 5/ and the trust placed in him grants 2/3 of the 200A tract. ... Gordon Howard ... Sealed and delivered in the presence of Conrad Weiser, and James Gallespie ... Ack'd none ... Rec'd none ... Cert'd deed was recorded Benjamin Longenecker.

B-616 - THIS INDENTURE - 13 Feb 1748 - Susanna Connolly, here after called Susanna Ewing of Manor Township, widow to John Kogy of Conestoga Township, yeoman, £500 for 1/2 of 300A, enfeoff release. The land is located in Conestoga Manor, neighbors - late of Peter Sholleberger. John, Thomas, and Richard Penn under the hand of Thomas Penn on 21 Mar 1739 granted to Thomas Ewing of Lancaster yeoman, since dec'd, and Susanna his wife a tract of 300A. Deed is recorded in Bk A, vol 9, pg 201. Susanna is the only surviving heir, she is entitled to the 300A. ... Susanna Connolly ... Sealed and delivered in the presence of Thomas Cookson and George Smith ... This day above I have received £500 from John Kogy, Susanna Connolly ... Teste - Thomas Cookson ... Ack'd 16 Feb 1748/9 Thomas Cookson ... Rec'd none ... Cert'd deed was recorded Benjamin Longenecker.

B-618 - THIS INDENTURE - 13 Feb 1748/9 Susannah Connolly of Manor Township widow to John Kogy of Manor Township, yeoman £100 for 200A. Land is located in Conestoga Manor, neighbors - none mentioned. John, Thomas, and Richard Penn under the hand of Thomas Penn did by patent dated 21 Nov 1734 grant to James Patterson, dec'd, and Susannah his wife a tract in Conestoga Manor containing 200A. Patent is recorded in Bk A, vol 7, pg 5. Where as Gordon Howard of Lancaster Co., yeoman by several conveyances is seized of a share of 2/3 of undivided 200A. Gordon by indenture dated 12 May 1747 granted to Susannah Connolly all his 2/3, Susannah has agreed to let Benjamin Chambers of Lancaster Co., miller and Sarah his wife and daughter of Susannah Connolly purchase 1/3. Benjamin and Sarah had granted their share to Susanna Connolly. Susanna for £100 grants 200A the above tract. ... Susannah Connolly ... Sealed and delivered in the presence of Thomas Cookson and George Smith ... Ack'd 13 Feb 1748/9 Thomas Cookson ... Received of John Kogy £600 this day above, Susannah Connolly ... Witness - Thomas Cookson ... Rec'd 28 Feb 1748/9 no name ... Cert'd deed was recorded Benjamin Longenecker.

B-620 - KNOW ALL MEN - 13 Feb 1748/9 - That Susanna Connolly of Lancaster Co., widow is bound unto John Kogy of Lancaster Co., yeoman in the sum of £200. Condition, Susanna sold 200A to John Kogy in Manor Township. James Chambers Jr., a heir of Benjamin Chambers and Sarah his late wife dec'd was entitled to a undivided 1/3. James being under age, Susanna promises when James turns 21 he will receive his 1/3 share. Until then John Kogy can enjoy. ... Susanna Connolly ... Sealed and delivered in the presence of Thomas Cookson and George Smith ... Ack'd 13 Feb 1748/9 Thomas Cookson ... Rec'd 28 Feb 1748/9 no name ... Cert'd instrument was recorded Benjamin Longenecker.

B-621 - TO ALL PEOPLE - 13 May 1733 - Henry Damogar of Strasburg Township to Jacob Damogar of Strasburg, £93 for his share in 300A. Land is located in Strasburg Township, neighbors - Daniel Harmon, late John Evans, Peter Lemons, Joseph English and Martin Kendy. Michael Damogar received the 300A from John, Thomas, and Richard Penn under the and of Thomas Penn on 30 May 1733, recorded in Bk A, vol 6, pg 178. Michael died intestate leaving issue of Jacob eldest son, Henry, and Mary Damogar. Land was valued at £480, making each share at £93. Mary is not yet 21 years. ... Henry Damogar ... Sealed and delivered in the presence of John Hare, John Ronsharg ... Ack'd none ... Rec'd none ... Cert'd deed was recorded Benjamin Longenecker.

B-622 - TO ALL PEOPLE - Christopher Franciscus the elder of Lancaster Township, yeoman is possessed of land at Shenandoah Augusta VA, 3.000A. Christopher has contracted with several peoples for sale of part of the land.

THIS INDENTURE - 5 Dec 1739 - John Page of Austin Gayors London gentleman, William Allen of the city of Philadelphia, William Webb of Chester Co. Esq. and Samuel Powell of the city of Philadelphia merchant to Peter Feake of Plumton Manor, yeoman, £76 for 190A, in actual possession. Land is located in Plumton Manor, neighbors - soon to be granted to Christian Rulty, Peter Rood. Rent of 1 red rose on 23 Jun every year. John, Thomas and Richard Penn granted by patent on 17Sept 1735, 5,165A to John Page. Patent is recorded in patent Bk A, vol 7, pg 264. Rent of 1 red rose 24 Jun every year. Land is located on Tulpehocken Creek. John turned the land into Plumton Manor. John granted to William Webb, William Allen, and Samuel Powell full power of attorney to sell the land, instrument recorded Bk D2, vol 2, pg 196 on 17 Feb 1736. ... William Allen, William Webb, Samuel Powell Jr., for John Page ... Sealed and delivered in the presence of William Parsons, Michael Shefer ... Ack'd 30 Jan 1748 Conrad Weiser ... Rec'd 4 mar 1748/9 no name ... Cert'd deed was recorded Benjamin Longenecker.

B-625 - THIS INDENTURE - 2 Jul 1748 - John Dieter of Plumton Manor in Heidelberg Township yeoman and Catherine his wife to Peter Feak of Plumton Manor, yeoman, £30 for 55A, 104 perches, in actual possession, enfeoff. Land is located in Plumton Manor by other land of Peter, neighbors - George Terr, John Dietor. The land is part of a tract of 263A which John Page by indenture by his attorneys granted on 1 Jun 1748 to John Dietor. Rent of 1 red rose on 11 Jun yearly. ... Johannas Dietor, Catherine (X) Dietor ... Sealed and delivered in the presence of William Parsons, Valentine Hercklerod ... Ack'd

114

and release of dower 2 Jun 1748 Conrad Weiser ... Rec'd 4 Mar 1748/9 Cert'd the deed was recorded Benjamin Longenecker.

B-626 - THIS INDENTURE of mortgage - 2 Feb 1748 - Samuel Patterson of Strasburg Township, yeoman to William Coleman and James Pemberton both of the city of Philadelphia, merchants and executors of the will of Samuel Powell younger dec'd, £150 for 210A. Land is located in Lancaster Co., neighbors - Joseph Barnet, David Firy, George Mackeral ... Samuel Patterson ... Sealed and delivered in the presence of Joseph Golloway, Griffith Jones ... Received the sum of £150 consideration money, Samuel Patterson ... Teste - Joseph Golloway ... Ack'd 2 Feb 1748 John Kinsey ... Rec'd 13 Mar 1748/9 ... Cert'd deed was recorded Benjamin Longenecker.

B-628 - THIS INDENTURE - 31 Jan 1739 - Aaron Musgrove of West Sadsbury, yeoman and Elizabeth his wife to Joseph White of West Sadsbury, yeoman, £160 for 200A. Land is located in West Sadsbury, neighbors - none mentioned. Land is part of a tract of 340A granted by patent from the Proprietary on 13 Nov 1738 to Aaron Musgrove. ... Aaron Musgrove, Elizabeth (E) Musgrove ... Sealed and delivered in the presence of James McConnal, and Thomas Buller ... Ack'd 31 Jan 1739 Andrew Shaw ... Rec'd 25 Mar 1749 no name ... Received £160 on 31 Jan 1739, Aaron Musgrave ... Witness - James McConnal, Thomas Buller ... Cert'd deed was recorded Benjamin Longenecker.

B-629 - THIS INDENTURE - 20 Mar 1741 - Joseph White of Lancaster Co., yeoman and Jane his wife to James Miller, husbandman, £190 for 200A. Land is located in West Sadsbury, neighbor - Aaron Musgrave. Aaron Musgrave and Elizabeth his wife did by indenture 31 Jan 1739 convey the 200A to Joseph White. ... Joseph White, Jane (E) White ... Sealed and delivered in the presence of Patrick Shelld, and Moses McClenan ... Received £190 consideration money, Joseph White ... Ack'd 12 May 1741 John Kyle ... Rec'd none ... Cert'd deed was recorded Benjamin Longenecker.

B-631 - THIS INDENTURE - 21 Dec 1743 - Henry Carpenter of Lampeter Township, yeoman to Mary Firree, now wife of Daniel Firree of Lampeter Township and one of the daughters of Henry Carpenter, 5/ and love, affection, for 350A, enfeoff. Land is located in Cocalico Township, neighbor - none mentioned. The tract is part of a larger tract containing 700A, granted by John, Thomas, and Richard Penn. Deed is recorded in Bk A, vol 6, pg 300 on 22 May 1734. The other part of the tract was granted to Solomoa Wister. ... Henry Carpenter ... Sealed and delivered in the presence of John Hair, Emanuel Hair, and Christian Carpenter ... Ack'd 26 Dec 1743 Emanuel Carpenter ... Rec'd 4 Apr 1749 no name ... Cert'd deed was recorded Benjamin Longenecker.

B-632 - THIS INDENTURE - 29 Nov 1744 - Henry Carpenter of Lampeter Township, yeoman to Daniel Fierre of Lampeter Township, yeoman, £400 for 2 tracts. The first tract contains 150A and is located in Pequea Creek. Neighbors - Martin Bear, John Brown, George Snevley. The tract is part of a 350A tract granted to Henry by Thomas Hatton and Jane his wife by indenture of lease and release dated 29 & 30 Apr 1731. The second tract contains 150A and is also located on Pequea Creek. Neighbors - Henry Hoans, Valentine Milton, Martin Bear. Land is part of a tract of 350A which was granted to Martin Bear by lease and release dated 13 Apr 1731 by Thomas Hutton and Jane is wife. Martin and wife Elizabeth granted by lease and release dated 14 & 15 Dec 1738 to Henry. ... Henry Carpenter ... Sealed and delivered in the presence of Henry Zimmerman, Daniel Carpenter, Jacob Carpenter ... Ack'd 2 Dec 1744, Emanuel Carpenter ... Rec'd 6 Apr 1749 no name ... Cert'd deed was recorded Benjamin Longenecker.

B-634 - TO ALL MEN - John Steer of Lampeter Township, yeoman for £35 12/ paid by Daniel Harman the younger of Lampeter Township for chest of drawers, trunk, 2 walnut boxes, misc. household furniture, and farm animals. Animals are branded with W:E. ... John Steer ... Sealed and delivered in the presence of Thomas Cookson, and John Bushong ... Ack'd none ... Rec'd none ... Cert'd deed was recorded Edwin L. Reinhold.

B-635 -THIS INDENTURE - 29 Mar 1749 - John Steer of Lampeter Township, yeoman and Rachel his wife to William Hamilton of Leacock Township, yeoman, £430 for 200A. Land is located on Mill Creek, neighbors - William McNabb, William Evans, and James Smith. The land is part of a 500A tract which was granted to John by John, Thomas, and Richard Penn on 20 Mar 1734. John and Rachel are moving. ... John Steer, Rachal Steer ... Sealed and delivered in the presence of James Webb, James Wright, and Thomas Cookson ... Received £430 consideration money 29 Mar 1749, John Steer ... Witness - James Webb, and James Wright ... Ack'd 9 May 1748 Thomas Cookson ... Rec'd 12 Mar 1748/9 no name ... Cert'd deed was recorded Benjamin Longenecker.

B-637 - THIS INDENTURE - 11 Apr 1749 - William Hamilton of Leacock Township, yeoman and Jane his wife to Philip Eaken of Leacock Township, yeoman, £562 10/ for 200A. Land is located on a branch of Mill Creek, neighbors - William McNabb, William Evans, James Smith. Land was granted by John, Thomas, and Richard Penn on 12 Mar 1734 to John Steer. From John and Rachel to William Hamilton, recorded Bk A, vol 7, pg 106. ... William Hamilton, Jane (J) Hamilton ... Sealed and delivered in the presence of Thomas Cookson and George Landerson ... Ack'd none ... Rec'd 19 Apr 1749 ... Cert'd deed was recorded Benjamin Longenecker.

B-539 - THIS INDENTURE - 29 Mar 1749 - John Walker of Leacock Township, yeoman and Marllin his wife to Patrick Carrigan of Leacock Township, yeoman, £250 for 98A. Land is located in Leacock Township, neighbors - Richard Beeson, John Hildebrand, John Child, Robert Jefferies. Land was granted by patent from John, Thomas, and Richard Penn under the hand of George Thomas Esq. Lt. Governor on 13 Jan 1745 and recorded in Bk A, vol 12, pg 287. ... John Walker, Marllin (X) Walker ... Sealed and delivered in the presence of Martin Mylen and John Kendig ... Ack'd none ... Rec'd 25 Apr 1749 no name ... Cert'd deed was recorded Edwin L. Reinhold.

B-641 - THIS INDENTURE - 25 Jan 1748 - Jacob Bare of Manheim Township, yeoman and Barbara his wife to Sebastian Graff of Lancaster Co., gentleman, £80 for 45A. Land is located in Manheim Township, neighbors - John Long, George Nicholas Bucker, Isaac Bare, and Jacob Bare. The tract is part of large tract containing 213A and granted to Jacob by John, Thomas and Richard Penn on 12 Jan 1748/9. ... Jacob Bear, Barbara (X) Bear ... Sealed and delivered in the presence of Jacob Bare, and George Smith ... Ack'd

25 Jan 1748/9 ? ... Rec'd 20 Jan 1748 no name ... Satisfaction received in full of Sebastian Graff on 8 Jan 1759, Thomas Cookson.

B-642 - THIS INDENTURE - 14 Mar 1750 - Jacob Jacobs of Lancaster Borough, yeoman and Ann his wife to Honorable James Hamilton of the city of Philadelphia Esq., £250 for 15A. Land is located in Manheim Township, neighbors - James Hamilton, and Michael Myers. By indenture dated 9 Jul 1750 made or mentioned to be made between Henry Niseley, Jacob Niseley, Martin Niseley, Frona Niseley, Maria Niseley and Anna Niseley six of the children of Jacob Nutt alias Niseley of Manheim Township, yeoman dec'd granted 15A, which is part of a tract of 150A, to Jacob Jacobs. John, Thomas, and Richard Penn granted on 23 Jun 1747 to Jacob Nutt alias Niseley 150A located in Manheim Township, recorded in Bk A, vol 13, pg 226. Jacob now dec'd leaving 8 children - Henry, Jacob, Martin, Frona, Marie, Ann, with Barbara and Elizabeth infants. ... Jacob (I) mark has line thru center, Jacobs, Anne (e) Jacobs ... Sealed and delivered in the presence of Charles Morse, and Bernard Hubly ... Received consideration money, no signature ... Witness - Charles Moses, and Bernard Hubly ... Ack'd and release of dower 14 Mar 1750/1 Thomas Cookson ... Rec'd 19 Mar 1750 Thomas Cookson ... Cert'd deed was recorded Edwin L. Reinhold.

Lancaster County Warrants
1710 - 1742
Numbers 567 - 757

Number

567 13 of the 7th month 1717 - Jacob Neager and Foaln Landes
2,600A at Conestoga for £260

568 14 of the 12th month 1717/18 - Benedict Whitmer
300A no location for £30

569 29 of the 10th month 1718 - John Hendrick Sleins
150A at Conestoga for £15

570 5 of the 3rd month 1718 - Seld (Omri) ch (this is exactly as it is printed)
200A no location for £20

571 4 of the 7th month 1717 - no assignment

572 16 Oct 1710 - Reudolph Bundeli
1,700A near the head of Pequea Creek

573 16 Oct 1710 - John Rudolph Bundeli
500A no location given

574 28 of the 8th month 1713 - John Musgrove
600A for £60 no location given

575 5 of the 5th month 1713/4 - Samuel Guildin late of Canton of Bern in
Switzerland 800A to be laid out in Salisbury Chester Co. for £60
Paid within 6 months of survey

576 8 of the 5th month 1713/4 - Rebekah Shaw daughter of Robert Barron of
Kendel in Westmoreland Co., dec'd 300A no location

577 28 of the 11th month 1714/5 - Peter Miller
200A near Strasburg toward Susquehanna River

578 16 of the 12th month 1714/5 - Robert Hodgson and James Hendricks
1,500A on Conestoga Creek for £50, quit rent 1/ for every 100A's

118

579	16 of the 12th month 1714/5 - Robert Hodgson and James Hendricks 2,000A land in one regular tract on Conestoga Creek for £200
580	31 of the 11th month 1715/6 - Hans Graff 200A on Pequea Creek
581	22 of the 6th month 1716 - Richard Caster, wheelwright 200A between Pequea and Conestoga Creek
582	22 of the 6th month 1716 - John Foner of East Jersey 400A on south side of Conestoga Creek
583	22 of the 6th month 1716 - Alexander Bear of East Jersey 400A on south side of Conestoga Creek
584	24 of the 6th month 1716 - Philip Farre of Strasburg 300A near Pequea Creek
585	9 of the 12th month 1716/7 - John Gardiner Jr. of Philadelphia Co. 500A on south side of Pequea Creek
586	No date - John Harris 500A situated by the Indians
587 a	5 Nov 1714 - William Persey 500A on a branch of Pequea Creek
587 b	1 Mar 1717/8 - Richard Carter of Conestoga 20A on or near Conestoga Creek
588	27 of 6th month 1733 - Stephen Atkinson, clothier, granted liberty to settle and build a falling mill about 2 years since on land situated between the tract surveyed to Edmund Cartlidge on Conestoga Creek and also to raise a damn in the creek for his mill upon agreement that he pay after the rate of £25 per 1,000A's in order to survey land on which he is now seated.
589	1 of the 3rd month 1733 - Andrew Hamilton of the city of Philadelphia 500A where the Court House of the County now stands.
590	1 Sept 1733 - Aaron Vernon 300A on west side of Schuylkill £15 10/ for 100A quit rent 1/3 penny
591	1 Sept 1733 - Caleb Harrison 350A west side of Schuylkill £15 for 100A quit rent 1/2 penny

592   1733 - Thomas Lindsey
        480A on Pequea Creek

593   14 Dec 1733 - Mathew Adkinson
        200A head of Eastern branch of Conestoga Creek

594   3 Jan 1733 - Michael Shank
        290A on small branch of Conestoga Creek

595   3 Jan 1733 - Philip Hans Leman
        200A in Leacock Township

596   3 Jan 1733 - Michael Rynde
        300A on a branch of Mill Creek

597   3 Jan 1733 - Jacob Meyer
        215A on branch of Conestoga Creek

598   3 Jan 1733 - Oswald Hestator
        150A on Cocalico Creek

599   3 Jan 1733 - Sebastian Royer
        100A on south side of Mill Creek

600   4 Jan 1733 - John Verdan
        350A on Cocalico Creek

601   8 Jan 1733 - George Beard
        250A on Conestoga Creek

602   10 Jan 1733 - Nathan Evans
        300A on a branch of Conestoga Creek

603   11 Jan 1733 - John McGauby
        200A near Pequea Creek adjoining Thomas Stoney and Thomas Green

604   19 Jan 1733 - James Smith
        465A on Mill Creek

605   19 Jan 1733 - Michael Weilder
        185A on Conestoga Creek

606   19 Jan 1733 - Jacob Snevely
        200A on Mill Creek

607   19 Jan 1733 - Peter Forney
        250A on Cocalico Creek

608   19 Jan 1733 - Teeter Elwood
        300 A on a branch of Mill Creek

609   19 Jan 1733 - Jacob Rowland
        300A Cocalico Creek

610   19 Jan 1733 - John Smith
        335A on Cocalico Creek

611   19 Jan 1733 - George Wolf
        185A on Cocalico Creek

612   21 Jan 1733 - Patrick Moore
        460A on Pequea Creek

613   22 Jan 1733 - James McKaus
        240A on Pequea Creek

614   24 Jan 1733 - Henry Hoover
        160A on a branch of Pequea Creek

615   24 Jan 1733 - Mathew Limey
        150A on Mill Creek in Leacock Township adjoining Hatwell Vernon

616   8 Feb 1734 - John Noacve
        300A in Leacock Township between Samuel Jones and James LaRue

617   12 Feb 1733 - Felix Miller
        200A on Little Conestoga Creek

618   27 Feb 1733 - Hugh Brady
        150A in Paxton Township

619   1 Mar 1733 - Hans Shimooer
        250A on Cocalico Creek

620   4 Mar 1733 - Thomas Gardner
        500A in Paxton Township where he is already settled

621   7 Mar 1733 - Christian Shelly of Germantown
        200A at the head of little Conestoga Creek

622   14 Mar 1733 - James Treser Jr. (this one was really hard to read?)

200A on Beaver Creek

623 14 Mar 1733 - David Treser (this one was really hard to read?)
200A on Beaver Creek

624 14 Mar 1733 - James Treser (this one was really hard to read?)
200A on Beaver Creek

625 14 Mar 1733 - Robert Treser (this one was really hard to read?)
100A on Beaver Creek

626 20 Mar 1733 - George Kersner
200A on Casoosing Creek

627 26 Mar 1734 - Peter Smith
100A between Cocalico and Muddy Creek

628 4 Apr 1734 - Peter Lane
200A on Swartara Creek

629 4 Apr 1734 - Corneluis Lane
200A on Swartara Creek

630 17 Apr 1734 - Samuel Jones
150A in Leacock Township adjoining the land formally of Charles Jones

631 17 Apr 1734 - Jacob Hoover
300A about 3 miles to the East road of Chickaselugo Creek adjoining
Christian Bumberrias

632 22 Apr 1734 - Richard Larden
300A on Little Conestoga Creek

633 27 Apr 1734 - John Rubbel
150A on Muddy Creek near Philip Longs and Christopher Stannel

634 27 Apr 1734 - Peter Holler
150A on Muddy River near Philip Long and Christopher Stannel

635 1 Mar 1734 - Christopher Bumbarrie
300A near Chickaslunga Creek

636 1 Mar 1734 - Hugh Gilliland
400A on a branch of Paquea

637 1 May 1734 - John Kinnigh

164A near Chickaslunga Creek

638 3 Mar 1734 - Hugh Thompson
  205A where he has settled

639 19 May 1734 - James McClengahan
  200A on a branch of Octoraro Creek

640 3 Jun 1734 - James Massay
  200A on a branch of Octoraro Creek

641 12 Jun 1734 - William Cook
  100A on east side of Pequea Creek

642 27 Jun 1734 - William Dunlap
  250A between the forks of Swartara Creek

643 27 Jun 1734 - John Fridly
  150A in Robinson Township beyond the flying hill

644 27 Jun 1734 - Samuel Evans
  350A in Leacock Township near John Abys mill

645 28 Jun 1734 - Anthony Pretter
  200A on Conestoga Creek lying continuos to land whereon he now dwells

646 13 Aug 1734 - Dennis Milr
  150A between Pequea and Conestoga Creeks

647 16 Apr 1734 - Roger Hunt
  400A on a branch of Swartara Creek

648 16 Aug 1734 - John McNab
  150A in Manheim Township adj to Michael Baughman

649 16 Aug 1734 - John McNab Jr.
  150A in Manheim Township adj to Michael Baughman

650 17 Aug 1734 - Frederick Elveashed
  300A between Tulpehocken and Cocalico Creeks

651 17 Aug 1734 - Hersey Pastler
  300A between Tulpehocken and Cocalico Creeks

652 17 Aug 1734 - Thomas Howard
  100A in Chestnut lead adjoining John Stewart

653	22 Aug 1734 - Felix Landus 200A in Lebanon Township adjoining John Frederick
654	22 Aug 1734 - Martin Harrist 300A between Pequea and Conestoga Creeks adj Jacob Meris
655	22 Aug 1734 - Thomas Starp 200A on the south side of Swartara Creek
656	22 Aug 1734 - Michael Towner 200A Lebanon Township
657	23 Aug 1734 - James Logan 200A in Conestoga Manor
658	30 Aug 1734 - William Richey 300A between Octoraro Creek and Susquehanna River where he now dwells
659	31 Aug 1734 - Benjamin Webb 200A beyond Pequea Creek
660	4 Sept 1734 - Jacob Shelley 300A on a branch of Little Conestoga
661	11 Sept 1734 - Christian Long 150A on Mill Creek adj to Orber Long
662	11 Sept 1734 - Orber Long 150A on Mill Creek east of John Aby's mill
663	11 Sept 1734 - Christian Neasty 200A on Mill Creek
664	16 Sept 1734 - Samuel Ferguson 300A in Lebanon Township near Donegal Township
665	20 Sept 1734 - Alexandar Montgomery 200A on Octoraro Creek
666	27 Sept 1734 - James Lewis 200A in 2 tracts in Robinson Township
667	27 Sept 1734 - Benjamin Owen 150A in Robinson Township

| 668 | Oct 1734 - George Graff |
| | 200A in 2 tracts on Mill Creek |

| 669 | 2 Oct 1734 - John Adlum |
| | 300A east side of Chickaselunga Creek |

| 670 | 2 Oct 1734 - Jonas LaRue |
| | 350A in Leacock Township adj to Philip Ferre |

| 671 | 3 Oct 1734 - John Clawson |
| | 100A on a branch of Pequea Creek |

| 672 | 3 Oct 1734 - George Haine |
| | 100A on Cocaosin Creek |

673	5 Oct 1734 - Rudolph Carrode
	300A in Warwick Township between Hans George Kissel, Hans
	Hoover and Lawrence Hoff

| 674 | 5 Oct 1734 - Hans George Kissel |
| | 200A in Warwick Township |

| 675 | 10 Oct 1734 - Ulrick Lype |
| | 200A in Manheim Township |

| 676 | 10 Oct 1734 - Abraham Steiner |
| | 200A in Warwick Township |

| 677 | 22 Oct 1734 - Philip Schaffer |
| | 250A in Earl Township adj to Peter Graff and John Musslen |

678	22 Oct 1734 - Samuel Miley
	300A about a mile this side of Conestoga Creek Between Michael Miear
	Jacob Funk

| 679 | 24 Oct 1734 - Maria, widow of John Diteher |
| | 100A in Hempfield Township where her late husband was settled |

| 680 | 25 Oct 1734 - John Moore |
| | 200A near Tulpehocken |

| 681 | 25 Oct 1734 - John Seller |
| | 50A on Mill Creek |

| 682 | 25 Oct 1734 - Henry Selbr |

100A near Mill Creek

683	26 Oct 1734 - Peter Allen 400A in Paxton Township
684	31 Oct 1734 - Jacob Cocghnarder 200A adj to John and Jacob Sneaely
685	2 Nov 1734 - Peter Erubb 200A in Lebanon Township
686	6 Nov 1734 - Michael Meiser 50A adj to a tract of 100A he bought of James Logan
687	6 Nov 1734 - Andrew Saltsehiean 100A in Heidelberg Township in Mill Creek
688	6 Nov 1734 - Henry Seller 200A between Tulpehocken and Swartara Creeks
689	6 Nov 1734 - Peter Glubb 200A between Tulpehocken and Swartara Creeks
690	15 Nov 1734 - Fitus Dimmiay 100A on a branch of Pequea Creek
691	28 Nov 1734 - Michael Neif 250A above Mill Creek adj to Michael Breitts
692	2 Dec 1734 - John Douglas 200A in Salisbury Township
693	3 Dec 1734 - William Sherrein 200A on a branch of Beaver Creek
694	3 Dec 1734 - James Smith 150A on a branch of Mill Creek
695	5 Dec 1734 - John George Swab 150A on Mill Creek in Earl Township adj to William Lewis
696	5 Dec 1734 - John George Swab 150A on Mill Creek adj to William Lewis
697	23 Dec 1734 - James Whitehill 100A on Pequea Creek

| 698 | 28 Dec 1734 - John George Arnold |
| | 150A on Cacoos Creek |

699   30 Dec 1734 - Samuel Robinson
150A on a branch of Pequea Creek

700   30 Dec 1734 - Peter Reisht
300A in Warwick Township between Ulrick Bankherds and Abraham Sleiver

701   2 Jan 1734 - William Richardson
200A about 1 mile beyond Pequea Creek

702   2 Jan 1734 - Thomas Steinman
140A about 1 mile beyond Pequea Creek

703   8 Jan 1734 - Robert Aruner
200A near Pequea Creek

704   8 Jan 1734 - William Wilson
200A on Pequea Creek

705   8 Jan 1734 - James Galt
400A at the head of Pequea Creek

706   11 Jan 1734 - Erasmus Buckenire
150A Mill Run near Tulpehocken

707   14 Jan 1734 - John Deaer
200A where he now dwells on Octoraro Creek

708   16 Jan 1734 - Leonard Fesller
200A Earl Township beyond Conestoga Creek

709   20 Jan 1734 - Alexander Miller
150A on Conestoga Creek adj to Christopher Franciscus and Michael Miller

710   21 Jan 1734 - George Haine
400A lying on a branch of Schuylkill River

711   21 Jan 1734 - Thomas Jackson
175A on a branch of Pequea Creek

712   22 Jan 1734/5 - John Scott

200A on Octoraro Creek where he now dwells

713   27 Jan 1734/5 - Casper Filler
        150A in Earl Township adj to Christian Seusiney

714   27 Jan 1734 - Christian Seusiney
        150A in Earl Township adj Jacob Miley and Christian Martin

715   27 Jan 1734/5 - Christian Seusiney
        150A in Earl Township adj Edward Owen and David Davis

716   28 Jan 1734/5 - Patrick Jack
        200A west of Sadisbury Township

717   29 Jan 1734/5 - John Leusman
        150A near Cocalico Creek

718   29 Jan 1734/5 - Daniel Acker
        100A upon Cocalico Creek adj to John Leusman

719   31 Jan 1734/5 - Evan David
        200A on a branch of Conestoga Creek

720   1 Feb 1734 - Joseph Gray
        200A Earl Township on Octoraro Creek

721   10 Feb 1734 - William Houston
        200A in Sadisbury Township on Octoraro Creek

722   17 Feb 1734 - Nicholas Pasley
        200A near Conestoga Creek

723   18 Feb 1734 - John Mucklevaue
        200A Earl Township

724   18 Feb 1734 - John Ewards
        400A Aligacy Creek about 3 miles above John Lewis

725   18 Feb 1734 - Badaur Davis
        150A in Earl Township adj to Christian Sneider and Andreas Graff

726   19 Feb 1734 - Matthias Stauffer
        150A in Earl Township on Cedar Run

727   19 Feb 1734 - John Divendarwer
        200A north of Mill Creek adj to Jacob Mixell

728	19 Feb 1734 - Jacob Mixell 200A about 1 mile north of Mill Creek
729	19 Feb 1734 - Conrad Debois 100A on Mill Creek
730	19 Feb 1734 - Henry Stouffer 100A on a branch of Cocalico Creek
731	19 Feb 1734 - Jacob Miley 200A on Mill Creek adj to Rees David and Martin Livingston
732	19 Feb 1734 - Anthony Pneiter 50A on a branch of Mill Creek adj to his other survey
733	19 Feb 1734 - Andreas Meixell 250A on a branch of Mill Creek
734	20 Feb 1734 - Michael Andreas 100A between Cocalico and Muddy Creeks
735	20 Feb 1734 - Jacob Bear 150A in Earl Township adj to Henry Bear
736	20 Feb 1734 - Henry Bear 50A on a branch of Mill Creek adj to his other survey
737	20 Feb 1734 - Jake Wolfsparier 100A between Cocalico and Muddy Creeks
738	20 Feb 1734 - Michael Deal 200A on Conestoga Creek Adj to Jacob Bear
739	27 Feb 1734 - Abraham Tea 200A between Cocalico and Muddy Creeks
740	20 Feb 1734 - John Geer 150A between Cocalico and Muddy Creeks
741	27 Feb 1734 - George Swab 200A between Cocalico and Muddy Creeks
742	27 Feb 1734 - Thomas Heaning 300A between Cocalico and Muddy Creeks

743	20 Feb 1734/5 - Conrad Webb
	200A between Cocalico and Muddy Creeks
744	21 Feb 1734 - William McNealy
	200A on west branch of Cattauing Creek in Drumore Township
745	21 Feb 1734 - Henry Coffman
	100A near Little Conestoga Creek adj to Christian Steiner
746	21 Feb 1734 - Hans Niseley
	300A on a branch of Little Conestoga adj to Jacob Shell
747	22 Feb 1734 - John Schieffer
	150A on Cocalico Creek
748	25 Feb 1734 - John Nicley
	150A on a branch of Conestoga
749	26 Feb 1734 - John Anderson
	100A on west head branch of Brandywine near Jason Cloud
750	27 Feb 1734/5 - James Hughes
	225A on west head branch of Brandywine near Jason Cloud
751	26 Feb 1734/5 - Hans Rude Negler
	100A in Earl Township adj to Hans Meir
752	26 Feb 1734/5 - Widow Anne & Catherine Lesley
	100A on Cocalico Creek
753	27 Feb 1734/5 - John Landis
	150A between Christian Steiner and Hans Scheiffer
754	27 Feb 1734/5 - Joseph Lethar & Samuel Goath
	100A between George Wolf and Christian Seivers
755	27 Feb 1734/5 - Mathias Uland
	150A on Cocalico Creek adj to Hans Schieffer
756	27 Feb 1734 - Rudolph Fallinger
	125A adj to Adam Moser and Mathias Uland
757	27 Feb 1734 - John Berger
	100A in Earl Township
758	no assignment

759   27 Feb 1734 - John Kitzmiller Jr.
              100A on Cocalico Creek

760   27 Feb 1734 - Henry Musselman
              100A on a branch of Little Conestoga

761   27 Feb 1734 - Mathias Levingston
              200A in Earl Township between Jacob Miley and Jacob Meisal

762   27 Feb 1734 - Andrew Boyer
              150A in Heidelburg Township

763   28 Feb 1734 - Philip Satand
              150A in Earl Township on Mill Creek adj to Anthony Breddes and Leonard
              Elbucker

764   28 Feb 1734 - Robert McLalland
              200A West Sadsbury Township

765   28 Feb 1734 - Leonard Elbucker
              150A in Earl Township on Mill Creek adj to Anthony Breddes and James
              Young

766   26 Feb 1734 - Hans Bushan
              200A near Mill Creek adj to Andreas Boichiney

767   27 Feb 1734 - Jacob Swyther
              100A near Cocalico Creek adj to John Miners and Thomas Hain

768   29 Feb 1734 - John Shevash
              200A in Chestnut Level

769   29 Feb 1734 - Conrad Roode
              200A near Mill Creek adj to Hans Good and Hans Pudingley

770   29 Feb 1734 - William Porter
              200A West Sadsbury Township

771   28 Feb 1734 - John Keller
              200A near Cocalico Creek adj to Nicholas Adams and Holzinger

772   28 Feb 1734 - Hans Meir
              100A near Cocalico Creek adj to Michael Adams and Samuel Bear

773   28 Feb 1734 - Nicholas Adams

200A near Cocalico Creek adj to Samuel Bears and John Keller

774 28 Feb 1734 - Hans Good
150A near Mill Creek adj to the tract of 400A formally surveyed to him

775 28 Feb 1734 - Samuel Bear
150A near Cocalico Creek adj to Elias Mier and Nicholas Adams

776 1 Mar 1734 - Andreas Scroop
250A lying on Cocalico Creek

777 3 Mar 1734 - Jacob Slough
200A ca 3 miles north of Lancaster

778 3 Mar 1734 - Hans Goode
200A near Mill Creek

779 3 Mar 1734 - Henry Kreiter
200A ca 3 miles north of Lancaster

780 4 Mar 1734 - John Leonard Hyde
100A on Cocalico Creek adj to John Zimmerman

781 4 Mar 1734 - Michael Bear
150A on Cocalico Creek

782 4 Mar 1734 - Paul Henshaver
100A on Cocalico Creek

783 4 Mar 1734 - Martin Frank
226A on Cocalico Creek adj to John Bowmans

784 4 Mar 1734 - John Bowman
200A on Cocalico Creek

785 4 Mar 1734 - Henry Miller
100A on a branch of Conestoga Creek

786 7 Mar 1734 - Alexander Davison
400A on Pequea Creek

787 7 Mar 1734 - Casper Stover, Lutheran Minister
200A on a branch of Mill Creek adj to John Hoover

788 7 Mar 1734 - Ludwick Hockenbach
100A on a branch of Mill Creek

| 789 | 8 Mar 1734 - George Miley |
| | 300A on a branch of Swartara Creek |

| 790 | 8 Mar 1734 - Thomas Thompson |
| | 100A on a small branch of Tulpehocken Creek |

| 791 | 10 Mar 1734 - Jacob Graff |
| | 200A on a branch of Cocalico Creek |

| 792 | 10 Mar 1734 - Henry Stouffer |
| | 50A Cocalico Creek |

| 793 | 12 Mar 1734 - Henry Saunders |
| | 200A on the north west side of Chickaslunga Creek |

| 794 | 12 Mar 1734 - Jermiah Wolf |
| | 150A near Cocalico Creek |

| 795 | 12 Mar 1734 - Hans Adam Moser |
| | 300A near Cocalico Creek |

| 796 | 12 Mar 1734 - Weitig Pence |
| | 200A on Cocalico Creek |

| 797 | 12 Mar 1734 - Francis Clark |
| | 150A on Cocalico Creek |

| 798 | 13 Mar 1734 - Casper Bouman |
| | 50A adj to a tract of 300A surveyed to him in Strasbury Township between Beaver Creek |

| 799 | 20 Mar 1734 - Philip Ranch |
| | 150A on Cedar Run in Earl Township |

| 800 | 20 Mar 1734 - Michael Ranch |
| | 150A on Mill Creek adj to William Lewis |

| 801 | 21 Mar 1734 - William Fisher |
| | 200A near Goshen Hill adj to George Hain |

| 802 | 21 Mar 1734 - George Hain |
| | 100A near Goshen Hill adj to the tract he now lives on |

| 803 | 27 Mar 1734 - Hanry Caldwell |
| | 100A on the upper land of Chestnut Level |

804 28 Mar 1735 - Jacob Sheart
200A in Strasburg Township on a branch of Pequea Creek adj to the widow Feree

805 29 Mar 1734 - Matthias Sheremaker
150A near Pequea Creek

806 31 Mar 1735 - John Price
300A in Robinson Township on Schuylkill River

807 3 Apr 1735 - Jacob Keyer
100A in Warwick Township

808 7 Apr 1735 - Hans Jacob Bear
300A on Cocalico Creek adj to Henry Carpenter

809 7 Apr 1735 - Peter Shank
300A on a branch of Cocalico Creek adj to Christian and Jacob Krop

810 7 Apr 1735 - John Shank
300A on a branch of Cocalico Creek

811 7 Apr 1735 - Ulrick Shank
300A on a branch of Cocalico Creek

812 9 Apr 1735 - William Wright
200A on the western branch of Cocalico Creek

813 9 Apr 1735 - John Wright
200A on a western branch of Cocalico Creek

814 9 Apr 1735 - James Hamilton
200A between Conestoga and Pequea Creeks

815 15 Apr 1735 - Michael Betsley
200A on Chickaslunga Creek

816 15 Apr 1735 - Philip Sweiger
200A between Cocalico and Muddy Creek adj to George Swope

817 21 Apr 1735 - John Paxton
200A in West Sadsbury Township

818 23 Apr 1735 - Henry Muller
100A near Cocalico Creek

819	23 Apr 1735 - John Evans 100A Carnarvon Township
820	25 Apr 1735 - Daniel Hammond 200A where he has already made settlement near Octoraro Creek
821	30 Apr 1735 - Philip Lung 250A on Cocalico Creek
822	1 May 1735 - Thomas Edwards 200A in Earl Township
823	1 May 1735 - Annie Roger 200A near Pequea Creek adj to Bastian Roger and Adam Lydener
824	1 May 1735 - Annie Roger 200A near Pequea Creek
825	1 May 1735 - Edward Owen 200A in Earl Township
826	7 May 1735 - Thomas Davis 300A near Mill Creek
827	7 May 1735 - William Evans 200A in Earl Township between his fathers Nathan and Mathias Stouffer
828	14 May 1735 - Anthony Morris of the city of Philadelphia 1,000A in 4 tracts in Robinson Township
829	14 May 1735 - Henry Appaley 200A on the middle branch of Conestoga Creek
830	15 May 1735 - Hans Musselman 200A where he now dwells near Middle Creek
831	16 May 1735 - Philip Trout 100A ca 1 mile beyond Cocalico Creek
832	21 May 1735 - Michael Meir 500A in Manheim Township
833	21 May 1735 - John Hare Jr. 250A head of Chickaslunga Creek

834   22 May 1735 - Peter Hayes
100A on the Great Spring in Tulpehocken Township adj to his fathers, George Hayes

835   29 May 1735 - Werrig Pence
100A on Cocalico Creek

836   4 Jun 1735 - David Jones
100A in Robinson Township

837   12 Jun 1735 - Michael Breith
100A in Heidelburg Township near Christopher Stump

838   14 Jun 1735 - David Stephens
100A in Robinson Township

839   4 Jul 1735 - Adam Rainber
100A in Earl Township adj to Hans Graff and Hans Good

840   30 Jul 1735 - Christian Shetler
100A on Cocalico Creek

841   1 Aug 1735 - Michael Bower
150A on Conestoga Creek

842   2 Sept 1735 - Christian Wyland
150A on a branch of Conestoga Creek

843   12 Sept 1735 - Hans Michael Fouts
150A in Lampeter Township

844   12 Sept 1735 - Christopher Soleirger
150A in Earl Township on Conestoga Creek

845   10 Oct 1735 - Hans Henry Pochwan
150A on a branch of Cocalico Creek adj to Jacob Brunners

846   10 Oct 1735 - Jacob Brunner
150A on a branch of Cocalico Creek

847   23 Oct 1735 - Jacob Heller
100A in Leacock Township adj to John Line

848   23 Oct 1725 - Hans Groff
200A in Leacock Township

849   23 Oct 1735 - Peter Goode
100A in Earl Township adj to Hans Graff

850   29 Oct 1735 - Matthew Paxton
200A on the land he has for some years settled on by Octoraro Creek

851   15 Nov 1735 - Moses Martin
300A in Carnarvon Township

852   no assignment

853   17 Nov 1735 - Jacob Hains
100A near Pequea Creek

854   19 Nov 1735 - John Peter Salling
250A on a small branch of Conestoga Creek

855   25 Nov 1735 - Baltzer Ont
300A ca 4 miles to the farm of ? ? Creek adj to Michael Baughman and
Michael Towne

856   25 Nov 1735 - Woolrick Soak
250A on a branch of Chickaslunga Creek

857   25 Nov 1735 - Michael Baughman
300A on a branch of Swartara Creek

858   25 Nov 1735 - Wooley Reeger
250A on a branch of Conestoga Creek

859   28 Nov 1735 - Christian Winger
150A in Leacock Township adj to John Rine

860   28 Nov 1735 - Jacob Bowman
150A in Earl Township upon Conestoga Creek

861   3 Jan 1736 - Matthias Vewrick
150A on a branch of __ Creek

862   1 Mar 1735/6 - Martin Groff
200A in Earl Township

863   4 Mar 1735/6 - Jacob Rullvean
100A on a branch of Pequea Creek

864   13 Mar 1735/6 - George Shalleberger

125A in Hempfield Township

865   17 Mar 1735/6 - Jacob Lloyd
       250A at the head of Little Conestoga Creek

866   18 Mar 1735/6 - David Thomas
       100A in Robinson Township

867   11 mar 1735/6 - Joseph Higginbottom
       130A in Conestoga Township

868   24 Mar 1735/6 - Samuel Moorhead
       200A on Muddy Creek

869   24 Mar 1735 - Casper Walter
       250A in Leacock Township

870   24 Mar 1735/6 - Jeremiah Evatt
       300A in Leacock Township

871   31 Mar 1735/6 - James Crawford
       200A between Fishing Creek and the Susquehanna River in Dunmore
       Township

872   23 Apr 1736 - Alexander Creighead
       300A in Sadsbury Township

873   28 Apr 1736 - Michael Fickle
       100A in Strasbury Township

874   19 May 1736 - Edward Davis
       300A in a branch of Conestoga Creek in Carnarvon Township

875   26 May 1736 - Peter Toreider
       250A on Pequea Creek

876   26 May 1736 - Falladerie Brandison
       200A on a branch of Conestoga Creek

877   29 Jun 1736 - Philip Showfelbergar
       150A in Lampeter Township

878   9 Jul 1736 - William Makin
       200A in Sadsbury Township

879   2 Aug 1736 - Jacob Haigy

150A on which he settled about 3 years ago on Cocalico Creek

880   15 Sept 1736 - Garven Miller
        250A in Sadsbury Township

881   5 Oct 1736 - John Powell
        100A on Conestoga Creek

882   3 Nov 1736 - William Evans
        200A near Cocalico Creek

883   Nov 1736 - Jacob Rem
        300A on Muddy Creek

884   2 Dec 1736 - Hans Carvend
        150A on Muddy River

885   17 Nov 1736 - Edward Rem
        100A on Cocalico Creek adj to the other land he holds

886   15 Dec 1736 - James Kimeson
        200A on Tulpehocken Creek

887   24 Jan 1736 - Conrad Foy
        200A on Conestoga Creek

888   23 Feb 1736/7 - Charles Hudson
        200A on the south side of a branch of Conestoga Creek

889   23 Feb 1736/7 - John Nisbet
        100A on a branch of Pequea Creek

890   23 Feb 1736/7 - James Davies
        150A at the Springs of Pequea Creek

891   26 Feb 1736/7 - Peter Summy
        300A on Little Cocalico Creek

892   4 Mar 1736/7 - George Boyd
        250A in Sadsbury Township

893   9 Mar 1736/7 - Peter Kraie
        200A on the south branch of Muddy Creek

894   15 Mar 1736/7 - Anthony Pretter
        600A in Swartara Valley on the south side of the creek

895   15 Mar 1736/7 - Jacob Nisley
       100A on Conestoga Creek

896   22 Mar 1736/7 - Hans Conner
       200A in Cocalico Township

897   25 Mar 1737 - Barthalomeu Salinger
       100A in Manheim Township

898   2 Apr 1737 - Hugh McLallan
       200A in Salisbury Township

899   5 Apr 1737 - Andreas Wagner
       300A on Mill Creek a branch of Conestoga Creek

900   9 Apr 1737 - David Dadwalader
       200A in Robinson Township

901   15 Apr 1737 - Cornelius Land
       200A in Manheim Township

902   15 Apr 1737 - Peter Lane
       200A in Manhiem Township

903   15 Apr 1737 - Henry Lane
       200A in Manheim Township

904   19 Apr 1737 - Adam Neartin
       100A in Carnarvon Township

905   20 Apr 1737 - Richard Smith
       100A on the south branch of Hay Creek in Carnarvon Township

906   22 Apr 1737 - Robert Matthews
       100A in Sadsbury Township near Octoraro Creek

907   25 Apr 1737 - Samuel Buchanan
       200A near the head of Pequea Creek

908   3 May 1737 - Thomas Thomas
       100A in Carnarvon Township

909   4 May 1737 - Jacob Beheue
       150A on a branch of Pequea Creek

910   4 May 1737 - Rees Pritchard
100A at the mouth of Beaver Creek

911   5 May 1737 - Evan Thomas
350A on a branch of Schuylkill River called Beaver Creek

912   11 May 1737 - John Bishop
150A in Strasburg Township

913   11 May 1737 - John Sensiney
100A in Earl Township adj to Jacob Sensiney

914   17 May 1737 - Joseph Barnett
150A on Pequea Creek

915   17 May 1737 - Robert Hughey
425A on a branch of Brandywine

916   18 May 1737 - David Jones
100A in Carnarvon Township

917   24 May 1737 - Timothy Douglas
150A in Sadsbury Township

918   24 May 1737 - Frederick Becker
150A in Leacock Township adj to Hans Swope and Jacob Helless

919   26 May 1737 - Henry Martin
200A on a branch of Swartara Creek

920   8 Jun 1737 - Benjamin Wittmer
500A in Lampeter Township

921   28 Jun 1737 - John Hastings
350A in Salisbury Township

922   24 Aug 1737 - Michael Amwagh
150A near Cocalico Creek adj to Ushly Gelier and Jacob Brummers

923   5 Oct 1737 - Abraham Steiner
60A adj to a tract of 300A already confirmed to him

924   19 Oct 1737 - John Smith
300A in Earl Township on Cocalico Creek

925   23 Nov 1737 - George Gibson

50A in Salisbury Township

926   15 Feb 1737/8 - Jenkin Jenkins
        350A in Earl Township

927   2 Mar 1737/8 - George Gibson & Archibald Little
        150A in Salisbury Township

928   28 Jun 1738 - Henry Worke
        200A on the north side of Valley Mountain in West Sadsbury Township

929   18 Jul 1738 - Samuel Bethel
        70A in Manheim Township

930   10 Jan 1738/9 - Henry Landus
        50A on a branch of Conestoga Creek in Warwick Township

931   22 Feb 1738/9 - Jacob Hoover
        150A in Warwick Township

932   3 Dec 1739 - John Wister of the city of Philadelphia
        100A in Warwick Township

933   7 Dec 1739 - John Wister of the city of Philadelphia
        350A in Warwick Township

934   10 Jan 1739/40 - Michael Emmit
        50A in Manheim Township

935   6 Feb 1739 - William Rogers & John Henderson
        200A on which settlement was made about 13 years ago in Upper Octoraro

936   13 May 1741 - Thomas Falkner
        100A in Salisbury Township, vacated and now granted to John Jones, and
        Charles Bruket in Salisbury Township

937   8 Jun 1741 - John Lyon
        200A in Leacock Township

938   6 Oct 1742 - Hans Koch
        150A in Warwick Township adj to Hans Crup

4 Index

Made in the USA